The Unfinished Project

Twenty-five large cardboard boxes dominate my office in the sociology department. The outdated building feels uninspiring, and the room is small and drab. Classes start in just a few weeks, and I need to get ready for the fall semester. The late-summer heat seeps into the room, making the daunting task ahead feel even heavier. When I moved from Evanston, Illinois, to Philadelphia to begin my faculty position at the University of Pennsylvania, I had the boxes shipped directly to my new office.

After my father's passing and my mother's devastating stroke and subsequent death a few years later, my sister Evelyn had sent me the boxes from our parents' home. Back then, I was living in a spacious old house near the Northwestern University campus, where I was teaching. As the only sibling with a basement big enough to store them—and the only academic among us—I became the natural custodian of this archive. For nearly a decade, the boxes had gathered dust in my basement while I continued putting off the overwhelming job of sorting through the papers they contained. But when I relocated to Philadelphia, the stack of boxes looming in my office forced me to confront the inevitable.

I reach for a pair of scissors from my desk drawer and slice through the tape sealing one of the boxes. Inside, I find piles of yellowed papers held together with rusty staples, their edges brittle with age. The text on the pages had been created with an old-fashioned typewriter, the kind that went clickity-clack when you pecked at the keys. It hits me. These must be transcripts of interviews my father conducted with interracial couples while I was growing up in Chicago in the 1960s. As far back as I can remember, my father, an anthropology professor, was consumed by writing a book about interracial marriage. His obsession with documenting the lives of Black-white couples for his book was a constant presence in my childhood. In the rambling Victorian house in the Kenwood neighborhood, where I grew up with my twin sisters, only a year younger than me, my father's book suffused our family life. Daddy spent countless hours cloistered in his third-floor study, engaged in the research that defined his career. The mixed marriage project was his life's work, a passion that seemed to permeate every corner of our home and every memory of my upbringing.

Yet for all his intellectual intensity, my father had a genial, easy-going warmth about him. He was devoted to spending time with my sisters and me, balanced between lecturing us about his work and having fun with us—howling with laughter on a roller coaster or showing family movies in the living room on Saturday evenings. He was quick to chuckle. Slow to anger. Everyone felt comfortable in his company. He wasn't strikingly handsome, but he had a pleasant, approachable look, with soft edges and a twinkle in his greenish-gray eyes.

Now, in my hands for the first time, are the original interviews—the very ones that sent Daddy roaming Chicago neighborhoods in search of Black people married to white people, found their way into our dinner-time conversations, drew him into his study afterward to labor over his book, brought unforgettable couples into our home, taught my sisters and me enduring lessons about race, family, and love. In an instant, what minutes before had felt like an arduous chore transforms into an exhilarating if uncertain expedition.

I pull the top transcript from the pile. Its thin, crackling pages are so aged that they've turned a dingy beige, the edges of the first sheets chipped away. At the top right corner of the first page is a four-line caption. I sink into my desk chair, captivated, and begin to read.

Interview with Mrs. ALBERTS. The original typewritten name has been scratched out with black ink and *ALBERTS* is written in longhand—a pseudonym. My heart jumps when I recognize my father's handwriting.

32-- Prairie Avenue. The last two numbers of the address have been erased and replaced with two handwritten dashes.

ONE SIGNAL
PUBLISHERS

ATRIA

ALSO BY DOROTHY ROBERTS

Torn Apart
Fatal Invention
Shattered Bonds
Killing the Black Body

The Mixed Marriage Project

A MEMOIR OF LOVE, RACE, AND FAMILY

Dorothy Roberts

**ONE SIGNAL
PUBLISHERS**

ATRIA

NEW YORK   AMSTERDAM/ANTWERP   LONDON
TORONTO   SYDNEY/MELBOURNE   NEW DELHI

**ONE SIGNAL
PUBLISHERS**

ATRIA

An Imprint of Simon & Schuster, LLC
1230 Avenue of the Americas
New York, NY 10020

First One Signal Publishers/Atria Books hardcover edition February 2026

ONE SIGNAL PUBLISHERS / ATRIA BOOKS and colophon are registered trademarks of Simon & Schuster, LLC

Simon & Schuster strongly believes in freedom of expression and stands against censorship in all its forms. For more information, visit BooksBelong.com.

For information about special discounts for bulk purchases, please contact Simon & Schuster Special Sales at 1-866-506-1949 or business@simonandschuster.com.

The Simon & Schuster Speakers Bureau can bring authors to your live event. For more information or to book an event, contact the Simon & Schuster Speakers Bureau at 1-866-248-3049 or visit our website at www.simonspeakers.com.

Interior design by Davina Mock-Maniscalco

Manufactured in the United States of America

1   3   5   7   9   10   8   6   4   2

Library of Congress Control Number: 2025944914

ISBN 978-1-6680-6838-0
ISBN 978-1-6680-6840-3 (ebook)

Let's stay in touch! Scan here to get book recommendations, exclusive offers, and more delivered to your inbox.

In memory of my parents, Iris and Bob
For my sisters, Evelyn and Helen

The Mixed Marriage Project

By Robert Roberts
February 19, 1937

As far as I know, my father had conducted the interviews in the 1960s. This date must be when Mrs. Alberts got married. I retrieve more transcripts from the box and skim the notes at the top. All have dates in 1937. At first, I wonder if all the couples he interviewed were married in that year, but that seems an unlikely coincidence. Suddenly, it occurs to me: *Daddy spoke to these couples in 1937.* Computations spring into my head. My father was born in August 1915. That means he was only twenty-one years old when he interviewed Mrs. Alberts, while he was a graduate student at the University of Chicago.

I clutch the stack of transcripts to my chest, unable to move. I feel faint. The date these interviews took place upends the story I have always known about my father's research. For my entire life, I thought that my white father had first started studying interracial relationships when he met my Black Jamaican mother in the 1950s. His obsession with mixed marriages was supposed to have been motivated by his falling in love with her when she was his student at Roosevelt College. As a child, I saw my father's research as a reflection of the love my parents had for each other. I believed that my father's faith in the promise of interracial marriage grew from the steadfast devotion they shared. Turns out that he had begun interviewing Black-white couples more than a decade before he met my mother.

My mind races. How did my young father, the son of Welsh and German immigrants raised in a whites-only neighborhood, become so intrigued by marriages between white and Black people? In deeply segregated Chicago, his childhood neighborhood of Logan Square had been violently protected from the influx of Black migrants. My father had been four years old at the time of the notorious Red Summer of 1919, when mobs of white people beat, stoned, and shot Black residents and burned down their homes and businesses. I wonder if he even knew any Black people growing up.

My father's mother and brother were far from open to interracial relationships. Daddy waited until his own mother passed away to marry my mother, as he didn't want to upset her. I barely knew my uncles, even though they lived in Chicago. His younger brother, Edward, disowned him after the wedding, and I never met him.

More unsettling questions flood my mind. This new timeline suggests that an academic interest in mixed marriages might have prompted my father to pursue one himself. Did he marry my mother because of his obsession with interracial intimacy, rather than the other way around? Overwhelmed by this notion, I decide to ignore the boxes a little longer.

So it was that the boxes containing my father's papers stayed stored away in my sociology office throughout the fall and spring semesters, while I spent most of my time working from my more comfortable office in the law school. When summer arrived, I finally had the time and emotional fortitude to deal with them. With the help of two Penn undergraduate students, I sorted through the interview files, along with photographs, letters, newspaper articles, and lecture notes. Six of the boxes were filled with transcripts of interviews conducted with Black-white couples in Chicago, nearly five hundred interviews in total, spanning from 1937 through the 1980s. My father had given all the couples pseudonyms to protect their identities. The breakdown was remarkable: 138 interviews from the 1930s, just 1 from 1940, 63 from the 1950s, 234 from the 1960s, 20 from the 1970s, and 10 from the 1980s. The interviews were numbered, and it was immediately clear that many were missing. A large chunk of the 1950s interviews—likely half—had been lost. As for the 1940s, I suspect there had only ever been that one interview: my father served in the army during World War II and had been stationed in Europe during that time.

Over the next several years, I dipped into the boxes—leafing through interviews, lingering over old photographs, perusing various papers—until I decided to devote an entire summer to reading all of my father's interview transcripts. I wanted to immerse myself in this project while staying in my childhood neighborhood, so I began searching for summer rentals in Hyde Park–Kenwood and nearby areas. Through a website for academics, I found a miraculous listing. A couple with ties to the University of Chicago, currently living overseas, was renting out their apartment just two blocks from the house I grew up in. From the living room windows, I would be able to see my old elementary school and the street leading to my childhood home. It felt like fate.

The rental apartment seemed instantly familiar. Decorated with items from the couple's travels—brass trays, Middle Eastern carpets, and intriguing drawings—it mirrored the aesthetic of my childhood home. A spacious room at the front served as a study, lined with bookshelves and furnished with a comfortable chair and a desk, perfect for reading and taking notes. A large brown leather chair to the side provided a cozy spot for reflection. I packed lightly for myself, but I shipped six large boxes of transcripts, labeled by decade, to arrive the day after I moved in.

On a sweltering June afternoon, the boxes were delivered intact, save for one with a gash that thankfully hadn't damaged the papers. I hauled them up three flights of stairs, drenched in sweat by the time I finished. Midway through, a neighbor introduced himself with a cheerful "Let me know if I can help with anything" before bounding off—leaving me to chuckle at the irony of his offer as I continued to tackle the task alone.

I turned the dining room into my depot, stacking the boxes neatly against the walls. I started with the interviews from the 1930s, laying the transcripts in piles on the dining room table in chronological order. Once I finished reading that decade, I returned the transcripts to their boxes and moved on to the 1950s and then the 1960s, following the same method. My daily routine became a rhythm of simplicity and focus: a light breakfast of yogurt and tea, a jog around the schoolyard and the block I grew up on, and hours in the study with a stack of transcripts carried from the dining room. Often, I would lose myself so completely that lunchtime came and went unnoticed. Even after dinner, I would return to the transcripts, reading late into the night. Sometimes I would go an entire day without speaking to another human being. My daughter suggested, quite seriously, that I should set a timer to remind myself to stand up, eat, and take bathroom breaks. But the interviews were so absorbing that I would ignore the timer, and I eventually abandoned it. Each morning, I woke up eager to continue, and by the end of the summer, I realized it was the most pleasurable reading I had ever done in my life.

I was awestruck by the breadth of the interviews. My father had opened a window into the extraordinary lives of couples who had dared to cross Chicago's racial boundaries at the turn of the twentieth century. Their stories stretched across the city's shifting racial landscape—through the start of the Great Migration, the aftermath of World War II, and the seismic changes of the civil rights movement. But the interviews didn't just illuminate history; they pulled me headlong into mysteries that shattered my settled understanding of my family. They unearthed vivid memories of engaging my father in discussions about his research and forced me to confront my evolving identity as a Black girl with a white father. Reading his conversations with Black-white couples sparked new, imagined conversations with him—questions I hadn't known to ask when he was alive, questions I now sought answers to in the transcripts he had left behind.

In one of the boxes, I found a manila folder bulging with correspondence between my father and editors at various publishers, including both trade and university presses. I had no idea he had made so many attempts to publish his book. I remember only one publishing arrangement from my childhood—when my father signed a contract with the major New York publishing house Simon & Schuster. It was the biggest news we celebrated in our Kenwood home. Bigger than my father receiving a Fulbright fellowship to teach in Cairo, Egypt. Bigger than my mother becoming a U.S. citizen. Bigger than my eighth-grade graduation. When my father announced the book contract, a wave of jubilation had swept through our house. Buzzing with excitement, our whole family piled into our sky-blue Rambler and drove to Kon-Tiki Ports, a restaurant in the Sheraton Hotel in downtown Chicago, for a celebratory dinner.

Despite his lofty aspirations and our encouragement, my father failed to deliver the manuscript to Simon & Schuster. The details are hazy, but I remember that Daddy had to return the advance he received. The joy that filled our home when he signed the contract was replaced by a pall of disappointment when he breached it.

I don't know why my father struggled so much to complete his manuscript. Perhaps, by trying to do too much, he managed to accomplish too little. Overwhelmed by the multitude of topics his work inspired, he lost focus on what was the most compelling aspect of his research: the face-to-face interviews he—and later, my mother—undertook with hundreds of interracial couples who shared their stories of crossing Chicago's color line. These stories, stored away for decades in cardboard boxes, were left for me to explore.

At first, I thought I might finish the book my father never published. But as I explored the transcripts, I realized a different story was unfolding—the story of my parents themselves, woven through every interview. It was their story I wanted to follow, traced through the lives of the couples they had met. I would read those intertwined accounts not just to piece together their project but to solve the deeper mysteries the boxes had stirred—about my parents, my family, and ultimately, about myself.

CHAPTER 1

Origins

Transcript of Mrs. Alberts interview, February 19, 1937

Mrs. Alberts
February 19, 1937

The first box of interviews from the 1930s is unpacked, stacks of transcripts spread in chronological order across the dining room table. A cup
of green tea in hand, I carry the first pile to the study—the space that
will serve as home for the rest of the summer. My eyes close as I let out a
deep sigh, a steadying breath before the expedition begins. In my hands,
the fragile pages feel almost sacred, holding the essence of a life's work
that once shaped my childhood and wound itself deep into the fabric of
who I have become. From the top of the pile, I remove the interview
with Mrs. Alberts, careful not to damage its yellowed and brittle pages.

Six months shy of his twenty-second birthday, my father arrived at a
building on Prairie Avenue in a Black neighborhood of Chicago, where
he hoped to interview a white woman whom he learned was married to
a Black man. He walked up the stairs to the second-floor apartment and
knocked on the door. A young "colored" man opened the door and left to

summon Mrs. Alberts. A few moments later, she appeared at the entryway. *She is a white woman, apparently about twenty-five years of age,* my father noted, also commenting that *the appearance of the room was very unattractive and dirty-looking.* He could see two little children playing on a bed inside. Remaining at the entrance, he explained that he was from the University of Chicago and helping to conduct a study of the neighborhood. He had heard that Mrs. Alberts might know about a club that he was interested in. She asked, "Who told you about me?"

"Mrs. L. said that you might know of a club called the Mannasses Club, which is composed of Negroes who have married white persons," my father replied.

Mrs. Alberts said she had never heard of this club. Instead, she was eager to tell my father about the Young Democratic Club she belonged to. She excitedly recounted her efforts to win her predominantly colored precinct over to the Democratic Party. "The people here used to be all Republicans, but we got a lot of them at the last election," she boasted. "I told the people, 'Roosevelt's your man. Do you think there'd be any WPA if Landon got in? You don't want to see the boys loafing in pool halls and saloons and your girls out hustling again.'"

President Franklin Delano Roosevelt had been elected to his second term the previous year after defeating Alf Landon, the Republican governor of Kansas, in a landslide victory. Roosevelt had introduced a sweeping series of reforms and social welfare programs, collectively known as the New Deal, aimed at bringing immediate relief from the economic devastation of the Great Depression. The New Deal included massive public works initiatives, like the millions of jobs dispensed by the Works Progress Administration, WPA for short, which Mrs. Alberts had referred to. To win another election, Roosevelt needed votes from Chicago residents.

The 1930s marked a turning point in the racial dynamics of presidential politics. Before Roosevelt, the majority of Black Americans sided with Republicans, the party of Abraham Lincoln and Frederick Douglass. Convincing them to shift their allegiance to the Democratic Party was crucial. For many recent migrants from the South—who represented a growing share of Mrs. Alberts's precinct—this election was their first opportunity to vote. Mrs. Alberts's enthusiasm for Roosevelt was part of the groundswell of popular sentiment that ultimately propelled FDR to an unprecedented third term three years later, making him the longest-sitting president in U.S. history.

My father, undeterred, pressed Mrs. Alberts about the Mannasses Club.

Might her husband know about the organization? When she said that he might, my father proposed to return in a week to speak with Mr. Alberts.

"Perhaps you would be interested in this club if I can get some information about it," my father offered.

At that moment, one of the children, a three-year-old boy, ran over to Mrs. Alberts. *He appeared to have only the slightest trace of Negroid features,* my father observed. *His hair was rather wavy and light brown.* A baby, which Mrs. Alberts identified as hers, slept in a cradle, at first obstructed from view. Two colored children played with Mrs. Alberts's son in the apartment and a colored girl my father estimated as ten or eleven years old came and went from across the hall behind where my father was standing. My father wasn't sure if any of the darker youngsters was also Mrs. Alberts's. *I didn't learn who these children were, but they seemed to be perfectly at home there.*

Before taking his leave, my father walked into the room to get a better look at the baby, seemingly anxious to inspect the infant's appearance.

The baby appeared to be about a year or a year and a half old. I didn't ask whether it was a boy or girl. It had reddish hair and light skin. I could see no trace of Negro in the baby's hair or skin. Its face did seem to be slightly Negroid but I am sure that I wouldn't have thought so if I hadn't heard that Mr. Alberts is colored. Neither would I probably have noticed any trace of Negro in Mrs. Alberts' three-year-old boy if I hadn't been looking for it.

This was the earliest interview I found in my father's papers and reading it left me aghast. *No trace of Negro? Slightly Negroid?* I didn't recognize my father in these words, given his outspoken admiration for my dark-skinned mother, his love for my sisters and me. I was baffled until I recalled the era in which he wrote it. He was being trained as an anthropologist at the University of Chicago in the 1930s. I imagine the professor leading Daddy's ethnographic methods class had instructed the students to take meticulous note of the racial traits of their research subjects. He was probably taught those words to describe Black people in his anthropology lectures.

One of the Black men my father interviewed later that year tried to impress him by reciting the five races. "I learned them in school many years ago," he boasted. "There's the Caucasian, the Ethiopian, the Mongolian, the Malay, and the Red Race, or American Indians." He added, "I can name the five senses, too."

The man had been reciting the racial classifications described by German professor Johann Friedrich Blumenbach in the third edition of his influential treatise, *On the Natural Varieties of Mankind*, published in 1795. Blumenbach was the first to lend scientific credibility to the racial category Caucasian, derived from the people who inhabited the Caucasus Mountains, which he deemed the most beautiful. He postulated that Caucasians, encompassing the white populations of Europe and neighboring regions, represented the ideal from which the other races "degenerated." While it should be obvious that Blumenbach fabricated this scheme for categorizing human beings, most Americans today would probably respond similarly if asked to name the races, though perhaps using language that seems less offensive to modern ears.

My alarm dissipating, I reflect on other clues about my father lodged in his first conversation with Mrs. Alberts. Mixed with his fascination with the children's physical traits is his interest in the Mannasses Club, what drew him to interview her in the first place. In his first foray into interracial marriage there's a glimpse of an aspect of my father's research that would become more prominent in the future—his desire not only to study mixed marriages but to promote them. Barely in his twenties, my father had already veered away from the anthropological study of innate differences between races that dominated his field to embark on a quest to reveal their commonality.

It astounds me that my father felt so comfortable stepping into the homes of strangers—crossing Chicago's so-called color line—to ask deeply personal questions about their intimate lives. His fascination with interracial marriage, which was taboo at the time, had clearly begun when he was young, but what sparked it was a mystery to me.

Daddy was born in Chicago on August 17, 1915. Professionally, he went by Robert E. T. Roberts, but my mother and his friends simply called him Bob.

Among the items I found in the boxes was a book with a light blue cloth cover, titled *Baby's Life* in gold lettering. Published by Barse and Hopkins, its copyright dates to 1913. On the first page, a printed inscription reads "This Book Is a Record of the Baby Life of," followed by my father's full name, Robert Edward Thomas Roberts, handwritten in black ink. Inside, there's an old-fashioned illustration of a white baby with light hair, rosy cheeks, a thumb stuck between red lips. On the "Baby's Birth" page, someone recorded my father's birthplace as 3222 Dickens Avenue in Chicago and his birth weight as eight and a half pounds.

The "Mother's Notes" section provides small glimpses into his early life. His first bank account was opened at Illinois Trust and Savings Bank with a $10 deposit made by his uncle Paul Reinert. At just a month old, he took his first automobile ride to attend his mother's cousin's birthday party. His first word, "Dada," came at six months of age.

On the pages labeled "Family Tree," names are recorded all the way back to his great-grandparents on both sides.

I never met my grandparents on my father's side. Both had died before I was born, even before my parents were married. Daddy's father, Alfred Roberts, was Welsh and grew up in Devauden, a small bucolic village in Wales near the border with England. His family owned two homes there in the 1800s, one called "the Well," and the other "Beaufort House." I inherited a painting of one of the homes, which depicts a simple two-story house made of tan stone or stucco, featuring a slate roof, brick chimneys on both ends, three windows on the second floor, and two windows flanking the front door. Alfred, born in 1884, was the ninth child of Thomas Roberts, a stonemason and landowner, and Emily Morgan. Historical records locate his birthplace of Monmouthshire in either England or Wales. Daddy had once said something about Monmouthshire belonging for one hundred years to England and one hundred years to Wales. Even my father's pure British side is the subject of fuzzy boundaries.

As a teenager, Alfred left Devauden for Birmingham, England, to attend technical school and work as an apprentice in a photoengraving shop owned by his older sister's husband. Daddy told my sisters and me that his father, known as Alfie, was a star soccer player—what my father called a "footballer"—in England. I recall him saying that his father had played for the legendary team Aston Villa. That may have been apocryphal, for when I reported it to a professor from England I met at a conference, he told me the following day that he had checked the team's historical rosters and could find no Alfie Roberts on them. I suspected that this white professor couldn't believe that I, as a Black American, had a grandfather who played for a famous English soccer team. Roberts family lore also includes the story of Alfie shooting down an enemy plane with a rifle in Serbia during World War I. He was awarded a knife made from metal retrieved from the downed aircraft. The knife reportedly remains somewhere in the Roberts family.

When his brother-in-law sold the shop, Alfie, determined to find his fortune in America, made the transatlantic journey from Liverpool to New York in 1911. By the following year, he had settled in Chicago, where he swiftly secured a position as a photoengraver. I don't know much about my grandfather, except that he was a dedicated Mason and achieved the rank of commander, the highest office, in the Humboldt Park Commandery. This is corroborated by a large portrait passed down to me, depicting him in his Masons regalia. The jacket, embellished with medals and gold-threaded epaulets, along with the splendidly feathered hat, bears a striking resemblance to a British general's military uniform. On a cold winter day in 1944, when he was fifty-nine years old, Alfie returned home from work and collapsed, succumbing to a brain aneurysm.

The maternal side of my father's family was German. At the age of twenty, Daddy's grandmother, Dora Huch, my near namesake, set sail for New York from Hamburg with her family—Louis C. Huch, my great-great-grandfather; his wife, Louise; and their six children. The year was 1883. Louis had sold his tannery in Northeim with the aspiration of establishing a more profitable business in America. Among the heirlooms in my basement, I inherited the wooden chest that carried their belongings from Germany. Louis and his son George found work at a tannery in Chicago, where George befriended another German employee, Edward Reinert. Edward immigrated to the United States in the same year as the Huchs, arriving at the port of Baltimore from Bremen, Germany, aboard a ship named the SS *Braunschweig*. When Louis launched his own tannery business, Edward quit his job and went to work for him.

A frequent guest at the Huch home, Edward became close to Louis's oldest daughter, Dora. They tied the knot in the summer of 1890. Their daughters, twins like my sisters, were born two years later. One girl died at ten weeks; Johanna, my grandmother, survived. By 1907, Edward had saved enough money—perhaps with help from his father-in-law—to buy a solid graystone two-flat for the family. These sturdy two-story homes built of brick or graystone, with an apartment on each floor and bay windows overlooking the street, became a defining feature of European immigrant neighborhoods between 1900 and 1930, offering a foothold for families building new lives in the city. The dwelling, equipped with the modern conveniences of furnace heat and electric light, had recently been constructed on Wrightwood Avenue in the Logan Square neighborhood on Chicago's North Side. Established out of farmland in the mid-1800s, Logan Square attracted upwardly mobile Scandinavians and Germans like the Reinerts. This was the family home my father would live in until he married my mother.

Johanna was employed as a stenographer at the engraving company when Alfie came to work there. After they wed in 1914, Alfie and Johanna rented a five-room flat in Logan Square, where my father was born a year later. The family soon moved in with Johanna's parents on Wrightwood Avenue. So it was that my father, along with his younger brothers, Edward and Alfred, grew up in the Reinert household, which included their grandparents, Edward and Dora. On the first floor, where the children, their Welsh father, and their second-generation American mother resided, everyone spoke English. German was spoken on the second floor, where the immigrant grandparents lived.

Daddy would often regale my sisters and me with humorous stories about Dora, especially her struggles with the English language. He would burst into laughter after reciting the words she mangled, imitating her German accent. He told us that she called vitamins "wickateens." It was evident, though, that Daddy held the greatest affection for his grandmother. In a paper he wrote as a college student for Psychology 101, whose professor emphasized the importance of heredity, Daddy praised his seventy-one-year-old grandmother for her mental sharpness and loving nature. He wrote, "Whatever physical traits I may have inherited from her are assets, as her pep, endurance, and vitality are to be envied." It wasn't until I read my father's papers that I truly understood the meaning of my name. My father had told me as a child that I was named after our ancestor, Dora Huch, but I hadn't given it much thought. Now, knowing the name held a special significance drew me closer to my father. He had named me after the family member he cherished the most.

Raised in a bilingual household, my father spoke fluent German. In retrospect, I realize that German influenced my upbringing, too. Daddy used to recite jokes from his childhood that made witty uses of German words. For example, he often repeated a funny phrase that went along with flushing the toilet: *bitteschön, dankeschön*, pull the chain! When anyone sneezed in our house, the response was "*Gesundheit!*"—Health! My sisters and I learned to pronounce German words correctly. To this day, we say Volkswagen the way Germans do—*Folksvagen*. Daddy taught us several German children's songs. I can still recite my favorite lyrics in German.

Mein Hut, der hat drei Ecken,
Drei Ecken hat mein Hut,
Und hätt er nicht drei Ecken,
So wär es nicht mein Hut.

When I was in eighth grade, I enrolled in a German-language course at Kenwood High School and took early-morning classes before the start of my regular school day. I learned rudimentary German that year, but didn't continue to study the language, replacing it with French and Spanish in high school and college. All I remember now is the alliterative request *"Gib mir bitte das Brot und die Butter"* (Please pass the bread and the butter), probably because, unusual for German, it flows rhythmically off the tongue. I enjoyed learning a new language, and the pleasure I felt in speaking in a different tongue lasted into my adulthood. I don't recall thinking that learning German had anything to do with my heritage, though. Perhaps because I never met my paternal grandmother, I didn't think of myself as being part German. The German that accented my childhood was but one of many, many flavors in the smorgasbord of cultures that marked our Kenwood home.

Besides, Mommy preferred French and also taught my sisters and me phrases in that language. One of the first books she read to us was *La Vache Curieuse* (*The Curious Cow*), written in French, about a cow whose inquisitiveness gets her in lots of trouble. As with the German songs, we could recite all the words like little Parisians.

I try to imagine what my father's childhood community was like. Logan Square was a landing spot for immigrants arriving from Europe like his Welsh father and German grandparents, as well as assimilated ethnic Americans like his mother, in the early twentieth century. The neighborhood was on the white side of Chicago's infamous color line, the violently patrolled boundary dividing Black and white residents of the city. A *Local Community Fact Book* on Chicago reported that in 1930 there were only 19 Negroes and 67 people of Other Races living in Logan Square out of a population of 114,174.

My father probably had no Black friends, classmates, or neighbors when he was a boy. His high school yearbooks display photos of white students exclusively. The only Black individuals he would have encountered were likely servants. I wonder what he absorbed about Black people as a child. If anything, he probably heard disparaging stereotypes about them from the adults around him. The dominant images of Black women, men, and children at the time depicted us as lazy, stupid, and incompetent. The Mason lodge that my grandfather commanded most certainly excluded Black people. As historian Lynn Dumenil writes about white Masons from 1880 to 1930, "Not only did Masonry not admit blacks, but Grand

Lodges also denied that Prince Hall Masonry, a black Masonic order that had existed since 1774, was an authentic part of Masonry."

The decade into which my father was born was marked by a campaign of white terror designed to uphold the city's racist hierarchy and segregated landscape. Daddy was one month shy of his fourth birthday when the Chicago Race Riot of 1919 erupted. On Sunday, July 27 of that year, a Black teenager named Eugene Williams drifted across the invisible racial dividing line while swimming at Rainbow Beach. White men and boys, enraged by Eugene entering the whites-only section of the water, hurled rocks at him, causing him to fall off his makeshift raft and drown.

The murder ignited one of the bloodiest race riots in U.S. history. A police officer at the scene ignored demands by Black eyewitnesses to arrest a white man they identified as one of the rock throwers. Instead, he arrested one of the Black beachgoers. When Black residents protested the authorities' failure to arrest the perpetrators, white mobs retaliated by attacking Black communities, destroying homes and businesses. Black residents, including servicemen who had recently returned from fighting in World War I, defended their communities. Over seven days of violence, with tensions lingering long after, thirty-eight people were killed—twenty-three Black and fifteen white—hundreds more were injured, mostly Black, and thousands of Black residents were made homeless by arson. That summer, which saw similar outbursts of white terror across the nation, became known as the Red Summer.

Interracial romance had made sensational news in Chicago when my father was young. Jack Johnson, the first Black heavyweight champion, flaunted his celebrity with fancy cars, jewelry, and white women. His match with Jim Jeffries, who promised to "win back the title for the white race," became a well-publicized racial contest, dubbed "the Fight of the Century." Jeffries earned the moniker "the Great White Hope," which was adopted as the title of a 1967 play and 1970 movie, both starring James Earl Jones. On Independence Day 1910, the match drew more than twenty thousand spectators in Reno, and Americans across the country gathered at taverns to follow blow-by-blow reports via telegraph. Johnson defeated Jeffries in a fifteenth-round technical knockout. His victory triggered America's first nationwide race riot, as white men attacked Black celebrants in cities across the country, including Chicago.

In 1912, Johnson's marriage to white socialite Etta Terry Duryea sparked a new round of racial tensions in Chicago. The boxer returned one evening to the apartment they shared above his Café de Champion to find her dying from a self-inflicted gunshot wound to the head. While the Black-owned *Chicago Defender* offered some sympathy, the white *Chicago Tribune* blamed Johnson, accusing him of beating up his wife and tearing her away from her family and friends. Public outrage against Johnson intensified when within two months he began an affair with another white woman, Lucille Cameron, a nineteen-year-old whom the Chicago press sensationally branded as a prostitute. A mob hung him in effigy from a lamppost in downtown Chicago.

When the Black Appomattox Club subjected Johnson to an inquisition, he remained defiant. "I do want to say that I am not a slave and that I have a right to choose who my mate will be without dictation from any man," a witness reported him declaring. With the cooperation of a white former girlfriend, Belle Schreiber, federal prosecutors secured Johnson's conviction in 1913 under the Mann Act, known as the White-Slave Traffic Act of 1910, passed by Congress to criminalize trafficking of women, for transporting her across state lines. After seven years on the run, Johnson surrendered in July 1920 and was held in Leavenworth Prison for nearly a year.

The fury that white residents were unleashing in Chicago streets over Black encroachment on their property, beaches, and women must have reached my father's impressionable consciousness. Did his parents take the side of their white neighbors? Or did they express compassion for the Black people under attack? I wonder if the animosity many Americans directed against German immigrants during World War I might have shaped their attitudes. According to historian Frederick Luebke, after the United States declared war on Germany in 1917, "citizens of German origin were individually harassed and persecuted, German ethnic organizations were attacked, and serious efforts were made to eliminate German language and culture in the United States." A landmark U.S. Supreme Court case, *Meyer v. Nebraska*, decided in 1923, struck down the Nebraska Foreign Language Act of 1919, which prohibited teaching German in public schools. My father told my sisters and me that the church his grandparents attended stopped holding services in German after World War I.

An especially heinous act of anti-German violence occurred in 1918 when Robert Prager, a German immigrant, was lynched in Collinsville, Illinois, by a group of drunken men who falsely accused him of being a spy. I can imagine that the prejudice, discrimination, and attacks against Germans evoked empathy in the ethnically mixed Roberts-Reinert household toward the Black victims of injustice. But I can just as easily imagine that the family's unified white identity blocked any sense of camaraderie with the city's Black residents.

Daddy's brother Edward eventually developed dramatically different views about Black people compared to my father. Their differences were so pronounced that, as already noted, Edward disowned my father when he married Mommy, having nothing to do with our family. My father's other brother, Alfred, served as best man at my parents' wedding. I met Uncle Alfred, along with two of his children—my blond-haired cousins, Tommy and Tracey, twins who were born the same year as my sisters. While we weren't very close, they occasionally visited our house for my parents' backyard parties. From old photos of my father and Edward in their twenties, it is clear they once had a strong bond. In one picture, my father is embracing two of Edward's little boys—cousins I never even knew existed as a child.

When I was invited to lecture at the University of Oregon, I decided to reach out to one of Edward's sons—my cousin Bill, a neuroscientist at the university. His initial response was "I don't have a cousin named Dorothy." Once I explained our connection, he invited me to his home. When I arrived, a massive banner protesting the Iraq War hung across the front of the house. He greeted me at the door with an unguarded hug, as if no distance stood between us. Dressed in jeans and a T-shirt, with his hair tied back in a ponytail, he gave off a hippie vibe. I was struck by the uncanny resemblance to my father—and by how different he was from his own.

Among my father's papers, I found a card dated August 1980, with a handwritten message:

Birthday greetings to you, brother Bob. Our respective careers have progressed to a time where we can look back and sense some measure of accomplishment. But in life all is not sunshine—there are less pleasant situations too—the circumstances that have kept us apart for many years. I'm sorry to say that I have not yet been able to resolve these matters in my own mind and most likely never will. My position must be a reflection of early associations which are difficult if not impossible to erase. I trust that you can understand my feelings. I have always admired your sincerity, honesty and your ability to do what you believe in—along with your many other fine qualities. Best wishes for the future. Ed.

Those words were likely the first Daddy received from his brother in twenty-five years. Edward died from a brain tumor three years later. I don't recall the brothers having any contact with each other before Edward became fatally ill and my father visited him in the hospital. Perhaps the awareness of his impending death compelled Edward to seek as much of a reconciliation as his prejudices allowed. What strikes me most is his claim that their opposing perspectives stemmed from "early associations," formative experiences so indelible they drove a permanent wedge between brothers. Those experiences might have occurred during the era of white terror gripping Chicago. If so, why did my father emerge from it so profoundly different from his brother? A clue might lie in these boxes.

Aunt Ella, Daddy's maternal aunt, married a missionary named Paul Rostad. I remember meeting Uncle Paul when I was little. I have a black-and-white photo of him standing next to my mother before I was born, his arm linked affectionately in hers. The couple ran a mission in a village called Churachandpur in the hilly region of Manipur, in India's farthest northeast corner, bordering Burma and the Himalayas.

On August 17, 1931, his sixteenth birthday, my father embarked with his grandmother Dora on a voyage to India to visit her missionary daughter, Ella. Daddy had already graduated from high school that summer. The trip was what we now call a gap year before he started college. They spent six months living at the mission in Churachandpur. On their way to India and on their return to Chicago, my father traversed the globe with Dora, making stops in Shanghai, Hong Kong, Kyoto, Singapore, Manila, Colombo, Rangoon, Cairo, Jerusalem, Paris, Naples, and Berlin. I imagine Dora could afford such an extravagant trip with money from her father Louis Huch's tannery business, which had passed down to his sons upon his death in 1909.

Among my father's papers, I discover a folder with keepsakes from his year abroad. A brochure with a picture of a large ship and a sailboat on the cover proclaims in bold black type "$1295.00 ROUND THE WORLD/ CRUISE-TOURS/ DOLLAR STEAMSHIP LINES AND THOS. COOK & SON." Inside, the opening message tantalizes: "A journey of everlasting memories, of impressions never to be stamped from the mind. Too many of us have not seen them." The voyage must have made an indelible impression on my teenage father as promised.

There are three booklets labeled *Guest List* on the cover and titled *THE LOG of the President Liners to and* from *the Orient and Round* the *World* on the inside, one for each leg of the journey. The third booklet is for the SS *President Adams*, sailing from Bombay, April 8, 1932, with Dora and Robert listed under "Naples." Inside the booklet is a page from an old newspaper, the *Berlin News*, aged to the color of mustard. Its date, May 22, must be from 1932. The first column bears the headline "Americans in Berlin." I scan it for my father's and great-grandmother's names.

> Mrs. Dora Reinert and Robert Roberts arrived in Berlin recently after a trip to India, where Mrs. Reinert visited her daughter. She is now on her way to her old home in southern Germany. "We had a wonderful trip around the world," stated Mrs. Reinert when she registered.

The folder also contains a three-ring notebook with a cover page inscribed, "DIARY OF MY TRIP TO INDIA AND AROUND THE WORLD, August 17, 1931–June 4, 1932, by Robert E. T. Roberts." I can hardly believe my good fortune. Inside are yellowed three-hole pages with typed daily entries, beginning on the first day of the journey—the train ride from Chicago to San Francisco, where he and Dora boarded the SS *President Fillmore*. As the ship pulled away from the pier, the stewards passed out colorful paper streamers to the passengers on deck to be thrown toward the shore. "The hundreds of colored streamers floating in the air made a pretty sight as we left San Francisco," my father wrote.

Daddy meticulously chronicled his activities on board practically by the hour every day. He played ping-pong, shuffleboard, miniature golf, dominoes, and card games like Michigan rummy, poker, and pinochle with other passengers, mostly a girl named Helen. I wonder if my sister Helen was named after the girl he befriended at sea. He read detective stories and the *Radio News*, a folder distributed each day with reports on world events, baseball scores, and stock market prices; conversed with passengers and sailors; and stood at the bow to look for flying fish. He had a penchant for "talking pictures," like *Dishonored* starring Marlene Dietrich, viewing two or three every day, often going to another deck to watch one a second time. He seemed to be attuned to world news, mentioning, for example, discussing the fighting in Manchuria between Japan and China with another passenger. He bought newspapers, presumably written in English, at every port. His mother sent him a package of Chicago newspapers while he was living in India.

In his travel diary, I glimpse early signs of the investigative nature that propelled my father's interracial marriage research. He spent one afternoon helping the sailors perform a chore, had a lengthy conversation with the ship's doctor, who was from India and took my father to his office to show off his athletic medals, and asked the ship's electrician to take him to the engine room so he could see how the ship was powered. "We went down several flights of stairs and finally came to the furnaces where steam was being made," he wrote on a Saturday. "We also saw the ice plant and the water tanks. We then went to the stern and saw the screws which make the propellers turn. It was very hot in the engine room and I was glad to get back on deck."

My father detailed sightseeing with his grandmother at stops in Hawaii, Japan, China, and the Philippines. I search for a radical awakening in his entries, some epiphany my father experienced as he encountered people who weren't white like him, but I find only matter-of-fact observations. "We went through the country and the suburbs of Manila. Most of the native houses were on stilts and had thatched roofs. The chief crops seem to be rice and there are rice fields all over the country." Or "At 8:00 A.M. grandmother and I went out for a walk. The streets of Kyoto are crowded with bicycles. There are many more bicycles than automobiles in Japan." Or "Most of the people in Singapore are Chinese. There are also many Malayans and Indians. Most of the houses have thatched roofs. The Malayans who are fishermen catch fish in traps." I sense that even before this journey, my father had already developed a curiosity and openness that prepared him to imbibe the flurry of interactions with cultures so different from his own without the slightest indication that he found them strange or forbidding.

When Daddy and his grandmother arrived in Calcutta, they were greeted by his uncle and aunt. "Aunt Ella gave me a beautiful hand-woven bag which is a present from Thankai who is the interpreter at Chura-chandpur," he wrote. "The bag hangs over the shoulder and is used by the natives to carry their things in when they go out on a hike." He was perfectly happy to carry the bag over his shoulder as the "natives" did. As he traveled from Calcutta to Churachandpur, he described the Indian customs he witnessed with similar equanimity. Sacred cows roaming the streets and goats being slaughtered for sacrifice; men bathing in the muddy Ganges river and collecting some of the water to take back to their homes; snake charmers, magicians, and hypnotists performing in the street; sharing a berth with an Indian stranger on an overcrowded train, where reservations were disregarded; animal skulls hitched on poles at a village entrance to keep evil spirits away; Churachandpur boys sitting barefoot on the floor and scooping out handfuls of rice from a large bowl set between them, which they mixed with bits of fish and vegetables. He observed that he saw a white person other than his aunt and uncle only twice while living in the Indian village.

One entry, on a Sunday in 1931, stands out. That morning, my father accompanied his grandmother, aunt, and uncle to church. Uncle Paul delivered the sermon, which a local preacher translated into Lushei, one of the village's dialects. Afterward, a crowd of about thirty villagers gathered at the house to listen to phonograph records Aunt Ella played for them, a popular form of entertainment my father also enjoyed. He retired to his room after lunch.

In the afternoon while I was reading Treasure Island a Paihte boy, Henkai, knocked on my door. He entered my room and gave me a nice hand-woven cloth made by his sister. It was about five feet long and three feet wide. Cloths like these are used by the hill people as shawls or skirts (on the men). I thanked Henkai for the gift and gave him some chocolate. Then I played the ukulele and sang songs for him. Henkai told me that he wanted to learn English better so I let him read a book and corrected his pronunciation of words.

One of my father's prized possessions when I was growing up was a sheet of cotton fabric, tan with a brown geometric design, that he had brought back from India. He used to wear it around the house, wrapped around his waist, his chest bare, when he was lounging at home on hot summer days. I suspect that treasured cloth was the one that Henkai gave him.

According to the diary, Daddy continued to help Henkai practice his English by reading *Treasure Island* and American magazines together. In exchange, he began to teach my father Paihte, his native tongue. Daddy also showed Henkai and other village boys how to play baseball, using a wooden bat that Henkai had fashioned from a branch cut down from a tree. He organized a game with five players on each side. "The boys seemed to like baseball," my father reported.

The typed entries end on Saturday, December 5, 1931. That day, my father was joined by one of the Indian boys as he gathered nuts outside for his pet parrot. He played soccer with Henkai and other pals from the village. In the evening, he entertained about thirty men from the mission who were attending a tea party at Paul and Ella's house, playing phono-graph records and singing along to his ukulele. "Then I played 'Caro Nome' from *Rigoletto* on the phonograph," he wrote. "While Galli-Curci was singing on the record I sang the same notes to the amusement of the men." I had no idea my father had such musical—and comical—talents. Tucked in the back of the notebook are two notepads with my father's practically indecipherable scrawl recording events in 1932. I guess he tired of typing up his notes.

Later, in a college essay, my father wrote that what impressed him most about India were "the beauties of nature, the hardiness of the people, freedom from war and strife, primitive kindness and hospitality, and no worry about unemployment." I am convinced that his six months living in Churachandpur is what put him decidedly on the path toward a career in anthropology, sparking his interest in racial caste and curiosity about human diversity—though I can't tell if he had yet questioned the mission's colonial and religious underpinnings. Half a century later, he returned to India as a Fulbright senior lecturer, accompanied by my mother, to teach at the University of Rajasthan. On their way back, they traced the same journey around the world that Daddy had taken with his grandmother, their last overseas excursion as husband and wife.

In November 1922, when my father was seven years old, my mother, Iris Rosalie White, was born in Jones Pen, later renamed Jones Town, on the Caribbean island of Jamaica. We were never sure which day in November to mark as her birthday. She told us that she was born around midnight on November 22 and her father told the clerk the wrong date, but it was not clear if the correct date was the twenty-second or the twenty-third. We were celebrating Mommy's birthday when we heard the news that President John F. Kennedy had been killed, which was on November 22, 1963.

Jones Pen was a thriving corner of Kingston, Jamaica's capital, when my mother was growing up, a neighborhood where lovely homes, often owned by Black Jamaicans, lined the streets. From the way she spoke lovingly about her childhood house, I believe her parents owned theirs.

The area was renowned for its artisans—dressmakers, tailors, milliners, and carpenters—who fashioned refined clothing and handcrafted furniture. My grandparents were among them. A midwife delivered babies for the community, while rum bars run by Chinese businessmen offered spaces of respite after long days of work. Over time, economic and political shifts, along with waves of migration to Europe, Canada, and the United States, frayed the oasis in the city. As one Jamaican journalist later wrote, it left "homes to become tenement yards."

My mother's father, Alexander Nathaniel White, was born in St. Mary Parish on the northeast side of Jamaica in February 1891 to Francis White and Caroline Hamilton. Her mother, Rebecca Smith, was born diagonally across the island in St. Elizabeth, on the southwest side, on Christmas Day 1894. Her parents' names were George Smith and Jane Campbell. I suspect my grandparents met and married in St. Andrew Parish, where Kingston is located. Mommy had five siblings, an older sister, Violet, and the younger Carmen, Alfred, Carlton, and Herbert, whom we called Uncle Bertie. She also told us about two sisters—one named Ivy, who died before she was born, and Marion, the youngest, who succumbed to typhoid—and a beloved little brother called Neville, who died when a wheelbarrow he and his brothers were playing with fell on him, leaving a bad cut on his leg. Mommy said the boys weren't supposed to be playing, so hid the cut from their parents. The wound became infected and eventually caused his death. Now thinking about the story, I wonder if Mommy exaggerated some parts of it to impress on my sisters and me the potentially fatal dangers of disobedience.

I knew my grandparents on my mother's side. They lived with us in Kenwood for two years, when I was between eleven and thirteen. My mother called them Dada and Mama. They were a lopsided pair, Grandpa, wire-thin, stern, straight-backed. He always looked like he was standing at attention. Grandma was plump and cheerful with a ready smile and generous spirit. Dressed simply in a cotton frock, she stood wider and taller than her mate. My mother got her slender figure from her father, her height from her mother, and her dark brown skin from both. Mommy told me she weighed only ninety-nine pounds when she met Daddy and used to drink half-and-half to put on extra weight. As she got older, she veered more toward her mother's physique, never losing her graceful appearance. Grandma and Grandpa had the African features and salt-of-the-earth disposition of couples in black-and-white photographs of Black people in the American South emerging from slavery and sharecropping.

My maternal grandparents, Rebecca and Alexander White, at our Kenwood house, c. 1968

As an adolescent, I didn't think to ask my grandparents about my Jamaican ancestors. I have no excuse for failing to ask my mother as an adult about what she remembered of her grandparents. So, I know nothing about the generations on my Jamaican side that preceded Mama and Dada. From 1655, when the British took control of the island, until slavery was abolished in 1838, most Jamaicans of African descent were enslaved—which means my mother's great-grandparents may have been born in bondage.

My grandfather was a cabinetmaker, another word for carpenter, though the former serves better, for he built beautiful pieces of furniture out of wood. My grandmother was a skilled dressmaker who sewed garments for her family as well as for customers. From what I can tell, Mommy had a happy childhood. Whenever she got together with her brothers and sisters, my Jamaican aunts and uncles, their favorite pastime was to repeat words of wisdom their parents would say, savor memories of Mama's delicious meals and meticulously sewn shirts and dresses, and recall Dada's remarkable woodworking skill. I never saw my mother laugh so hard as when she was reminiscing about Jamaica with my aunts.

When my grandparents came to live with us, my parents prepared special places to make them feel at home. They set up a woodworking shop for Grandpa in the basement, where my sisters and I sometimes sat beside him, watching as he crafted intricate furniture for the house. Grandma claimed a side of the kitchen table for her sewing—outfitted with a modern sewing machine and an ironing board—where she softly hummed hymns as she created clothing for the family. As a child prone to headaches, I remember how Grandma would gently anoint my forehead with oil and murmur prayers over me. "You don't have a headache because you lack aspirin," she'd say. To her, healing came from faith and touch, not pills.

My grandparents belonged to another era—not ones to engage in long talks with children. Though I loved them dearly, we never shared the kind of closeness I now enjoy with my oldest granddaughter. Their love showed in what they made for us—jewelry boxes with finely inlaid wood from Grandpa, and soft cotton housecoats tailored to fit from Grandma.

At some point after my mother left Jamaica, her parents had become Seventh-day Adventists. They were strict adherents to the doctrine and followed many of the Old Testament rules religiously. They kept the real Sabbath day, and my father would drive them to church on Saturday mornings. My mother could no longer prepare foods that the Mosaic law forbids. I knew that Orthodox Jews refused pork, but learned that creatures that ate from the bottom of the ocean were also considered unclean. My mother stopped cooking shrimp. My father had to give up bacon.

Two of my cousins on my mother's side had been raised by my grandparents in Jamaica. My cousin Edwin, Aunt Carmen's son, and my cousin Neville, the son of my uncle Alfred in Toronto, grew up together under my grandparents' care. Sending children away to spend their childhoods with relatives "back home" was a common practice in the Jamaican immigrant community. It gave the parents who had immigrated to the United States or Canada or England more freedom to work long hours at multiple jobs. The grandparents received a steady income from remittances sent by their children working hard across the sea. I suppose that was a fair bargain. But I remember thinking how lucky I was that my parents hadn't sent me away. Edwin told us frightening stories of life under the strict discipline that our grandparents enforced. Having to get up early to do grueling chores. Obeying their commands without grumbling or talking back. Enduring harsh punishments for what seemed to be minor infractions.

Although my mother retained some aspects of the strict child-rearing approach she learned in Jamaica, I was relieved she forsook the custom of sending children back home.

As a young child, my mother was an exceptional student. She earned coveted admission to the prestigious Wolmer's Preparatory School and Wolmer's High School for Girls in Kingston, whose origins date back to 1729. That year, John Wolmer, a white goldsmith, bequeathed most of his estate for the establishment of a free school open to Jamaican students regardless of race, class, or gender. Its motto, "Age quod agis," a Latin phrase meaning "Do well whatever you do," perfectly captures my mother's approach to life. At Wolmer's, she received a first-class British education that rivaled the best schools in London. Her studies included British and European history, mathematics, botany, French, Latin, and Scripture. That must be where she got her melodious accent—a lovely blend of British and Caribbean tones. She spoke with the precise enunciation of the Queen's English, softened by the charm of a delightful West Indian lilt.

Growing up, there was no historical event, no esoteric word, no natural phenomenon I brought to my mother that would not elicit a crystal clear explanation. She could help with every homework assignment, no matter the subject. Whenever I learned something new in elementary school, Mommy would claim she had learned it at Wolmer's when she was much younger. She could recite entire sonnets by the British poets Wordsworth, Keats, and Shelley. In her final years, weakened by a stroke, when she frequently confused which city she was in or what she'd had for breakfast, she would recall all six stanzas of Alfred, Lord Tennyson's "The Charge of the Light Brigade" she'd memorized as a child in Jamaica. *Theirs not to make reply, / Theirs not to reason why, / Theirs but to do and die.* She would chuckle at the absurdity of Jamaican schoolchildren forced to repeat poems written by Englishmen about snow.

Mommy's intellectual prowess was demonstrated daily in her invincible skill at word games and puzzles, which were her favorite hobbies. She completed the *Chicago Tribune* crossword puzzle every evening after dinner with remarkable alacrity. In hard-fought family Scrabble contests, she was the inevitable victor, winning with a word unfamiliar even to my father, but proven accurate when we checked the dictionary. She would have been delighted, I mused, when I learned I was the answer to the clue in a crossword puzzle: 42 across, author of *Shattered Bonds: The Color of Child Welfare*, in the *New Yorker* on June 28, 2023.

One night, before going to bed, I signed up for Ancestry.com on a whim. I stayed up until two in the morning clicking on the leaves called hints that promised to reveal records about my ancestors. Like magic, records appeared detailing my father's lineage. Among them was a photo of my paternal grandfather, grandmother, great-grandmother, and uncle uploaded by one of my Welsh relatives. I don't recall ever seeing a photo of my grandmother before that moment, though my sisters remember my father showing us a wedding photo of his parents. I liked how she looked—diminutive, chubby, and kind. She seemed to embody the tenderness of a loving mother, and I found myself imagining the bond she shared with my father. Until that night, I hadn't given much thought to their relationship—or to hers with me.

From right: my paternal grandparents, Alfie and Johanna Roberts; great-grandmother, Dora Reinert; and uncle Alfred Roberts, Chicago, c. 1942

Later, I discovered five photos of her with Uncle Edward's firstborn son. In one of them, she stands with Uncle Edward, who is holding the baby boy, while she looks on with admiration. The inscription on the back reads "Milwaukee Fair, Aug. 10, 1948." In the other photos, she is alone with the infant, holding him lovingly on her lap, both looking happy. I could see her sweet smile more clearly. It felt such a shame that the prejudice she harbored had kept my parents from marrying sooner—and perhaps from giving her the chance to hold her oldest son's first daughter.

The website turned up no records at all about my mother's ancestry. Only a single document surfaced—Mommy's petition for naturalization as a U.S. citizen in 1961. Online, it was my father's side—the side that had been muted all my life—that suddenly rose into focus, while my mother's side, so central to my childhood, barely left a trace.

Passport photo of my father, Robert Roberts, and his grandmother Dora Reinert, 1931

CHAPTER 2

The Master's Student

Robert (Bob) Roberts, c. 1937

Mr. and Mrs. Alberts
February 25, 1937

Morning light spills across the study as I finish reading my father's interview with Mrs. Alberts. From across the hall, the neighbors' big black Lab barks—his signal that it's time for a walk. Clipped to the first transcript is another, its pages just as fragile with age, this one labeled with both spouses' names. I slip into the kitchen for another cup of tea, then return to the study, ready to see what unfolds next.

As promised, my father returned to the Alberts's apartment the following week to interview the couple together. It would be the second of four visits he made to the Alberts home between February and April that year. This time, he brought along his friend and colleague Mike, *who was interested in Negro-white mixture from the point of view of physical anthropology.* Mike carried with him several instruments *to take anthropological measurements.* I picture a black doctor's bag filled with calipers and a small scale, harkening back to the days of phrenology and to Samuel Morton's collection of crania to measure racial differences in intellectual capacity. It conjures up the scene in Quentin Tarantino's film *Django Unchained,* when the vicious enslaver played by Leonardo DiCaprio holds an enslaved person's skull in his hands. I'm relieved that my father distinguished his interest in the sociological aspects of interracial marriage from Mike's concentration on its corporeal dimensions.

The two researchers were admitted into the apartment. Once inside, my father encountered Mr. Alberts face-to-face—*a colored man with apparently about fifty percent of white blood. His features were about half white and half Negro, his hair was rather curly, black, and grown long, and his color was tan.* He was dressed "poorly" in an old sweater and dirty overalls. My father observed many people milling around the apartment. *During the entire two hours I spent there the room was filled with from about eight to a dozen persons, all of these individuals were obviously colored. They were of all ages and, from time to time, some left the room and others entered.*

In due course, my father discovered that the cast of characters were all part of the Alberts household. Mr. and Mrs. Alberts and their three children, Raymond, four, Ronald, three, and Robert, thirteen months (I assume my father assigned them these alliterative names); Mr. Alberts's mother-in-law from a prior marriage; the mother-in-law's husband; and two children from his prior marriage—Rosemary, thirteen, and Roberta, fifteen. Roberta was already married and her husband also lived in the apartment. The pieces were fitting together. The children with no trace of "Negroid blood," whom my father met on his first visit, were the ones born to the current, white Mrs. Alberts. The two older colored children he saw had been born to the first wife, who had died, and must have been colored, too, as was her mother.

I try to make sense of the cacophony of ages, races, and kinship ties crammed together in the Alberts's apartment. It occurs to me that their extended family was living in one of the tenement flats that journalist Isabel Wilkerson describes in *The Warmth of Other Suns,* her Pulitzer Prize–winning book chronicling the Great Migration. She recounts the living conditions faced by Ida Mae Brandon Gladney, a Black migrant from Mississippi, upon her arrival on the South Side of Chicago in August 1938—the same time my father was interviewing Black migrants with white spouses. With thousands of Black southerners seeking housing in an increasingly segregated city, Wilkerson writes, "[m]any rooms sat airless and windowless, packed with so many people that some roomers had to sleep in shifts."

The bedroom and living room were one combined space. My father sat on the bed, which doubled as a couch, next to Mrs. Alberts. He explained to Mr. Alberts the research project that occasioned his visit in greater detail than he had to Mrs. Alberts. To my surprise, he did not identify it as a study focused on interracial marriage. Instead, he told the couple, "We are testing relationships to find out if we have a caste system here in Chicago as was found in Natchez, Mississippi."

I find it fascinating that my father called the racial hierarchy in Chicago a "caste system" and that he compared the system in the North to the one in the South. I imagine that his year living in a village in India, where caste structured social relationships, helped him to view racism in America similarly and to recognize its presence in Chicago. Understanding how caste in India dictated suitable marriage partners may have sparked his interest in exploring the connection between interracial marriage—and its prohibition—and this system of racial domination.

My father had gone to college without his parents' financial support. Unable to afford an elite college's tuition, he had enrolled in the humble Central YMCA College. At first, he worked in the Reinert tannery during the day and attended classes at night. I suspect it was in college where my father first became acquainted with Black people. When Central YMCA College closed in 1945, a quarter of the student body was Black and a third was Jewish.

From the time he arrived at college at age seventeen, Daddy had been questioning dominant views about race. In the essay he wrote during his first year for Psychology 101, he opposed the professor's views about the importance of inherited traits in determining psychological fitness. Recognizing that his ancestry as far back as could be traced was northern European, my father dispelled the popular opinion that "the Nordic sub-race is mentally superior to any other group." "If this were true (I think the idea of Nordic innate superiority is false), the mere fact that I belonged to the superior group would give me a decided advantage over the members of other racial groups," he wrote.

Instead, he went on to discredit the myth of inherited superiority. "It is very probable that, being of German-English ancestry, I will be favored in many ways over persons actually my equal in every way, because of discrimination against persons of non-Nordic and, particularly of non-European ancestry." He added, "Being male will also give me certain privileges not accorded to women." I sit with this for a moment, letting the words sink in. My father—a white teenager living long before the civil rights and feminist movements were mainstream—was already writing about his white male privilege.

Along with the psychology paper, I find a handwritten draft of an essay that may have been part of his college application or another assignment for the course. He wrote that he planned to major in sociology and anthropology and to teach as his career. He concluded by asserting that hatred, militarism, and patriotism were threatening to cause another world war, and he recommended several ideals that would make the world a better place. After extolling honesty and rational thought, he wrote: "Next, all racial and nationality prejudices must be eliminated. Men should be judged only on their individual merits. Nationalism and patriotism should succumb to world peace ideals. Militarism should be ended and trade barriers lifted." His eloquent expression of his humanitarian principles at such an early age continues to amaze me.

Graduating in just three years with a BA in sociology, my father began his graduate studies in the University of Chicago's anthropology department in 1936 at age twenty-one. He was one of twenty graduate students, most of them white, serving as primary investigators on the first large-scale sociological study of a Black community in the North. The research team was led by Lloyd Warner, a University of Chicago anthropology professor, and Horace R. Cayton Jr., a Black sociologist who had taught at Fisk University and was employed by the federal WPA, which funded the project.

Originally intended to study juvenile delinquency in Black neighborhoods, the Cayton-Warner project expanded into a comprehensive investigation of racial discrimination and Black culture in the city, running from 1935 to 1940. The project employed more than 150 people, including administrative staff, typists, and statisticians, in addition to the graduate student investigators. Among the investigators was St. Clair Drake, the renowned Black anthropologist, who would become my father's lifelong friend and closest colleague at Roosevelt College (renamed Roosevelt University in 1954). The interviews collected during the project, including those conducted by my father, served as the foundation for Drake's classic book, *Black Metropolis*, coauthored with Cayton.

My father joined the Cayton-Warner research team shortly after arriving on campus. It must have been exhilarating to step into a research project so closely aligned with the perspectives he had developed during his time in India and college. I can see him eagerly seizing the opportunity to conduct fieldwork on racism, caste, and interracial marriage. Likewise, Professor Warner—one of the first anthropologists to conceptualize race as a form of caste—must have been thrilled to hire a graduate student who already had such relevant experiences and insights. My father was preparing to become an unconventional anthropologist for his time, focusing on inequitable social structures in a major U.S. city rather than on so-called "exotic" cultures abroad. I think he diverged even further from traditional anthropology than his professors, for his goal wasn't just to study these inequities but to end them. He wasn't simply examining the taboo against interracial marriage as a symptom of Chicago's racial caste system—he was investigating interracial marriage as a potential means to dismantle that system entirely.

It also occurs to me that his probing about the Mannasses Club might have stemmed as much from his own curiosity about interracial relationships as from the research assignment he was given. I wonder if his specific focus on Black-white marriages was his own initiative or an existing part of the project. As I reflect further on his interest in the Mannasses Club, another possibility emerges: Was Daddy seeking out the interracial club for more personal reasons? Perhaps he wanted to find a space where Black and white people mingled freely—a space he could explore for himself. Regardless, he chose a strategic site to study America's racial caste system. His very first interviews with Mr. and Mrs. Alberts already revealed how exploring interracial intimacy can shed light on state mechanisms for enforcing racial hierarchies, as well as how individuals' private choices can either perpetuate or challenge them.

Mr. Alberts, who would be thirty-eight in April, was born in St. Paul, Minnesota, in 1899. He told my father that his parents left him with another family, but didn't say why. Maybe they were too poor to care for him. Or, given my father's description of his biracial appearance, he might have been the product of a mixed-race romance that had to be hidden. Mr. Alberts ended up in a school for dependent children, from which a woman retrieved him at age eleven, with nothing more than a promise that she would give him $500 and two suits when he turned eighteen. "She indentured me out," Mr. Alberts said. He ran away a year later, eventually coming to Chicago on his own in 1916. Working during the day and going to school at night, he completed his high school education. When World War I broke out, he enlisted in the army as a mechanist's mate, but when he was assigned to be a mess cook, he walked away, going AWOL. "I knew my rights and I refused to be bullied," he told my father defiantly. Now he worked for the streets department collecting garbage.

When my father resumed his inquiry into the Mannasses Club, Mr. Alberts, like his wife, had no information to offer. Regarding Chicago's racial caste system, however, Mr. Alberts had much to say. He launched into impassioned accounts of the racism he encountered in Chicago despite the city's lack of official segregation as was enforced under Jim Crow laws. "I would say there's more prejudice up here than in the South, only they don't let you know about it," he told my father. "The only difference between the way they treat a Negro in the North and in the South is that they're honest about it in the South."

Mr. Alberts posited an interesting take on northern hypocrisy. "On the streetcars, in the theaters, and all over they have a place where colored people know they can go," he said, referring to the southern form of segregation. "Here you can go almost anywhere and sit where you please if you stand up for your rights, but they let you know you are not welcome."

He borrowed from his experience working on segregated railroads in the South to illustrate his point. "Down there a colored person can always sit in the place reserved for him in the streetcars," he elaborated. "Here you can sit any place you want to, but they may step on your toe in the streetcar to let you know that you're a nigger."

Mr. Alberts then gave examples of unofficial segregation in downtown Chicago. "Suppose I take a notion tonight to take in Wayne King's orchestra. They have to let me in because we have a law that forbids them to bar me. But do you think they'd welcome me?" he asked rhetorically. "Or suppose I go to the Canton's teahouse for something to eat. They might make me wait and then serve my meal cold. They'll probably spit on the steak first."

Mr. Alberts spoke angrily against other forms of racial discrimination in Chicago—the barriers to colored people getting jobs, finding housing, and being treated equally. He mentioned a Negro man named

Dr. Robinson, who invented a type of wheel used on streetcars and trains who was unjustly arrested and jailed forty times.

I am impressed not only by Mr. Alberts's comparison of racism in the North and South but also by his prophetic views about challenging both forms of inequality. He told my father that Negroes traveling by railroad from Chicago to the South must move to segregated cars once the train crosses the Mason-Dixon Line. Nearly two decades before the Montgomery bus boycott, Mr. Alberts advocated nonviolent resistance as a means of contesting racial segregation in train cars.

"I like the method used by Gandhi in India to get what he wanted," Mr. Alberts said. "By passive resistance he was able to win some of the things he wanted for his people. He gained some respect, and, at the same time, lost less lives than he would have had he fought."

Turning to his mixed-race marriage, Mr. Alberts described the hostility he had encountered in Chicago. The problem began when he had applied for a marriage license and told the clerk that his intended bride was German. "They don't like it that I married a white woman here in Chicago," he recounted. "When I got the license, the clerk turned his nose up.

"I can take my wife around anywhere here where the people are colored, but let me take her to a white neighborhood. The people stare at us and wonder what is wrong with my wife," he carried on. "I don't think a man should marry out of his race unless he has a lot of intestinal fortitude. Everybody wouldn't be able to do it because of the disapproval of others."

Like Mr. Alberts, many of the people my father interviewed reported having to endure the inquisitive or disapproving gazes of strangers when out and about in Chicago. "Sometimes I go on the streetcar with my wife. She enters and I pay the carfare and follow her in," a Negro husband told my father later that year. "As we walk down the aisle, people turn around and stare at us." He said his response was to bow to them and say, "How do you do?" One white wife said she knew couples who, when traveling in the city together, board the streetcar separately, each paying his or her own fare, then find seats apart until they reach their destination, so no one detects they are married. Some of the interviewees wondered why people still stared at mixed couples when there were so many residing in the city.

My father's interview with Mr. and Mrs. Alberts shifted from the barriers to interracial marriage to its benefits—a conversation punctuated with sexual innuendos. "But let me tell you! Any poor white girl, if she has any character at all, will do better if she marries a colored man,"

Mr. Alberts bragged. "He'll treat her much better than a white man would. He knows that he is getting something that has always been forbidden to him and he'll treat her good. It's like whiskey was during Prohibition. People wanted it because it was forbidden them."

"I think a colored man and a white woman make the best marriage because they both got enough of the devil in them," Mrs. Alberts added. Although neither spouse said it explicitly, their allusions to forbidden desires and devilish behavior suggest a belief in a special sexual attraction between Black men and white women.

In a later interview, I discovered a superstition about interracial sex I had never heard before. A white wife told my father that, when she was a waitress, she had an especially lucrative day, receiving far more tips than usual. Another waitress said to her, "I bet you slept with a nigger last night."

"What makes you think so?"

"Because you are so lucky today" was the reply.

Mr. Alberts continued to praise the superiority of marriages between colored men and white women. "Strange as it seems, more white women marry colored men than white men marry colored women," he said. Then he turned to the depravity of sexual liaisons between white men and colored women.

"All through the South Side you have white men who live with colored women. But they come after dark and leave before it gets light."

Mrs. Alberts chimed in, "That's right. That's the truth."

Mr. Alberts went on to criticize the wealthy white men from Chicago's Gold Coast who frequent South Side cabarets to mingle with colored women, giving the example of a municipal court judge who was secretly keeping a colored woman, yet ruled with intolerance from the bench.

"I've never been able to understand how white men can condone the intermingling of the races in cabarets, brothels, and houses of prostitution and yet won't permit their mixing under the banner of Christ," he said.

Mr. Alberts made a good point about the hypocrisy of white men who engage in interracial sex under cover while condemning interracial marriage in the open. But I am also beginning to sense his hypocrisy in implying that intimate relationships between Black men and white women were inherently preferable.

My father interjected his opinion, proposing that the reason white men were so secretive wasn't always because they disrespected colored women, "but because the relationship they are having was one frowned upon in our society."

Mr. Alberts responded by lambasting white men for cowardly concealing their colored lovers, adding that he only hid his marriage to a white woman to protect his job. "I don't care what other people think," he declared. "If I took a notion to a baboon in the zoo, I would buy it and take it out and marry it. What right do people have to make you do what pleases them?" Indeed, he recommended mixing the races to "get a finer type," like breeding animals. "It's only the false idea that the Negro is inferior that prevents this," he opined.

Mr. Alberts elaborated further on the biological implications of race mixing. "Now you can see that it is impossible for a man of my color to be full-blooded Negro. Yet if you have one-tenth of Negro blood you are still considered a Negro," he pointed out.

"There are a great number of Negroes who look like they are white. You even find some platinum blondes," he continued. "If I would tell you some of the places where Negroes are working, you wouldn't believe me. There are thousands of colored people in this town that wouldn't have the jobs they have if it was known."

Mr. Alberts was referencing the concern that had fueled anti-miscegenation laws in the South. Laws banning interracial marriage were part of the Jim Crow legal regime that took hold after the Civil War and officially separated Black people from white people in every aspect of social life, including schools, hospitals, buses, restaurants, hotels, swimming pools, and drinking fountains. From 1874 to 1913, at least twelve states and territories enacted legislation against interracial marriage. At the anti-miscegenation regime's peak, from 1913 to 1948, thirty states prohibited sexual and marital relationships between Blacks and whites.

At the time my father started his research, the intertwined policies of Jim Crow and eugenics were at their zenith. A striking example is the "Act to Preserve Racial Integrity," passed by the Virginia state legislature in 1924. This law prohibited white people in the state from marrying anyone who wasn't white. This was the statute struck down by the U.S. Supreme Court in its 1967 landmark decision, *Loving v. Virginia*, which declared laws criminalizing interracial marriage unconstitutional.

In the summer of 1958—three and a half years after my parents' wedding in Chicago—twenty-four-year-old Richard Loving, a white bricklayer, drove from Virginia with his eighteen-year-old childhood sweetheart, Mildred Jeter, to Washington, D.C., to marry. Richard was barred by Virginia law from marrying Mildred, who had Black and Cherokee ancestry, because she was not white. After their wedding, the Lovings returned to Caroline County to live with Mildred's parents. But just five weeks later, they were awakened in the middle of the night by the county sheriff and two deputies, who arrested them for unlawful cohabitation. Their marriage certificate, the sheriff declared, was meaningless in Virginia. Indicted by a grand jury for attempting to evade the state's interracial marriage ban, the couple pleaded guilty. A judge suspended their one-year sentence—but only on the condition that they leave Virginia and not return together for twenty-five years. Determined to fight back, the Lovings, represented by the American Civil Liberties Union, challenged their convictions all the way to the U.S. Supreme Court.

The Racial Integrity Act was passed on the same day as another law authorizing the forced sterilization of individuals confined to government asylums because they were deemed "feebleminded," a vaguely defined condition claimed to be hereditary. This eugenic sterilization law was upheld three years later by the Supreme Court in *Buck v. Bell*, where Justice Oliver Wendell Holmes wrote his infamous declaration: "Three generations of imbeciles are enough."

To enforce the ban on interracial marriage, the Racial Integrity Act erected an intricate administrative scaffolding. It mandated that local and state registrars keep certificates documenting the "racial composition" for everyone born in the state and required marriage license applications to include precise "statements as to color of both the man and woman."

The racial classification system was overseen by Walter Ashby Plecker, Virginia's state registrar of vital statistics. A physician with strong ties to both eugenicists and white supremacists, he believed that sexual intermingling by Black and white individuals would degrade the white race. He was particularly alarmed by the perceived threat posed by people with mixed ancestry. "I would feel somewhat easier about the matter if I thought that these near-whites would not produce children with the negroid characteristics," he wrote in a 1931 letter to prominent eugenicist Harry Laughlin.

In his preface to the Racial Integrity Act, Plecker advocated for the state to use "radical measures" to prevent the "intermarriage of the white race with mixed stock." He feared that growing numbers of "near white" people were surreptitiously accessing white privileges while concealing their "intermixture of colored blood." To Plecker, the Racial Integrity Act was not only an anti-miscegenation measure but also an anti-passing one.

"Race-mixing proves that races can mix—and in a lot of cases, *want* to mix," writes Trevor Noah, the child of a Black South African mother and Swiss father, in his memoir. "Because a mixed person embodies that rebuke to the logic of the system, race-mixing becomes a crime worse than treason." In apartheid South Africa, as in Jim Crow Virginia, Noah was "born a crime." Marriages between white people and Negroes were especially taboo because Blackness was considered absolutely contaminating of white purity. The Virginia law created an exception for white men who married Native women. But any amount of discernible African ancestry was enough to constitute a Negro. Hence Mr. Alberts's point about Negroes with only "one-tenth of Negro blood."

Mr. Alberts was living in Chicago, not Mississippi. The Illinois legislature had repealed its anti-miscegenation law in 1874 and prohibited racial discrimination in public places. Illinois was an outlier—at the time of my father's interview, most states in the nation had laws banning interracial marriage. Yet Black and white residents of Chicago were separated in every aspect of life, including marriage and housing, by what historian Thomas Lee Philpott called the "unwritten law of the 'color line.'" Nor were white supremacist and eugenicist ideologies confined to the South. Dominant scientists teaching in elite northern universities claimed that race mixing was biologically dangerous and the hybrid humans it produced would be defective. In a fourth edition of the bestselling book *The Passing of the Great Race*, released in 1923, New York eugenicist Madison Grant called interracial marriage a "social and racial crime of the first magnitude." The *Saturday Evening Post*, hardly a southern rag, praised the book's reflection of "recent advances in the study of heredity and other life sciences" and recommended it as something that "every American should read."

"Now look at my little Bobby over there," Mr. Alberts said, pointing to the baby my father had inspected on his first visit. "He's a little Dutchman. He's even lighter than his mother. That's a case where a dark and a light produced something still lighter. It's like mixing blue with white to get a bright white paint."

When my father asked what Bobby would grow up to be, Mr. Alberts speculated that he might become a chauffeur to one of the wealthy industrialists in the Vanderbilt dynasty. From there he spun out a fantasy of his son's future. Vanderbilt's daughter would meet Bobby while he was driving her father's fancy car. She would fall in love with Bobby and marry him, not realizing he was a Negro. Mr. Alberts imagined the headline in the *Chicago Tribune* if the Vanderbilts discovered that he, a Negro, was Bobby's father: "Negro Marries Rich White Girl."

Mr. Alberts's tall tale brings to mind a true story from a decade earlier in New York City—a scandalous trial that captivated the public in 1925. The trial involved Leonard Kip Rhinelander, a wealthy socialite, who sought to annul his marriage to Alice Beatrice Jones. What made tabloid headlines and packed the courtroom with curious spectators wasn't the couple's fortune but the controversy surrounding Alice's race. Leonard claimed that Alice had deceived him into believing she was white when, in fact, she was Black. If the jurors agreed that Alice had perpetrated this racial fraud and that Leonard would not have married her had he known the truth, their vows would be declared null and void. Rumors swirled that Leonard was madly in love with Alice, but had filed the lawsuit under pressure from his millionaire father, who strongly opposed their union.

At trial, witnesses presented conflicting evidence regarding Alice's racial identity. For instance, Alice had been admitted into prestigious hotels alongside Leonard, suggesting she was perceived as white. But Dr. Caesar McClendon, a colored doctor, testified that Alice had been his patient—if Alice were white, she would have been treated by a doctor of her own race. In a surprising move, Alice chose not to prove she was white. Instead, she admitted having some colored blood, but insisted that Leonard had always known the truth. She pointed out that before their wedding, Leonard had met her family, spent many nights with her at the Hotel Marie Antoinette, and even bathed her.

The trial reached a climax when the judge, lawyers, jurors, and Leonard gathered in the jury room while Alice prepared for a dramatic demonstration. Stripping down to her underwear in an adjoining lavatory, she emerged covered only by a coat. At her lawyer's direction, a weeping Alice dropped her coat to reveal her body to the all-white male jury so they could see for themselves how obvious her race was. Her attorney concluded his defense with a pointed question to Leonard: "Your wife's body is the same shade as when you saw her in the Marie Antoinette with all of her clothing removed?" Leonard reluctantly admitted, "Yes."

The jury found in favor of Alice. They believed that Leonard knew that Alice was colored before he married her. But the verdict was hardly a victory for Alice, who paid a dear price in the humiliating act of disrobing in the public courtroom and, in the end, losing her husband because of her race. W. E. B. Du Bois expressed the outrage of the Black community when he wrote, "If Rhinelander had used this girl as concubine or prostitute, white America would have raised no word of protest. . . . It is when he legally and decently marries the girl that Hell breaks loose and literally tears the pair apart." Alice and Leonard never reunited after the trial.

At first, I find Mr. Alberts's wry commentary on definitions of Blackness to be insightful. The U.S. understanding of who counts as Black, as having any amount of "Negro blood" or, to use the modern lingo, "African ancestry," is opposite of the standard for who counts as white. To be white, one must be pure, having no amount of anything other than "Caucasian" blood or European ancestry. That contradiction demonstrates that the rules defining race are completely made up. They are determined by politics, not by any objective science. There is no natural division of human beings into races, no built-in way of telling who is Black and who is white.

Yet Mr. Alberts veered off base as he continued to pontificate about the physical outcomes of racial mixture. "Don't forget that you can find a colored person that looks like anything you want him to look like," he said. "Some have light hair and eyes, and many women, especially, have European features. If you mate a white man and a colored woman, their children will invariably have straight hair."

I chuckle to myself, thinking that twenty years later my father would have children with a colored woman. They would have a daughter with unmistakably Negroid hair—proving Mr. Alberts's pronouncement to be false.

Still lecturing, Mr. Alberts sent my father off with guidance for his research. He told the young academic that he hoped the study would improve relations between the races. "I wish you could get others to understand that colored people are as human as they are and knock the ego out of some people," he said.

Mr. Alberts also offered sage advice for my father's potential book.

"Now, when you get this research done, don't write a dry book," he counseled. "Probably only those in the universities who are interested in such studies will read it and it won't get to the public. It will probably be filled with charts and graphs and a lot of technical stuff. Put all that dull stuff in the introduction and then write something interesting."

Well, I think to myself as I put down the transcript, *my father never wrote his book, but what he left me with certainly isn't dry.*

I spend most of the morning poring over the Albertses' interviews, trying to piece together what they reveal about my father. As lunchtime approaches, the summer heat begins to creep into the study, and I switch on the ceiling fan to find some relief. The interviews with the Albertses leave me curious about the mysterious organization my father kept asking about—the Mannasses Society. I had never heard of it before. Nor had I known that there were social clubs in the early 1930s that catered to inter-racial couples. Just as I'm turning these questions over in my mind, I pick up the next transcript from the pile—and find myself pulled into a story that begins to offer answers. Lunch can wait.

CHAPTER 3

Finding Manasseh

Bob, left, and unidentified man at Ladies Manasseh Club No. 1 monument, Chicago, c. 1965.

Dr. Andrews
March 1, 1937

Shortly after meeting with the Albertses, my father walked into the South Side office of a physician named Dr. Andrews, *a dark-skinned Negro of medium height and with thinning Negroid hair* who sported a small mustache. When my father told Dr. Andrews that he was interested in "a club, which I understand had been formed by white and Negro couples who were intermarried," the doctor gave a helpful response. "Yes, it is called the Manasseh Club," he replied, correcting my father's "Mannasses" pronunciation and spelling. "That isn't anything new."

Dr. Andrews was born in 1893 in Sandusky, Ohio, and raised in a predominantly white neighborhood, where he said there was very little racial discrimination. Although he was the only colored pupil in his high school, he experienced no friction with his white classmates, playing on the football team and attending school dances. His first encounter with prejudice occurred when, as a teenager, he got a job busing dishes at a restaurant in a Toledo department store and began giving piano lessons to several white girls who worked there. When his supervisor found out, she told him to stop the lessons if he wanted to keep his job. He persuaded the store manager to retain him, but his supervisor retaliated by giving him burdensome tasks and the white chefs messed with the food they served him, possibly even spitting in his meals. His manager rescued him again when he threatened to quit, transferring him to another position at the store, with a $2 raise.

In 1919, Dr. Andrews moved to Chicago, where he met his wife, a woman with Irish, Scotch, and German heritage, who worked as a social service nurse at Hull House, the pioneering social settlement founded by Jane Addams and Ellen Gates Starr in 1899. She had come to the hospital where he was an intern to visit a white friend whom he was treating. They married in 1922. "Neither of us was conscious of the difference of color," Dr. Andrews told my father. Their only worry was whether their marriage would threaten his medical business. "The type of person who objects to intermarriage is not the type I would want anyway." Dr. Andrews believed he was the only physician in Chicago married interracially, but he said it was impossible to be sure: "So many doctors have bright [light-skinned] wives that it is hard to tell whether they are colored or white."

Dr. Andrews had bought his home in Morgan Park four years earlier from a white man for $4,000. In the 1930s, Morgan Park, a predominantly white neighborhood on Chicago's Far South Side with Irish, German, and Scandinavian residents, had a distinct racial divide. Like much of the city, Black residents faced housing restrictions and discrimination, living primarily in areas closer to neighboring Washington Heights and Beverly. My father asked the doctor to make a list for him of any other interracial couples he knew who lived in Morgan Park or were members of the Manasseh Club.

As my father left the office, he handed Dr. Andrews a gift—a book, *The Negro in Chicago*, which he had bought on sale at the University of Chicago bookstore for twenty-five cents. I wonder if there might be a further clue here as to my father's interest in the topic.

I look up the book online and discover that its full title is *The Negro in Chicago: A Study of Race Relations and a Race Riot*. It is a comprehensive report of more than six hundred pages prepared by the Chicago Commission on Race Relations and published in 1922 by the University of Chicago Press. The first chapter, fifty-two pages long, investigates the Chicago Riot, July 27–August 2, 1919. The second documents other outbreaks of white terror in Illinois—clashes in Chicago preceding the 1919 race riot, as well as similar riots in Springfield, Waukegan, and East St. Louis. There is also reference to the Abyssinian Affair, June 20, 1920, and the Barrett murder, September 20, 1920. Subsequent chapters detail aspects of Negro life in Chicago, beginning with the mass migration from the South, followed by housing, employment, crime, and social interactions. The book ends with opinions expressed by Negro and white citizens and recommendations by the commission.

I had wondered whether, as a little boy, my father had been affected by the Red Summer of 1919. Although he would have been almost four years of age at the time, and likely shielded by his parents from the violence occurring nearby, his gift to Dr. Andrews tells me that he cared enough to learn the details of those racist incidents. Knowing how much he opposed violence when I was growing up, I imagine he was angered by the atrocities. I see in his parting gift to Dr. Andrews an effort to convey his desire that his research, which his interviewee viewed skeptically, would in some way contest the continuing hostility that scarred their city.

Seven months later, when my father interviewed a white wife named Mrs. Lane in October 1937, she showed him a blue pamphlet with the following words on the cover: *Little Blue Book No. 1387. Racial Intermarriage in the United States: One of the Most Interesting Phenomena in Our National Life*. The pamphlet was authored by the well-known Black journalist George S. Schuyler, who wrote for the *Pittsburgh Courier*. It was published by the Haldeman-Julius Company in Girard, Kansas, in 1929. Schuyler called for mixed marriages as an answer to America's racial inequality. Mrs. Lane seemed to have adopted Schuyler's view because she told my father how these marriages would change white people's prejudiced ideas about colored people. "Don't you think that if a good friend of a white person married a Negro that person would think more of colored people?" she asked. "They would think that some colored people must be worthwhile or their friend wouldn't have married one."

My father asked to borrow the pamphlet until the next time he visited. *As Mrs. Lane hadn't heard of the author before, I told her who he was*, he noted.

This is the first source my father mentioned that might have influenced his beliefs about the positive potential for interracial marriage. Perhaps he had been following the journalist's articles on race. I recall encountering Schuyler while researching the history of birth control in Black communities for my book *Killing the Black Body*. I set aside the transcript and reach for the copy I brought with me to Chicago. Settling into the large leather armchair in the study, I look up Schuyler in the index and turn to the pages where I discuss him. Alongside W. E. B. Du Bois, Schuyler had championed family planning as a way to combat the devastating rates of maternal and infant mortality among Black Americans and to enhance their quality of life. In a 1932 scholarly article, he had written: "If anyone should doubt the desire on the part of Negro women and men to limit their families, it is only necessary to note the large scale of 'preventive devices' sold in every drugstore in the various Black Belts and the great number of abortions performed by medical men and quacks." Reading that passage again—and realizing my father had engaged with Schuyler's work in his own research decades before I did—moves me deeply. In that moment, I feel an unexpected connection with my father's younger self.

As the summer progresses and I read the 1930s transcripts, I begin to grasp my father's methods for finding what became a snowballing collection of interracial couples to interview. I do not know how he encountered Mrs. L., the source who initially told him about the Manasseh Club and pointed him to his first interviewees, the Albertses. After that, my father would ask each couple he interviewed for names and addresses of any other Black-white couples they knew. He then tracked down the couples, showed up at their homes without warning, and knocked on the front door or rang the doorbell. If someone opened the door, he introduced himself as a student at the University of Chicago assisting with a research study and mentioned the name of the couple who had provided their address.

Sometimes the person answering the door had already heard of my father's study from their mixed-couple friends and welcomed him. Others feared he was a bill collector, a salesman, a proselytizer from the Moody Church. "To tell you the truth, I didn't want my husband to let you in at first," one white wife confessed. "I thought you were connected with the Ku Klux Klan." If no one answered, my father returned, sometimes multiple times, until he found someone at home. He told one couple that he was aiming to interview one hundred pairs in an effort to compile a representative sample. He handed out a questionnaire for each spouse to fill out, but many failed to comply. He had far better luck engaging them in conversation.

A second method my father adopted was less precise. If a research subject reported that a mixed couple resided on a particular street in Chicago, he would walk up and down the street asking anyone standing outside a home if they were aware of the couple and request their address. On one evening in September 1937, for example, my father was stationed on Warren Boulevard when he stopped *an elderly Negro of dark complexion* walking in his direction. "Yes!" the man replied to my father's inquiry. "My wife is white and is at home now." Similarly, if he learned that a particular venue—a dance hall, tavern, or hotel—catered to interracial couples, he would frequent it, hoping to accost someone willing to give him their address or the address of others who were married across racial lines. At one point in his research, he located several mixed couples in a Black suburban community on the Far South Side known as Lilydale and made several trips there by streetcar. The reason for his dogged search for the Manasseh Club, I imagine, was to acquire the names of its members to interview.

There were also many letdowns. Some people rebuffed my father quickly, despite his mention of the University of Chicago and assurances of confidentiality, with snubs such as "I don't open my door to anyone I don't know" and "I have much more important things to do." Sometimes he found no interracial couple living at the address he was given. Sometimes he found no building there at all. He might ask a mailman he chased down on the street for help locating a missing couple. He might cajole a cooperative couple he had interviewed to persuade their reluctant friends to meet with him. But it didn't always work.

Dr. Andrews directed my father to the Communist Party as a promising point of entry. "Now you have a lot of interracial contact among communists," he reported. "There is more communism here than you would think. The intelligent Negro believes in nearly all the things that communism stands for." When Mrs. Raymond, a white wife my father interviewed in November 1938, told him that she had an aunt, a member of the Communist Party, who was also married to a Negro, she discouraged him from pursuing the lead and refused to give him her aunt's address. *Mrs. Raymond said that her aunt considers her marriage "her sacred problem" and would be angry if I tried to talk to her about it.*

Despite the warning, my father asked about the aunt among the mixed couples active in Chicago's Communist Party he had interviewed, all white wives and Negro husbands. After a year of persistent detective work, he eventually permeated the interracial network within the radical organization and had become acquainted with many of its members. They had heard of Mrs. Raymond's aunt, whom they identified as Mrs. Rose, the daughter of Lithuanian Jewish immigrants, soon to turn thirty years old. Her husband, they informed my father, was currently in Spain, where civil war was raging, serving as an ambulance driver with the Abraham Lincoln Battalion, the racially integrated American combat unit that joined the global effort to stop a fascist takeover in Europe. The communist wives promised to introduce my father to Mr. Rose when he returned to Chicago at the start of the new year.

As I continue to read the transcripts over my first month in Chicago, I discover that by the close of 1938 my father had helped to organize a discussion of "interracial and other social problems" at the apartment of one of his interviewees with about fifteen people in attendance. He invited his friends, and one of the communist wives brought two other interracial couples to the gathering. The couples had formed a closely knit circle in Chicago's communist movement—all of whom were eventually interviewed by my father. It occurs to me that Daddy was building a network of interracial spouses—and he and my mother would join them when they married more than a decade later.

At the end of an interview my father had conducted in October 1938 with a white wife named Mrs. Johnson, she had urged him to buy tickets she was selling to a dance hosted by a neighborhood athletic association her family belonged to, to be held at the Ambassador Club. *I could hardly say no to Mrs. Johnson after she has been so willing to help me with the information I asked and because I wanted to see what kind of affair they would have and how she was accepted by the colored people.*

Two weeks later, my father arrived at the Ambassador Club at 11:45 p.m. *with a Negro girl (dark brown) as my guest.* Was the girl who accompanied him—whose presence was inserted as part of his research notes—an aspect of his study or was his study becoming an aspect of his personal life? Did he mention his date's skin color as an anthropological notation or to emphasize the color he found attractive? Everyone at the dance was colored except Mrs. Johnson, my father, and two other white men. There was only one more brief mention of the young lady my father brought to the dance: *After I had danced with the girl I came with a couple times, and sat in the dancing room which was filling with cigarette smoke for an hour or so, we went to the bar and got two Coca-Colas which we drank at one of the tables.* My father's three pages of single-spaced typed notes on his observations of the partygoers and conversations with several of them make me wonder if his date felt neglected by his incessant pursuit of research subjects.

My father left the party with the dark brown girl at 3 a.m., giving no further clue to her identity or their relationship. But what is clear is that, by age twenty-three, my father was dating Black women.

Not long after the Ambassador Club dance, my father purchased two tickets for eighty-three cents each from a communist couple to attend the New Year's Eve ball hosted by the *Daily Record*, a left-leaning local newspaper. When he arrived an hour before midnight at the Ashland Auditorium, in a shabby neighborhood on the white side of town, Don Fernandez and His NBC Trocadero Orchestra, a swinging big band staple of 1930s nightlife, were on the stage, later to be replaced by several skits ridiculing fascism. In a room dedicated to Spain, chili was being sold to benefit the Abraham Lincoln Battalion as dancers swayed to Spanish music. In a smaller room, Chinese curios and chop suey were for sale as young Chinese activists distributed anti-Japanese literature.

My father estimated that, of about two thousand people attending the ball, only 5 percent were Negroes, 80 percent of those were men, and half of those men were with white women. He bemoaned the dearth of Negro women at affairs thrown by the communists. Despite buying two tickets, he seemed to have arrived alone. I suspect that, in addition to more subjects for his research, he had hoped to find a Negro girl to dance with.

At the New Year's Eve ball, my father recognized several couples from his interviews and maneuvered through the revelers to procure fresh ones for his study. He enlisted one of the communist wives to help him find Mr. Rose, who had recently returned from Spain. His search was successful. Mr. Rose agreed to be interviewed and gave my father his address.

My father visited the Roses at their home on two occasions that month, drawing out lengthy stories about their backgrounds—meeting at a Young Communist League dance on a sweltering summer night in 1931, their marriage several months later, Karl Marx's view that labor in white skin can never be free while labor in Black skin is enslaved. *Then we had a discussion of communism, war, and other topics which I shall not include in this account. I found them rather interesting. Mr. and Mrs. Rose said I could come and see them anytime I wanted to. Mrs. Rose was very willing to speak about whatever I asked her.* Once again, Daddy had converted someone who considered marriage "her sacred problem" into a willing participant in his study—and had made a new friend.

As the summer wears on, I keep to the same steady rhythm. Each morning, I pick up a fresh stack of transcripts from the dining room table and read late into the night. My reward is a cup of pistachio ice cream and a movie on my laptop—there is no television in the apartment. My only other diversions are a weekly walk to the supermarket, returning with a bag in each hand after asking the clerk to balance them evenly; nightly phone calls with my husband to catch up on the small updates that keep us connected; and a monthly Zoom call with my sisters, where I report on my progress with Daddy's papers. Evelyn is living with her husband, John, in upstate New York; Helen has just returned from Liberia and is staying with her oldest son in Maryland until she decides where to settle for her retirement years.

With this routine firmly in place and half the 1930s interviews now behind me, I begin to reflect more deeply on what these documents reveal about the couples of that era. My father interviewed many of them over two, three, or four visits. At times, he spoke with the husband and wife together. At other times, he caught one or the other alone. He started by asking a series of demographic questions—about their birth and upbringing, their parents' backgrounds, their education, their occupations, their children. Then he would dive into questions exploring their marriage—how did you meet, what race are your friends, how do your families feel about your marriage, what do your neighbors think, are you embarrassed to go out together, would you prefer for your children to marry a white or colored person, to what extent do you agree or disagree on handling family finances, table manners, recreation, religious matters, demonstrations of affection.

He always ended with the most revealing question: If you had your life to live over, would you marry the same person? Most said that, despite the hardships thrown at them, they would marry their partner again. The wives were more likely to express dissatisfaction with their husbands when interviewed by themselves. "Put down we almost always disagree," one white wife told him. "He doesn't even have enough sense to take his hat off in the house." Another disclosed that she was contemplating divorce. Some couples had separated or divorced, often because of the husband's gambling or drinking, sometimes because of the adversities that stemmed from being married interracially. Some had even grown bitterly opposed to mixed marriage.

The couples had met in various and sundry ways, no different from any other couples of their era, an era when the city had erected fewer barriers between its Black and white residents than in years to come. They were high school classmates. They were introduced by acquaintances. They met at dance halls and taverns. They met playing cards at a friend's house. They met riding the elevated train or a bus. They met at Democratic and communist political meetings. They met at Baha'i spiritual gatherings. They met shopping in a candy store or when a salesman stopped by their home. They met at work—in hotels, hospitals, laundries, factories, and restaurants.

"My husband worked at the same restaurant as me. He was cook and I was pantry girl," Mrs. Jackson told my father.

"I worked in the Plankinton House, the largest hotel in Milwaukee," Mrs. Slade said. "I was a scrub girl. That's how I met a colored man."

"I was a governess at a place where he was a chauffeur," Mrs. Owens recalled.

"The hotels had colored waiters and white chamber girls," said Mrs. Carroll. "That's how we met each other. It was all decent."

My father had heard rumors about the indecent kind of interracial partnering—white prostitutes who married Negro panderers for protection, and white men from the South who brought their colored mistresses with them to Chicago, where they were permitted to wed—but he didn't meet any couple that fit those descriptions.

Mrs. Pierce, whose mother was white and father colored, said she knew of white spinsters who were so economically desperate during the Depression that they married hardworking colored men who could support them. "I'm sure that isn't true of my mother," she began, qualifying the type of white woman she was referring to, "but I know women who've been around, if you know what I mean, and couldn't get anybody but a colored man to marry them."

The husbands, Black and white, came from all walks of life. Some were doctors and janitors, business owners and garbagemen, pharmacists and Pullman porters, chauffeurs and social workers. Many were still recovering from the Depression and were on relief or working on a WPA job. One white husband was a peddler who rented a horse and wagon from a small stable and sold fruits and vegetables in the summer and coal and wood in the winter, mostly to the Polish community on the West Side. It seemed that most of the women became housewives when they married, though some were secretaries, stenographers, bookkeepers, seamstresses, shop clerks, and telephone operators. When my father informed a colored wife that he read that persons who marry interracially are "of low type," she took offense.

Some people answered each question curtly, while others delivered a sermon. Upon opening the door, Mrs. Kruger, a light-brown-skinned woman married to a white man from Holland, stated, "We're just like any other married couple—husband and wife. We've been married twenty-three years and still love each other," and swiftly bid my father goodbye. But most of the couples seemed anxious to share stories about their unorthodox unions to the young researcher, as if he had opened the spigot to a well of pent-up thoughts and emotions. "At first, I thought I would not get very much response on a ticklish subject like this," my father revealed to a couple. "But I have been getting as much information as if I had asked persons about their cats or dogs." My father wrote the responses to his inquiries on a pad of paper. I figure he must have typed up the conversations and his notes when he returned home from each interview. Those are the typed transcripts on yellowing sheets of paper I am reading seven decades later.

I marvel at how successful my father was as a master's student at not only collecting the names of more than one hundred Black-white couples but also persuading them to tell him their stories. They often had lengthy conversations with him that lasted late into the evening. They invited him to share meals with them and to return as often as he liked. Conjuring my father as a young man, appearing uninvited at the doorsteps of apprehensive residents, I can picture him coaxing them to let him in. I knew him to have an affable disposition; he put people at ease. Though his looks weren't especially remarkable, his gentle manner and pleasant expression drew others in.

In some old photos, Daddy looks surprisingly stunning. On her bedroom dresser, my sister Evelyn keeps a small, yellowed black-and-white photo of my father in a delicate gold frame. He looks to be in his twenties, likely taken during his years as a master's student, around the time he was conducting the 1930s interviews. His thick dark hair is parted slightly off-center, and he wears an appealing mustache with a closely trimmed beard. His eyes, fixed on the camera, are intense but kind—conveying both seriousness and gentleness in a single glance.

There's another photo of my father displaying an impressive full beard that he grew for a contest when my family was living in Liberia in the 1950s. He would have been forty-two when the photo was taken, when I was a toddler. Our home movies from that time include a scene that begins with my father showing off his beard, grooming it with a small comb, and preening for the camera. Then he lifts a razor to his face with a dramatic flair and shaves off all the whiskers. My father loved to boast to my sisters and me that he won that beard-growing contest, though the contestants must have been few. In his passport photo for the journey to Liberia, my father is clean-shaven, his hair parted on the side and slicked back. He strikes a pose that gives him the dashing good looks of a movie star.

And, oh, Daddy loved to talk. My mother frequently complained that he talked too much at parties. "Your father has diarrhea of the mouth," she used to grumble to my sisters and me. Those gregarious character traits must have been an asset to him when he was doing his research in his twenties. They likely intensified by the time he became my father, nurtured by decades of conversations in strangers' homes.

In time, as my father gathered more and more information about the Manasseh Club, he finally met one of the charter members. Mrs. Brown, an elderly gray-haired woman of German origin, told him the organization dated back to 1890, and the first meetings were held in a member's home. Her husband of fifty years was the only survivor among the founding men. Mr. Brown, a colored man in his seventies, had come to Chicago from Virginia before the Great Migration. He called himself a "miscellaneous man" because he had worked waiting tables, on the railroad for the Pullman Company, and as a janitor in shops—"anything I could get." By 1920, the club had one hundred members. Mrs. Brown refused to consider the children of mixed couples as colored. "I always call those girls Manasseh," she told my father. "The children are the real Manasseh people. That's what the word means."

Manasseh. The word sounds vaguely familiar, but I can't put my finger on its origin. I put aside the transcript I'm reading to dig into its roots. My search takes me to the Old Testament. According to the book of Genesis, Manasseh was the name that Joseph, who was sold into slavery in Egypt by his jealous brothers, gave his first son. Manasseh was born to Asenath, the Egyptian woman Pharoah bestowed to Joseph as his wife, a reward for Joseph's loyal and wise management of Egypt's economic fortune. According to the biblical story, Joseph's father, Jacob, adopted

Manasseh and his brother, Ephraim, so they could share in Jacob's inheritance. So, the Manasseh Club founders named their organization after the offspring of a mixed couple of sorts—a Jewish husband and his Egyptian bride. Their son represented a reconciliation between feuding siblings and nations. Manasseh means "God has made me forget." He was blessed with an inheritance from his Jewish grandfather, an acceptance not all interracial couples my father interviewed were granted by their relatives. Learning this origin story, I turn back to the transcripts.

My father tracked down additional charter members and prior officers of the Manasseh Club. A different Mrs. Pierce, a white woman from England who married a Negro tinsmith in 1894, retrieved a satchel with copious records from the club—the "Charter, Constitution, and By-laws of the Ladies Court of the Manasseh Society No. 1"; "Ritual of the Ladies Manasseh Club No. 1, including Opening, Initiation, Installation, and Funeral Ceremonies" (dated 1915); programs for an annual memorial service, the thirty-third annual May Ball, and the Grand Prize Masquerade Ball (dated February 9, 1924); and obituaries of several members. My father learned that the Manasseh Club imposed strict qualifications for its members. To be eligible for membership, couples had to show their marriage license, and it cost $5 to join, in addition to monthly dues.

The Club offered sick payments and burial coverage, benefits many former members highlighted as its most important function. It even maintained a separate section of a cemetery for the graves of its members. Others remembered fondly the glamorous balls the club hosted. When someone speculated the Manasseh Club still might host dances, my father eagerly asked, "Do you think it would be possible for me to go to the next Manasseh Club dance?" But he was disappointed to learn that the interracial social club had disbanded.

My father heard multiple explanations for the Manasseh Club's demise. It strayed from its original purpose, having become "a radical red organization" full of communists. It was the fault of the National Interracial League, which, out of envy, poached Manasseh members. Its membership waned over a scandal when one member ran off with another member's wife. No, the feud was over the younger members resenting that their dues were paying the burials of older members. Other members pointed to a lawsuit: when the club failed to pay death benefits because of questions surrounding a decedent's membership, the husband threatened to sue. Rather than pay up, the organization folded, the story went. Mrs. Brown said it was a legal technicality: according to its attorney, the society needed five hundred members to acquire a new charter, and "we didn't want to take everybody."

The Slades, a Negro husband and white wife, were especially helpful to my father's quest. This was Mrs. Slades's second marriage. Her first husband was a colored man who had been dragged off a streetcar and beaten to death in the 1919 race riot. They told my father that the club dissolved in 1932 because the Depression wiped out its capacity to afford the expenses. Mrs. Slade went into the bedroom and returned with a gold mine—a little notebook labeled "MEMBERS RECEIPT BOOK, Ladies Court of Manasseh Society," where she had recorded the wives' names and their dues payments, thirty-five cents per month, while the club was still in operation. My father asked Mrs. Slade about the individuals listed in the book and she reported her recollections about each one.

"Who is Mrs. Wick?" my father inquired.

Mrs. Slade replied that Mrs. Wick was the daughter of a mixed couple who were members, adding, "Her husband was colored and so was she."

My father was confused. He thought only interracially married people were eligible to join.

"Children of interracial marriages could get in and so could their husbands and wives," Mrs. Slade explained. "Two colored people couldn't get in, though, unless their parents were mixed."

"I couldn't have joined unless I married a colored girl, could I?" my father responded. The question followed so quickly that it seems obvious he had hoped to join the interracial club.

"No, but you could visit as much as you wanted to," Mrs. Slade offered.

The next morning, I wake up thinking about the Manasseh Club. It pre-occupies me. On one hand, I am happy that my father had managed to track down details about the elusive interracial social club. Although it was too late for him to attend its dances, the roster of former members acquired from Mrs. Slade would offer tremendous help in locating more Black-white couples. As a researcher myself, I can understand the value of a coup like that. On the other hand, the more I read, the more I am infuriated by the members' treatment of Black women. And disappointed by my father's desire to be directly involved.

Dr. Andrews had emphasized the exclusivity of the Manasseh Club, noting that most of its members "are from the higher element of both Negroes and whites." Although he and his wife were not members, they appeared to consider themselves part of the elite social circle. As I read more interviews, I learn that eligibility for membership was determined by an intersection of race and gender criteria: Black women—and their white husbands—were largely excluded from the club. Several former members my father interviewed counted seeing only three or four Black women and their white husbands ever being admitted.

One white wife candidly explained, "Most of the Manasseh women don't want to have anything to do with colored women." She attributed the rarity of interracial marriages among white men to her own prejudiced belief that "the morals of colored women have been looser. They don't have to marry them."

She wasn't the only one to blame Black women for white men's reluctance. "Colored women especially are prejudiced. They don't like intermarriage and yet they will have all sorts of white men," stated another white wife, named Mrs. Wells. "Many dark colored women have light babies and don't think anything of it. They like to have light children." As if her disparagement of colored women wasn't enough, she went on to bemoan the greater affliction that white women endured. "Who are the slaves of the South?" she asked dramatically. Her answer: "A white woman and a colored man."

Dr. Andrews declared as the solution: "If colored women would say to the white men of the South, 'You can't have me until you put a ring on my finger,' the southern white man would be the first to favor intermarriage."

As became evident in many of my father's conversations with white wives and Black husbands, Black women were categorically barred from what was considered the "the higher element" of society—and from membership in the Manasseh Club.

To me, the social club's exclusivity shows that interracial marriage itself—even an association dedicated to racial mixing—does not necessarily advance racial equality. The club members who disparaged Black women were reinforcing Chicago's racial hierarchy, not challenging it. I wonder what the white wives were saying about their husbands—and their husbands' Black mothers, aunties, and sisters. I wonder what Black husbands felt when they attended Manasseh events and saw only white women there. Didn't they realize that the absence of Black women was a rejection of an essential part of themselves?

It had become clear to me that, for members of the Manasseh Club, the gender of the spouses mattered just as much as their race. They revered marriages between white women and Black men, while looking down on those between Black women and white men. I wonder what my father made of this double standard. As a white man who dated Black women, he likely disapproved of the Club's hostility toward Black women and their partners. Yet he never seemed to grapple with the contradiction that unsettles me. As I sit down to read another stack of transcripts, I find myself swept deeper into questions about how the entanglement of hierarchies and stereotypes shaped the interracial relationships my father was studying—and whether it ever gave him pause.

CHAPTER 4

Excluded from the Higher Element

Interview with Mrs. (███████) O'ROURKE
17== Fulton Street
September 14, 1937
By Robert Roberts

I went up the stairs of the old brick house in which the O'Rourkes
live and rang their bell. After waiting for some time and
receiving no answer I opened the front hall door and walked
to the second floor. Although I didn't know which floor the
O'Rourkes lived on I knocked on the door, again receiving no
response. While I was standing at the door an elderly colored
woman ascended the stairs. In answer to my query she said that
she was Mrs. O'Rourke. Upon stating my purpose in calling, Mrs.
O'Rourke invited me to be seated in the front room and sat down
opposite me.

Transcript of Mrs. O'Rourke interview, September 14, 1937

Mrs. O'Rourke
September 14, 1937

Six months after speaking with Dr. Andrews, my father interviewed a
dark-skinned elderly woman named Mrs. O'Rourke and her husband, a
gray-haired white man with blue eyes who earned a living fixing sewers.
Her mother, 102 years old at the time, had been enslaved, as had her father.
The O'Rourkes, both seventy years old, were born just two years after
the Civil War ended. They were one of the twenty-five couples my father
interviewed who were married before the turn of the twentieth century,
between 1882 and 1899.

Mrs. O'Rourke told my father that race had nothing to do with her
marriage. "At the time I married my husband I didn't think about his being
of another race," she said. "That never entered my mind, and I don't think
it ever entered his." She had heard in church that colored women marry

white men because these men are superior. She disagreed. "I didn't marry my husband because he is white but because he was a nice young man."

The topic of white men having sex with colored women quickly found its way into the conversation. "Do you know that rich men, bankers, and other white men like to ferret out some colored girl to live with?" Mrs. O'Rourke informed my father. "Even if they are married, they often have a colored mistress." She reported that some colored women objected to mixed marriages like hers, but these same women "will run after a white man if they can get one." These liaisons remained clandestine, however. "They wouldn't want anyone to know about it and they wouldn't marry a white man," Mrs. O'Rourke sneered. "But they will follow them around and go in rooming houses with them."

Mrs. O'Rourke reserved harsher words for the white men engaged in this skulduggery. "They say, 'Oh, that's terrible,' when they see a mixed couple together, but go off with a colored woman whenever they can in secret," she raged, my father noting her voice growing louder, her manner more aggressive. "They segregate themselves everywhere except in a bedroom. It makes me sick." She issued a final declaration before storming out of the room: "White people think they can stop intermarriage, but they can't. They've had it since the world began."

Around the same time, my father interviewed Mr. Benjamin, a short, thin Jewish man, whose "mulatto" wife had died three years before. He lived alone in the rear of a store in a colored neighborhood, where he sold used stoves and iceboxes that were polished so brightly they almost looked new. He complained that there were places that wouldn't have hired him had he revealed he was married to a Negro. My father described Mr. Benjamin as both a very fine and a very sad man, obviously still mourning the death of his wife. "I don't think any white woman could excel her," he said, his eyes welling with tears. "I will never give her up. I do wish I could go where she is."

Mr. Benjamin was also incensed at white men who sleep with colored women in the dark, yet refuse to marry them in the daylight. "So many of them that are turning up their nose at you will slip around with colored women. But to come out in the open they don't have the guts," he protested. "That is what I hate them for. It is just like throwing a rock and hiding your hand." I hear an admirable love in Mr. Benjamin's words— in his enduring affection for his wife, his staying in their colored neighborhood after she died, his indignation at the duplicitous tyranny of white men. I feel I have met someone in my father's papers who recognized the ugly chains of racism, but resisted being bound by them. I wonder if Daddy had begun seeking a way to love on those terms—setting out on the path that led him to marry my mother.

The gendered division within the Manasseh Club—its exclusion of Black women married to white men—reflects a preference among the couples for the opposite pairing that I detect throughout the interviews. This bias stems in part from the fact that most of the couples my father interviewed were composed of white women and Black men. It's not surprising that they would craft theories of interracial intimacy that cast their own relationships in a flattering light, while feeling less compelled to celebrate unions between white men and Black women. Perhaps this partiality also reflected the historical realities of race and sex throughout U.S. history. At that very moment, Black men were being tortured and lynched across the South for being accused of having sex with a white woman. In stark contrast, Black women were deemed innately lascivious and unworthy of protection—and therefore treated as unrapeable.

If I had to pick one early American document that fascinates me most, it wouldn't be the Declaration of Independence or the U.S. Constitution. It would be a 1662 Virginia law that determined the future of slavery and race. I picture white male enslavers in the Virginia House of Burgesses—America's first elected legislature—debating what to do about the light-skinned babies born to enslaved Black women. These children were the result of sexual violence, likely committed by the very men making the law. By British tradition, a child inherited the legal status of their father. But the colonists saw a problem: if these children were classified as white, they'd have access to freedom and privilege. That would disrupt the racial hierarchy and weaken the institution of slavery. Their solution was a simple but brutal law:

"All children borne in this country shal be held bond or free only according to the condition of the mother."

With that, they ensured that Black women's children—no matter who fathered them—could be enslaved. The law erased the family ties between white men and these children, while at the same time granting them power to sever the bonds between Black women and their children. It cemented white supremacy and made sexual violence even more profitable. White men no longer had to worry that their mixed-race children might claim an inheritance. Instead, they could rape enslaved women with impunity, increasing their own wealth in the process, as any resulting offspring would be their property from conception. As abolitionist Lydia Maria Child later observed, it was a "convenient game"—one that turned a white man's sins into financial gain.

Given this legacy, I understand how, at the time, Black men who loved white women may have felt like they were opposing white supremacy, while Black women who loved white men may have seemed to be upholding it. What continues to trouble me is how rarely some couples questioned the politics of attraction when it came to Black men with white women, while readily casting suspicion on white men with Black women. I still can't tell whether the double standard bothered my father. I remember his comment to Mr. Alberts, defending white men who failed to marry their Black mistresses "because the relationship they are having was one frowned upon in our society." But beyond that, his interviews and notes offer little insight into his views. Maybe he stayed quiet to avoid offending his interviewees. Or maybe he was still navigating his own attraction to Black women—a breach of a powerful societal taboo, and a complicated reckoning for someone only in his twenties.

Mr. Jacobs
June 1938

Nine months later, my father visited the Lilydale home of Mr. Jacobs, a well-spoken, loquacious janitor born in 1869, whose white wife had died and who described himself as composed of four races—Indian, Jewish, Negro, and Caucasian. Although he never graduated from high school, Mr. Jacobs spoke powerfully about multiple forms of racial injustice, ranging from lynchings taking place in the South to Hitler's claims that Germans were a superior race. He told my father that Alexander Hamilton's mother was a mulatto and that the duel that ended his life was over Aaron Burr calling him Black across a conference table. (As far as I can tell, neither is an established fact.) Mr. Jacobs unveiled to my father his ingenious plan for fostering Black political rights. If the forty-five thousand Negro churches in America took $2 each week from the collection box, compiled it in a general fund, and bought up deserted plantations in the South, Negroes could begin creating townships, annex the townships into counties, and go from electing county officials to electing state legislators.

He planned to propose his vision to George Washington Carver, the eminent Black botanist and inventor, on an upcoming visit to Tuskegee.

Mr. Jacobs recommended that my father read *Following the Color Line* by Ray S. Baker, the best book on Black Americans' political status, and *The History of the Conquest of Peru* by William H. Prescott, which demonstrated that the Indians were as civilized as the Spaniards. My father reciprocated by giving him a copy of *The Negro in Chicago*, which he had begun handing to interviewees who expressed an interest in racial politics. When my father returned to the Jacobs home in January 1939, Mr. Jacobs reported that he had spoken with Dr. Carver for more than an hour on the hospital grounds of the Tuskegee Institute, where Carver was convalescing, and had given him his copy of *The Negro in Chicago*. I smile at the thought that my father may have helped to expand George Washington Carver's awareness of racism in Chicago. As a schoolgirl, I was taught to revere Carver for his pioneering agricultural research and unwavering dedication to Black advancement, and I imagine my father admired him, too.

A good part of the conversation was devoted to Mr. Jacobs railing against white men's two-faced predilection for colored women. "I'll tell you something about the white man," he launched in. "You could put up a wall twenty feet high with white women on his side and a colored woman on the other side and he'd climb the wall to get the colored woman." He revealed that his own mother was forced to have sex with a white man when she worked at a hotel in Parkersburg, West Virginia. If she had resisted, she would have lost her job. "The result of that was me," he said. He learned through "grapevine telegraphy" that a white department store owner named Richard Todd stopped employing colored people after his daughter had a son by a colored coachman, yet he kept a colored mistress, who was "as black as my shoe."

Mr. Jacobs went on to recount a story from a time when he worked at the Cleveland Wheel Club in Ohio, a fancy establishment with a billiard room, eatery, and dance hall that boasted fifteen hundred white members. The male patrons persistently begged him to take them to see colored women. On one occasion, Mr. Jacobs acted as a guide as the white men drove around the city. When he directed them to stop the car by some white women, they told him, "We don't want those old white women; take us to some colored girls."

"What would you say if I ask you to take me to some of your white girls?" Mr. Jacobs replied.

I could tell my father grew close to Mr. Jacobs over their lengthy conversations. Daddy made six trips to Lilydale in the 1930s to speak with him and delve more deeply into his life story: his lineage in Virginia, beginning with his great-grandmother, a Russian Jewish governess who had a son with a colored servant working in the same house; his eclectic assortment of jobs before the Cleveland Wheel Club—as a coal miner, a shoeshiner in a Turkish bath, a porter in a barbershop—and his experiences in Chicago after marrying a white woman he met at a party in 1914. My father delighted in Mr. Jacobs's raucous laughter, which erupted whenever he made a particularly clever point exposing the absurdity of white prejudice. *Ha, ha, ha, ha, ha, ha. Mr. Jacobs laughed so loudly that his voice could be heard for blocks. I've never heard a man laugh so heartily before.* My heart melts, for Daddy also had a hearty laugh, often breaking into guffaws and *hee, hee, hee, hee, hee* at the dinner table.

I am happy to find among my father's papers notes from several visits with Mr. Jacobs and his new wife, another white woman, in the 1950s. Daddy recorded their conversations with the same care he brought to his earlier interviews from the 1930s, and he kept both sets of notes clipped together. I find myself wondering whether, by that point, these were still formal interviews or simply conversations between friends. When my father stopped by the Jacobs home in September 1963, Mrs. Jacobs shared that her husband had died of cancer four years earlier. I imagine he must have deeply felt the loss of the elderly gentleman who had become more than a research participant—someone he had remained close to for a quarter of a century.

CHAPTER 5

The Color Line

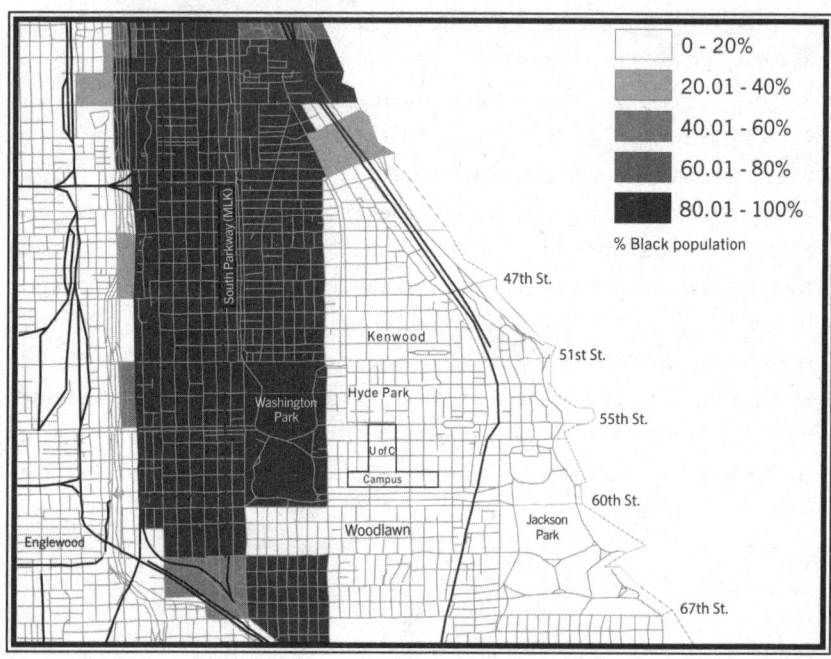

Map of Black Belt, Chicago, 1940

Dr. Andrews
September 1938

When my father visited Dr. Andrews a year and a half after their first conversation, he encountered a markedly different tone. Previously, Dr. Andrews had spoken freely, regaling my father with stories about his experiences, details about his relationship with his wife, and ideas on interracial marriage. Now he expressed suspicions about the motives behind the study, calling the University of Chicago "one of the most prejudiced places in the world" and the research questions "too personal." "Even if you try to be fair," he told my father, "I know that they are prejudiced there."

When my father probed why Dr. Andrews thought the university was biased, the response centered on housing. "The influence they have thrown into the question of Negroes living in white neighborhoods has been tremendous," he said. "They want the Negroes to stay in a congested area so that they can be exploited better. It seems to be the attitude of the university that a Negro shouldn't live in decent quarters."

Like Dr. Andrews, many of the couples my father interviewed in the 1930s remarked on Chicago's shifting racial landscape. They were witnessing the early waves of the Great Migration—the mass movement of Black Americans from the rural South to northern and western cities like Chicago, Detroit, New York, and Los Angeles. In *The Warmth of Other Suns*, Isabel Wilkerson captures the scale of this exodus, writing, "Over the course of six decades, some six million black southerners left the land of their forefathers and fanned out across the country for an uncertain existence in nearly every other corner of America." Fleeing the violent oppression of Jim Crow and seeking jobs in booming wartime industries, many migrants saw Chicago as a prime destination.

As I reflected on this migration, which spanned from 1915 to 1970, I realized that the marriages my father documented aligned with this transformative period. His interviews not only chronicled interracial relationships but also captured the largest internal migration in U.S. history—a movement that profoundly reshaped Chicago's social fabric for both Black and white residents. Interracial relationships formed and evolved within the social currents the Great Migration set into motion.

The couples were also witnessing a second, simultaneous phenomenon—a geographical shift within the city driven by white backlash to the arrival of Black migrants. Between 1910 and 1920, Chicago's Black population swelled from 44,000 to 109,000, and by 1934, it had surpassed 200,000. This rapid influx of migrants was met with intensifying residential segregation. Over the next three decades of continued migration from the South, Chicago became the most segregated northern city.

When my father began his study, Black Chicagoans were largely confined to a clearly defined area known as "the Black Belt," consisting of a narrow strip extending south of downtown. This recent racial segregation had reshaped the lives of Black residents, including members of the Black elite, who had once interacted socially and professionally with white communities. Now they were forced to live alongside newly arrived, unskilled migrants from the South in neighborhoods specifically designated to contain Black residents. With the Black population rapidly increasing, the Black Belt was bursting at the seams and its inability to expand led to severe overcrowding. By 1940, well into my father's research, Black neighborhoods were crammed with nearly four times as many residents per square mile as adjacent white areas.

The enforcement of this residential segregation required a colossal systematic effort carried out by realtors, banks, neighborhood associations, national organizations, and government officials as well as everyday individuals—all operating under legal authority. Chicago's racial boundaries were secured through white residents' use of violence, restrictive real estate covenants that barred sales to Black buyers, and federal housing policies that segregated public housing projects.

The Chicago Real Estate Board, for instance, voted in 1921 to expel any member who sold property to Black buyers in neighborhoods designated as white. The exclusionary practice faced legal challenges, including the landmark 1940 Supreme Court case, *Hansberry v. Lee*, which sought to enforce a covenant against Black homeowners. Carl A. Hansberry, a prominent real estate broker and father of renowned playwright Lorraine Hansberry, was at the center of this battle. In 1937, Carl had purchased a house in the South Park subdivision on Chicago's South Side, an all-white area bordered by Black communities to the west and south. This violated a racially restrictive covenant organized by the Woodlawn Property Owners Association, a group of white businessmen.

Although Hansberry prevailed in court, the Supreme Court's ruling rested on procedural grounds, neither confronting the discriminatory purpose of racially restrictive covenants nor overturning the precedents upholding them. It was not until the 1948 decision in *Shelley v. Kraemer* that the Court invalidated the enforceability of these covenants, holding they violated the Fourteenth Amendment. And while *Shelley* opened some white areas to Black residents, it did not result in an integrated city. South Park and Woodlawn, once fiercely guarded white territories, soon became segregated Black neighborhoods.

Initially, I had been surprised when the older couples my father interviewed told him that fewer people were marrying interracially than when they themselves had wed in the late 1800s. Mrs. Curtis, a white neighbor of Dr. Andrews in Morgan Park's desirable Negro community, told my father that discrimination against mixed couples had gotten worse. "Well, I believe in years gone by it wasn't a handicap," she reported in November 1938. "As times have gone on, thirty years has changed things. I believe it is a terrible handicap. Outside opposition makes it a handicap."

My father also noted the decline, attributing it to the intensifying residential and institutional separation between the races. In earlier decades, before the Black Belt had been established, Black people were scattered in predominantly white neighborhoods. By 1940, in contrast, most of the city's Black residents were concentrated in solidly segregated neighborhoods with limited social interactions with white people. Anti-Black sentiment and stereotypes intensified along with laws and policies that enforced racial segregation.

Mixed couples didn't just observe intensifying racial separation—they experienced it firsthand. Many described how interracial marriage collided violently with residential segregation. My father heard about the Blocks, a white wife and a Black husband, who once owned a home in a white neighborhood, but were forced to move after the 1919 race riot. "A mob was there and wanted to kill her," recalled another white wife, who knew the Blocks through the Manasseh Club.

White spouses who married Black partners had to leave their communities, friends, and families to live in areas where Black residents were confined. With rare exception, the couples my father interviewed in the 1930s resided in these segregated neighborhoods. They crossed two color lines—one dictating whom they could marry, the other determining where they could live.

As I read these stories, I'm struck by all the ways residential segregation shaped interracial marriage in Chicago. Segregated neighborhoods both deterred interracial relationships in the first place and penalized people who dared to defy the taboo against them. Forcing Black residents to live apart from white people constricted their opportunities to get to know each other intimately. Once married, residential segregation drastically limited where mixed couples could find housing. The geographic and social boundaries imposed by residential segregation also hampered the potential for the interracial marriages that did take place to have an impact on the racist order in Chicago. What the couples were telling my father in the 1930s confirmed my sense that the legal ability to marry across race operates within the racial caste system—it alone can't transcend it.

Even those couples who dared to marry across racial borders were still bound by them.

White wives and husbands who had been banished from the neighborhoods where they were raised found community with their spouses among Black people. Most white people my father interviewed were at least accepted in Black neighborhoods. Some, however, sensed disapproval from their new neighbors. "The white people don't want us at all. The colored people don't want us, but they tolerate us," was how Mrs. Wells put it. "Some colored people are prejudiced and some are not. It's about fifty-fifty in both races," she estimated. Mrs. Duckworth, sixty-nine years old, returned to a white neighborhood when her colored husband found work in New Mexico. "There aren't any women with colored husbands out here. If they knew I was connected I wouldn't be here," she said, conceding that her white neighbors would quickly boot her out if her mixed marriage were exposed.

My father tracked down a white widow, Mrs. Watts, who survived two Negro husbands and was one of the oldest living members of the Manasseh Club. He first located her daughter, hoping to secure the mother's address. The daughter, a light-skinned woman with wavy reddish-brown hair, agreed to speak with him.

"My mother has gone to the other side again. She's gone back now," the daughter informed my father. It takes me a minute to realize that she was saying that her mother had returned to the white neighborhood where she grew up, where she had lived before her marriages to Negro men.

"Your mother was with colored for a long time, wasn't she?" my father asked.

"Yes, since she was seventeen, and she will be seventy-four in January."

"Which side is your side?"

"My father's side," the daughter answered. By that she meant that she lived in a colored neighborhood.

"My mother comes and visits me, but it makes an awful gap between us," she said. "My brother is on the other side also. All the girls married colored and my brother married white." She explained that her brother was allowed to live in a white area with his white wife because he was passing as white.

My father's side. The other side. The words sting. I pause to think about this family tragedy caused by Chicago's racial divide, a hidden harm that had not occurred to me before. Residential segregation had split the Watts family apart geographically. The mixed-race daughters who "married colored" were forced to live in a different area of the city than their white mother and white-appearing brother, who had "married white." The color line had not only compelled Black families to live separately from white families. It had also compelled family members to live separately from one another. The daughter's story reminds me of the experience Trevor Noah recounts in *Born a Crime*, of being forced to grow up away from his Swiss father in apartheid South Africa, having to sneak around to visit him in a different part of town. The color line separated families as if they were living in nations ripped in two by war, like North and South Korea.

Armed with the address from her daughter, my father found Mrs. Watts in an apartment above a store on Cottage Grove Avenue in a white neighborhood. He noted her old-fashioned clothes. *Her full black skirt nearly reached her ankles.* He learned that she had immigrated with her parents to Chicago from Liverpool in 1872 at age seven and married her first husband, a coachman, ten years later. The couple had seven children, including the daughter my father had spoken with, all born before 1900. Mrs. Watts recounted her memories of the Manasseh Club founding, her two marriages to Negro men, the first one happy, the second spoiled by drinking, and her life as a white resident of a colored neighborhood.

As my father prepared to leave at six that evening, his attention turned to another daughter called Mrs. Cole, who was passing as white while she visited her mother. She had been lying on a couch, coughing, throughout the interview. *Mrs. Cole's cold seemed pretty bad and I asked her if I could buy her some medicine.* She replied with the type of remedy she needed. *I went to the drugstore and bought her a bottle which I gave her as a Christmas present.* I sense that my father seasoned his academic inquiries with a kindness that put his research subjects at ease. Another clue as to why so many were eager to welcome him back into their lives.

Residential segregation also harmed interracial couples by outing white spouses living in colored neighborhoods to their employers, jeopardizing their jobs. At the time, a white woman living among Negroes was a sure sign that she was sleeping with one of them. And that was cause for termination. "I never gave my right address," said another Mrs. Brown, a white wife in her forties living in Lilydale. (I'm not sure why my father sometimes gave two interviewees the same pseudonym.) "Once, I had a job, and told my right address, and it wasn't long and they let me out." From then on, she hid her husband's color because she knew that her boss would promptly fire her. That also meant she could never let her boss know where she lived. "No white woman can hold a job any place if it is known that her husband is colored. They would fire her immediately," Mrs. Wells told my father matter-of-factly. "It's too bad that they issue the license if they make it so hard for us."

Many white wives went to great lengths to conceal their marriages from their employers for fear of losing their jobs. Mrs. Lane always sat in the back seat when her husband picked her up from the office where she worked as a secretary. Once, when she offered her boss a ride to the train station, he got in the back with her, Mr. Lane acting as their chauffeur, the boss never suspecting they were married. One time she was sitting in the front seat with her husband, laughing together, when she noticed that a salesman from her office had spotted them. She told her husband to pull over so she could give the salesman an excuse. She told her coworker that the colored man she was with was merely giving her driving lessons.

"The only trouble I would have is if I would become ill and have to go to a hospital," Mrs. Lane said. "He couldn't see me then unless I didn't have my job." Apparently, Black men were allowed to visit their white wives in the hospital, but revealing their marriage could cost the women their employment.

"The husband doesn't visit her because he is afraid they won't treat the woman well if they know who her husband is," Mrs. Brown told my father in a later interview, offering a different explanation. "They don't find out that the woman has a colored husband till she dies and he calls for the body."

Once, Mrs. Lane was using an annual pass her husband had received from the railroad company that employed him. When the worker who checked the pass questioned her relationship to Mr. Lane, she responded that, despite looking white, she had colored blood. "I was telling the truth because I have red blood in my veins and that's colored," she told my father.

For some Black men, however, having a white wife brought unexpected advantages. Mr. Jacobs, for example, said it ensured a steady income. White employers, knowing his wife was "one of their race," wanted to make sure she was well-supported. During the 1919 race riot, Mr. and Mrs. Owens hid in their home while white mobs rampaged outside. Too afraid to leave, Mr. Owens relied on his wife to buy food. "No colored man could show his face on that street then," he recalled. "That's the one time my marriage helped me. If I didn't have a white wife, I would have starved."

Sitting in my rented Kenwood apartment decades later, reading these accounts—where white wives suffered for marrying Black men, while Black men sometimes benefited from their wives' whiteness—my thoughts, once again, shift to Black women. I wonder how they were treated in Chicago's segregated hospitals. Their same-race husbands had nothing to hide, so they could visit them—but I doubt it made any difference in their care. Did white bosses care whether their employees with Black wives earned enough to support their families? And when white rioters flooded the streets, did Black women dare leave their homes? I suspect they fared even worse than the white women who defied the color line to marry a Black man, regardless of whom they married.

Despite the absence of official Jim Crow laws, the interracial couples my father interviewed spent their lives maneuvering around the city's racist hurdles. In segregated Chicago, white spouses didn't just witness racism—they felt its impact. They were pushed into Black neighborhoods, risked losing their jobs, and feared neglect in hospitals. But this wasn't a special kind of discrimination against them, nor was it simply a case of seeing the world through their partner's eyes. Every hardship they faced stemmed from the same racial caste system designed to oppress Black people. And unlike their spouses, they had far more freedom to escape it.

To Mrs. Curtis, the white wife from Morgan Park, the children of mixed marriages suffered the most from being held back on account of their race. She gave the example of her son, nice-looking and smart as a whip, who was denied admission to the best schools. "It's like cutting me with a knife," she said.

"Don't colored children suffer the same handicaps?" my father asked. I am pleased that he thought to ask the very question that was on my mind. He recognized it was the discriminatory regime against Black people that held biracial children back—a regime that harmed Black children even more.

"The mixed child feels it more," Mrs. Curtis replied. "The hardest shock my children had was when they found out they were colored. We never wanted to tell them. People said things to them and finally we had to tell them and it was a terrible shock."

My parents never had a conversation like that with my sisters and me. There was no need for it. I don't recall my parents ever explicitly telling me, but for as long as I can remember, I knew that I was Black—and I knew that meant I'd be treated differently than if I were white.

CHAPTER 6

Passing

Bob swinging Dorothy, c. 1961

Dr. and Mrs. Everett
December 14, 1938

My father arrived at the well-maintained brick three-flat owned by Dr. Everett, a white physician, and his Black wife. Despite the prestige typically afforded a white man in his profession, they lived in a Black neighborhood like most of the other couples in my father's project. My father was greeted by an elderly man who was unusually agile for his years. Sporting a business suit and a full head of gray hair, Dr. Everett had a dignified appearance. The two men sat in a large parlor furnished with six or eight comfortable chairs and a large rug. My father noticed that all the pictures on the wall and atop the radio depicted white people.

Mrs. Everett soon joined them. She had straight black hair, combed up on her head, and her skin was very light, *but not as fair as most Europeans, her features show a trace of Negro blood.* When my father asked about portraits of two aristocratic-looking bearded white men hanging on the parlor wall, Mrs. Everett identified them as her father and uncle. "My father was one of the richest men in Tennessee," she said. "He raised me from the time I was six." She said her father was a doctor and her uncle a lawyer, but they were so wealthy they didn't need to practice their professions. Her mother, she continued, was born into slavery. Her grandmother was half Negro and half Indian, and her grandfather—a light-skinned enslaved man—was owned by her white great-grandfather.

"Mrs. Everett has a wonderful background," her husband interjected incongruously.

Mrs. Everett was born in May 1868, just three years after the Civil War ended. Her father took her from her mother to live with him when her mother married a Black man. Her father, himself a former enslaver, had owned vast properties across Louisiana, Mississippi, and Tennessee. "In slave times, he had thousands of Negroes on those farms," she re-marked, her words carrying a hint of pride in her father's ownership of human beings.

The nature of her mother's relationship with her father remained unclear at first. But when my father asked directly whether her mother had been enslaved before the war, she responded, "My mother belonged to Uncle Ted." She was referring to her father's brother, whose portrait hung in the parlor. Staunchly loyal to the Confederacy, Uncle Ted refused to swear allegiance to the Union or free the people he enslaved—until Yankee soldiers put a noose around his neck and threatened to hang him. Once freed, Mrs. Everett's mother married a Black man, who had also been enslaved by Uncle Ted. They had two children together before even-tually separating. She later moved near the area where Mrs. Everett's father owned a farm and married another Black man. "She came back down to where my father was, and that's how I came in between the two husbands," Mrs. Everett explained, leaving the circumstances of her conception unspoken.

It becomes clear to me that Mrs. Everett's father was one of those white men with a Black mistress whom so many couples had bad-mouthed to my father. He impregnated Mrs. Everett's mother, who had been enslaved by his brother, while he was married to a white wife. Given what we know about the social dynamics at the time, he probably raped her.

Yet, here was Mrs. Everett, painting her father as a hero for having rescued her from her mother and for raising her along with his white children. "My father was a wonderful man to have done that," she said. "He was a man of wealth and was not questioned." Dr. Everett embellished his father-in-law's extraordinary generosity even more. "In the colonial days the slaveholders did as they pleased," he explained. "To raise a colored and illegitimate child was not accepted, but a man like that was not questioned."

It wasn't her father's wife who cared for Mrs. Everett as a child, however. Her white stepmother had several children of her own and refused to rear her husband's illegitimate colored offspring. Instead, the little girl was raised by a special maid who lived in one of the cabins for the colored servants across from the plantation house. She even slept in the servants' quarters. "I would go across to where she lived in a log cabin and stay with her and come back to the big house in the morning," Mrs. Everett recalled. Sometimes she had to return to the cabin for a meal if her stepmother refused to feed her.

It was late in the conversation when my father screwed up the nerve to ask Mrs. Everett a question that had worried me from the start.

"Did your father live openly with your mother before he was married?"

"No, I'll tell you the truth," Mrs. Everett replied. "My mother says it was forced on her. She wasn't willing to and he forced her. It was just a forced thing, but I'm glad it was forced because of me. I'm so proud of my father."

Stunned, I drop the papers into my lap and stare into the quiet room. I can hardly bear Mrs. Everett's egregious disregard for her mother and equally appalling praise for her father. As I continue reading the transcript, my only consolation is learning that Mrs. Everett had eventually brought her mother, a woman who had never learned to read or write, up from Tennessee to live with her in Chicago. Her mother had come with the other children she had had with her formerly enslaved husband—Mrs. Everett's half-siblings. "My mother was with us all the time we were married, till she died here," Mrs. Everett said. I wonder if it was because of those relatives that they lived in a colored neighborhood. It seems that Mrs. Everett could have passed as white, so without them, she might have lived with her husband on the other side of the color line.

Mrs. Everett was sent by her father to study at Fisk University, a private liberal arts college for Black students in Nashville. Founded in 1866 as the Fisk Freed Colored School, part of the fleeting Reconstruction effort launched at the end of the Civil War, it was the first institution of higher education in Nashville, older than Vanderbilt. In 1930, it became the first colored institution to earn accreditation from the Southern Association of Colleges and Schools. Mrs. Everett was in the second generation of Fisk students, I estimate. There she met Dr. Everett, who was one of her professors.

Dr. Everett, born in England, boasted a prestigious pedigree as well. His father was a fencing instructor at the Royal Military Academy in Woolwich, England, before immigrating to America and teaching at Fisk, a position he eventually handed to his son, who was studying medicine at Vanderbilt. Dr. Everett bragged that his father trained the likes of King Edward, Lord Kitchener, and President Taft in the martial arts. While head of athletics at Fisk, Dr. Everett taught calisthenics to the student who would become his wife, later earning his medical degree and opening his own doctor's office. They traveled to Toronto, Canada, to wed in 1896, as interracial marriage was prohibited throughout the South and parts of the North at that time. Fifteen years later, they remarried in Chicago to acquire a U.S. record of their union. The couple had been married for forty-two years. "And we're more in love than ever," Mrs. Everett added.

When Dr. Everett proudly took a wedding picture of the attractive couple off the radio to show my father, my father noted that Mrs. Everett looked white.

"Could you tell that your wife was colored at the time you married her?"

"She had just a little colored cast," Dr. Everett replied.

"I didn't have him fooled. Is that what you mean?" Mrs. Everett retorted.

The couple then engaged with my father in a fascinating, if disturbing, repartee about the nature of racial mixing in the South. Mrs. Everett emphasized the extent of her white ancestry—her father was white and her mother's father, though enslaved, was almost white. Many of the colored girls at Fisk could pass as white, she added. Dr. Everett explained that the mixing of races could be traced to slavery, when enslavers fathered children with the women they held in bondage. He did not mention that the mixture resulted from sexual violence, that the enslaved women were raped by their enslavers, as had been the case with his mother-in-law. In fact, he put a positive spin on this horrific aspect of enslavement that I had never heard before. "It was not from the common people, but from the aristocratic slaveholders," he told my father, referring to the ancestry of Black individuals like his wife. "Some of the colored people have fine blood."

It seems that Dr. Everett's acceptance of Mrs. Everett as a colored woman worthy to be his wife hinged on her having descended from aristocratic slaveholders rather than from "ordinary colored folk," and on her being able to pass as white. I wonder if Dr. Everett would have considered marrying a woman with darker skin and if Mrs. Everett would have considered marrying a dark-skinned man, who might spoil the "fine blood" running in her family's veins. I feel weary from the obsession with whitening the Black race, with keeping the white race "pure enough," that I have encountered time and again throughout my father's interviews.

When my father asked his usual question about the Manasseh Club, the Everetts responded that they weren't familiar with the club. Perhaps this is unsurprising, given the club's exclusion of colored women with white husbands, despite the Everetts' very respectable home and pedigree. But Mrs. Everett flipped the rejection on its head. She said she wasn't interested in a club made up of white women married to Negro men, because—she claimed—most of them were "a low type." With those words, she turned their own insult back on them, deploying the very language they used to disparage women like her.

Mrs. Everett explained that she and her husband owned fourteen flats in the city's colored section, which they rented at a reasonable rate, unlike the white slumlords, who exploited tenants by charging them more than similar quarters cost in white neighborhoods. Only renting to choice tenants, she refused to lease her apartments to white women with Black husbands. "With the white woman's advantages, to lower herself to have a common Negro man, I wouldn't mix with them," she sneered. I almost smile at the way Mrs. Everett turned the tables on the white wives who had excluded women like her. But no one deserved to be called a "low type" for whom they chose to marry—not the white wives, nor Mrs. Everett.

My father had already donned his overcoat to leave when he asked a final question of Mrs. Everett, as if anticipating the concern I have. "Do you think you could have married a colored man?"

"No, I wouldn't marry a colored man," she answered, then thought better of it. "Maybe I could have married a real light one or if he was prominent."

"I don't think I would marry a girl as dark as her mother," Dr. Everett interjected.

Passing—Black people pretending to be white—came up repeatedly throughout the interviews my father conducted in the 1930s. It was a prominent topic in my father's very first conversations with the Alberts, and it arose in almost every exchange that followed. It was another way some couples crossed the color line, the Black spouses crossing into white neighborhoods instead of the other way around. Many of the couples seem fixated on whether their mixed-race children could pass as white. One white wife said her son could pass in winter but not in summer. If the couple didn't mention it, my father asked the question directly or, if the children were present, saw for himself. How light was their skin, European their facial features, straight their hair?

All the children are Caucasoid in racial characteristics although they show slight Negroid traces, my father observed about the four offspring of a white woman and Negro man, the Armstrongs, he interviewed in October 1937. *The two youngest boys can probably pass as white with little difficulty. The girl can almost do so*, he concluded his appraisal. There was no need to state the obvious about the oldest boy, for he was *the only one whose skin is definitely darker than that of a European.*

Mr. Barnes, also interviewed in October that year, claimed his two girls, ages nineteen and seventeen, could pass as white anywhere because they "are as white as I am." When the younger daughter, Betty, strolled across the room, however, my father noted, *I hardly thought so. Her features are European but her color is almost too dark for a Mediterranean type.*

I had never thought about my father's expectations for my sisters and me, at least not in terms of our physical appearance. He expected us to excel in school. He relied on my mother to keep us neat, tidy, and well-behaved. But, looking back on my childhood, I cannot think of a single time he remarked on our "racial characteristics." I suppose if he wanted to have children who could pass as white or whose features leaned toward European, he never would have married my mother, whose dark skin and African features made such desires a risky proposition.

Once, a Black wife complained to my father that her light-skinned son refused to pass as white. "Isn't that foolish?" she asked my father somewhat rhetorically. I appreciated my father's response: *I thought that Mrs. Boone wanted my opinion and replied that I thought his refusal to do so was a fine expression of devotion to his mother.*

My father may have remarked obsessively on the physical traits of his research subjects, but he never once in his notes or conversations suggested that the more European ones were superior, or the more African ones any less attractive.

One day in elementary school, a Black girl had cornered me in the girls' bathroom. She had discovered my father was white, perhaps from the time he chaperoned my class on a school field trip. "Are you Black or white?" she wanted to know. She was not satisfied with the answer my parents taught me, "I'm just human." "You have to be one or the other—Black or white," she insisted. When I refused to pick sides, she told me there were tests to figure out which race I was. "Do you have good hair?" she queried. This was a tricky one. My mother put my hair in braids and didn't straighten it, so I must have good hair. But it was obvious from its kinkiness that my hair texture didn't qualify as "good."

So the girl moved to the next test. "Do you have freckles?" she questioned me, inclining closer to inspect my face. My nose and cheeks were sprinkled with brown dots. "Freckles mean you're white," she pronounced. But we both knew I looked unmistakably like a Black girl, despite my freckles. She left the bathroom with a confused look on her face. I felt vindicated that her racial diagnostics didn't work as she intended. They only proved, as my parents always said, that I was just human, after all. I don't remember exactly when that bathroom interrogation took place, but it must have been in the early grades. By around fourth grade, I would have chosen one side. I would have said firmly, "I'm Black." I can't remember a time when I didn't think of myself as a Black girl. But when I was very young, I accepted my parents' emphasis on our shared humanity. I followed their lead, avoiding statements of racial identity. That changed as I learned more—about racism, about resistance, and about who I wanted to be in the world. As I began to think for myself and shape my own identity, I became more willing—and determined—to say, "I'm Black."

How we determine someone's race—especially when they don't fit neatly into categories—is now an area of study in psychology and sociology. While teaching at Northwestern, I had a graduate student, Destiny Peery, who researched how people classify racially ambiguous individuals. She showed college students computer-generated faces designed not to fit neatly in any racial category and asked them to determine the race of each one. She discovered that people rely on a mix of physical features, social cues, and ingrained racial norms, like the one-drop rule, which labels anyone with any African ancestry as Black. Skin tone, hair texture, the race of one's parents or friends—these all shaped how participants made their judgments. In the end, race wasn't a fixed identity, but a fluid, ever-shifting perception, one that defies any definitive rules.

Years later, at a symposium at the University of Pennsylvania, I learned that this research had evolved. Now scientists use databases of computer-generated faces and incorporate genetic ancestry data to study which factors influence racial identification. The question isn't just how we see racially ambiguous people—it's also how they see themselves.

Despite all this high-tech research, one thing hasn't changed: the old racial categories we inherited from slavery and Jim Crow still shape our thinking. The one-drop rule continues to influence how people define race, as does the reality that race isn't determined by biology but by social and cultural norms. Whiteness remains the most carefully guarded racial identity. The same questions my father studied in the 1930s are still driving research today. Either he was ahead of his time, or we're still stuck in outdated ways of thinking. I suspect both are true.

When my father interviewed Mr. Jacobs, the Negro man with a hearty laugh and impressive command of history, he had a few questions for his daughter, Mrs. Pierce. She lived in the same house along with her husband, also the offspring of an interracial marriage, and their two small boys. Mrs. Pierce, my father observed, *appears to be entirely white*, and I surmise from their exchange that her husband and children had a similar appearance. Mrs. Pierce told my father that she wanted to move away from Lilydale so her sons could associate with white people. "I'd hate to see my boys marry a black woman," she said. I wonder if she used the word "black" instead of "colored" to emphasize that she was referring to the dark shade that wouldn't produce a child light enough to pass as white—something she had achieved in her sons—like a dark sock that ruins a load of white laundry. I shudder to think that moving to a white neighborhood, passing as white, might deprive her sons of the rich heritage that their grandfather, Mr. Jacobs, had shared with my father.

Then, all of a sudden, she turned the table on my father, asking him if he could imagine his sister marrying a colored man. I perk up and turn the page of the transcript.

"How could a white woman with white friends just marry a Negro? The way they want to have you believe that out of a clear sky they fell in love with a Negro," she sneered dismissively. "I think they should be thrown in a sack and drowned."

"You ought to overcome your tendency to become upset when someone talks about intermarriage," my father advised her. His words catch me off guard—part deflection, part rebuke. I don't recall him ever scolding the husbands, like Mr. Alberts or Dr. Everett, when they said something foolish. But something about Mrs. Pierce's comment seemed to have touched a nerve. Maybe it was the way she had asked such a personal question. Or maybe it was the bluntness with which she had rejected the idea of marrying a Black person—condemning the very kind of marriage he was learning to value.

It appeared Mrs. Pierce had wished that her father had been white so she would have been born white. When Mr. Jacobs walked out of earshot, she whispered to my father that she wasn't sure he was really her father. "I used to think I was just unfortunate to be born this way, but now I have two children to think about," she said in a feeble attempt to defend her views.

It was the Manasseh Club's colorism that repelled a white wife, Mrs. Daniels, from becoming a member. When my father interviewed her at her apartment in Englewood, a neighborhood that would later change to all Black, she criticized the Manasseh members' fondness for light-skinned children. "They had the attitude that their children were a little better than the full-colored child," she explained.

Mrs. Daniels felt that this preference for biracial children backfired, however, because it instilled in the children a belief that colored people were incapable of high achievement. "That's why many of the Manasseh offspring haven't amounted to anything," she said. "They think that a colored person can't get anywhere."

Sitting in this rented apartment a lifetime later, only a couple neighborhoods away, I hear Mrs. Daniels to mean that the Manasseh parents had unwittingly given their children an inferiority rather than a superiority complex. Ironically, by disparaging children with two colored parents as inferior to their own children with one white parent, they had shattered their children's confidence in their own worth, for their children would soon learn that they, too, were considered colored.

I mull over these comments about the Manasseh children and am struck by how much they diverge from my father's views regarding the distinctiveness of mixed-race children. Daddy saw his research as contesting the belief that white people were innately superior to Black people, along with its corollary that children produced by racial mixing were destined to have biological, psychological, and social problems. While my sisters and I were growing up, he constantly told us that we were special because we were raised by parents of different races. He made it clear that we were expected to do well in school, to capably handle any conflict, and to be comfortable in any social situation. But he never indicated that we were better than other Black children. How could he when he so admired my mother, when we all knew that Mommy was the most gifted person in the family? My father's conviction that his daughters would not be tragic mulattoes filled me with confidence, not a sense of superiority.

My heart breaks for the Manasseh children who came out darker than their white mothers had hoped. A son or daughter who couldn't pass as white was born into disappointment. As a child of two parents who always loved me exactly as I am, I can only begin to imagine how painful that must have been.

As I continue to study the transcripts late into the evening, I am reminded of a highly publicized lawsuit brought by a white woman in 1990 against a fertility clinic for inseminating her with a Black man's sperm instead of her husband's, resulting in the birth of a Black child. The woman, who was the biological mother of the child, sought monetary damages, claiming her injury stemmed from the unbearable racial taunting her daughter endured in their white neighborhood. Reporters speculated that "[i]f the suit goes to trial, a jury could be faced with the difficult task of deciding damages involved in raising an interracial child." While the wrongful insemination was an injury in itself, as the child was not biologically her husband's, the fact that the sperm came from a donor of a different race allegedly compounded the harm. This second layer of harm, according to the mother, was tied to the clinic's failure to fulfill a crucial promise—providing her with a white child.

When I watch professional basketball games with my husband, I can't help but notice how many of the Black players have light skin and wavy hair. From what I can tell, many of them have white mothers. I've also noticed that many players—at rates higher than in the general Black population—date and marry white women. I'm not the only one who has observed this pattern. In June 2022, someone tweeted, "Modern NBA culture. #NBADraft," with a montage of video clips of the selected players walking onstage flanked by their Black fathers and white mothers. I speculate about the reasons behind this apparent phenomenon—whether Black basketball players and their fathers prefer to marry white women, or whether white women are seeking Black basketball players to marry.

I have no right to question their reasons for choosing a spouse. Yet, I recall former NBA player LaVar Ball claiming in an interview that he chose his tall, white wife for her physical traits, intending to "breed" children who would become basketball stars—and the success of two of his sons in the NBA was, to him, living proof of that theory. That kind of thinking sounds to me like the Manasseh ladies' disturbing desires for their children seven decades ago. There's no use in denying that such ideas continue to circulate in society today and influence some people's marital fantasies.

In that moment I admit to myself that when I first discovered that my father had begun studying interracial marriage long before he met my mother—and not *because* of meeting her—the thought had crossed my mind: Were my sisters and I part of his research? Living proof of his argument against the prevailing beliefs about children of interracial couples? But I had brushed that unsettling thought aside. My sisters and I used to joke that Daddy saw us as an extension of his theories. But we never believed he had married our mother with some larger purpose in mind. My father's love for us was too steady, too undeniable. There was never any doubt that we were the product of his love for my mother, not the result of a socio-logical experiment.

Although some of the 1930s couples relished their children's European appearance, the main motivation behind passing expressed in the interviews was economic, rather than athletic or aesthetic. Black people passed to live in a white neighborhood or to obtain and keep a better job. Mrs. Murphy was the white wife of a Black union leader known as a racketeer who was shot and killed by political adversaries in 1944. She told my father about a mixed couple that was living in a white neighborhood. "He is very light, though, and passes for white there," she said. "He comes here every day and is known to be colored by the colored people." She knew many colored people pretending to be white for "economic reasons," several of whom worked for the fancy Marshall Field's and Carson Pirie department stores, which refused to hire Black salespeople.

Mrs. Barnes, the Black wife whose husband claimed both daughters could pass, recalled going shopping when her older daughter was a baby. They were at a store together when several white women put the baby on a counter and formed an admiring circle around her, exclaiming how beautiful she was. "They thought I was her nurse and didn't know I was her mother," Mrs. Barnes told my father.

She said that her daughter, now grown, "only works as white" and has never done a "colored job." Contradicting my father's private assessment, Mrs. Barnes confided that her younger daughter, Betty, identified as white at her high school. "They think she is French or Italian." The fact that Mr. Barnes had appeared at the school corroborated Betty's whiteness. "They don't question that his children are white," Mrs. Barnes explained.

The opposite was true with my father when I was growing up. Once, my sister Helen and I had an appointment with an ophthalmologist in downtown Chicago. We had both been diagnosed as nearsighted and began wearing glasses in elementary school. My other sister, Evelyn, was blessed with perfect vision and spared the indignity. My mother brought us to the doctor's office and checked us in, but for some reason left us there for my father to retrieve. Maybe she had to get to work. Maybe she couldn't resist shopping close-by at Marshall Field's or Carson's—the name everyone used in the 1960s. They were still fancy department stores then. When Daddy arrived, he told the receptionist he was there to pick up his two daughters. "Your daughters haven't been here," the receptionist responded. As my father's confusion over his missing children mounted, Helen and I walked out of the exam room into the reception area. It was the receptionist who was confused. It never crossed her mind that the daughters of the white man standing before her were Black.

A photograph of my father and me when I was about five comes to mind. He's in a suit and tie, lifting me high into the air. I'm wearing a crisp cotton dress that flares at the waist, caught in mid-motion. It looks like he was spinning me around and the camera froze us in the middle of the fun. We're both laughing, my mouth open in a wide smile, my eyes bright with delight. The image feels slightly off. We're dressed too formally for that kind of play. It must have been taken at one of my parents' more elegant parties. I imagine the photo might strike others as even stranger, just my father and me, without my mother in the frame. In the dominant view of what a family is supposed to look like, we don't seem to belong together.

Other Black spouses passed to enjoy the better treatment afforded white people in Chicago's theaters, restaurants, and social clubs. "A colored person can go into any restaurant or hotel in Chicago and they have to serve you. If they don't you can have their license taken away," a white wife told my father. "I know because I was a waitress." But many of the Black interviewees reported otherwise. Mrs. O'Rourke, the Black wife of a white sewer fixer, referred my father to a mixed couple, but warned, "I don't know if she'll talk to you because she says she is white, but she's almost as dark as I am. She told me that she went with her father to a restaurant on Michigan Boulevard and they wouldn't serve him, but they served her." So much for restaurants losing their licenses if they refused Black customers!

Those who passed often shifted from Black to white and back again, depending on the circumstance. They might live in a colored neighborhood, where friends and family knew them as Black, then assume a white identity at work, school, or moving through the city. I imagine the psychological toll was staggering. The dual existence must have demanded constant vigilance—always watching your movements, your words, your accent. The code-switching alone must have been exhausting, compounded by the ever-present fear of being discovered. I imagine passing brought a deep ache—the pain of hiding parts of yourself, of never fully belonging to either world. Some interviewees, like Mrs. Wells's daughter, spoke of family members forced to break ties with loved ones to keep up the illusion.

I can understand why some Black people in the 1930s passed as white if they had the chance, as a form of subversion against the white supremacist order bent on denying them good jobs and entrance into public spaces. It's not the same as fighting to topple the racist regime, but it's a way to elude it. I can barely muster a shred of empathy, however, for the couples who took pleasure in having children who could pass as white—and who chose a partner with that objective in mind.

It dawns on me that some of the people my father interviewed had married because of their partner's color, not despite it. Some Black partners chose white spouses in the hope of lightening their children's skin, even imagining they might one day pass as white. Some white partners, in turn, selected Black spouses with light skin, hoping their children would turn out lighter than their spouse. I'm appalled by their obsession with color, especially when it was driven by the desire to look whiter—to lighten Black people generation by generation. It is precisely this kind of thinking that has always made it hard for me to see anything inherently positive in interracial intimacy. Why I've never been able to share my father's optimism, much to his chagrin.

CHAPTER 7

Coppers

Interview with
Mrs. Cadwell and
Mr. Downing
56-- S. Calumet Avenue
November 30, 1938
by Robert Roberts.

For the last year or more I had tried to locate Mr. and Mrs.
Cadwell without success. Mr. Cadwell is one of the leading members
of the Communist Party in Chicago. He is Negro and his wife is
Jewish. I was given four different address and two W.P.A. projects
where I might find Mr. Cadwell, but until today he had kept one
address ahead of me. Several persons had referred me to the Cadwells as the outstanding intermarriage in the Communist group. One
of my informants said that Mr. Cadwell had spent a year in jail for
his activities in the Communist movement.

Transcript of Mrs. Cadwell interview, November 30, 1938

Mr. and Mrs. Evans
September 17, 1937

My father was six months into his research when he arrived at the front desk of an unnamed hotel on Michigan Avenue whose customers were purported to be almost exclusively mixed couples. He told the clerk he was there to visit Mr. and Mrs. Evans. The clerk responded that he could proceed straight to a room at the end of the hall. When he knocked on the door, a female voice invited him in. He found Mrs. Evans, a dark-haired, thin, young white woman, lying in bed, clad in a bathrobe, *although it was mid-afternoon and she appeared to be quite well.* Her hair was styled in a straight bob; she wore glasses. Her husband should return soon, she said.

When my father explained he was studying mixed marriages, Mrs. Evans reported that the couple had recently been released from the Bridewell jail after being detained there for ten days "because of what you just mentioned." Apparently, she and her husband had been arrested for being an interracial couple. Evicted from their rented apartment, most of their furniture taken, they were living at the hotel temporarily.

"This was our first scrape with the law. The police and judges are very prejudiced against mixed couples," she told my father. "It's gotten so that they can't get married in Chicago anymore. The clerks won't issue licenses to mixed couples."

"If only one person needs to apply for a marriage license, how do the clerks know the race of the intended spouse?" my father queried.

"They've fixed it so that both persons have to appear now," Mrs. Evans replied. "If a mixed couple goes to the marriage license bureau, they can't get a license. Whatever the clerks decide to do is the law."

Mrs. Evans disclosed that, although she called Mr. Evans her husband, the two had lived together for seven years without formally tying the knot. People who loved across Chicago's color line were in a bind, she explained. "If you're not married, they want to know why you aren't and if you are married they want to know what's wrong with you."

The way clerks in Chicago policed marriage licensing to discourage interracial unions mirrored the legal apparatus Walter Plecker, Virginia's registrar of vital statistics, was overseeing to enforce the state's Racial Integrity Act. Even after the Supreme Court's *Loving* decision striking down interracial marriage bans, the racial regulation of marriage persisted at the local level.

Reading this transcript made me think of Ashley Ramkishun and Samuel Sarfo, who discovered the remnants of Plecker's handiwork when they tried to apply for a marriage license on a summer day in 2019. At the clerk's office in Arlington County, Virginia, Ramkishun, whose parents are of Indian descent, and Sarfo, a Black man who grew up in Ghana, were instructed to complete a computerized marriage registration form. The form included a mandatory "Race" field with a drop-down list of seven categories to choose from—American Indian / Alaskan Native, African American / Black, Asian, Caucasian, Hispanic/Latino, Pacific Islander, and Other. When the couple refused to click on a race category, the computer system blocked their application. They could not get married in Virginia without specifying their race. It wasn't until October of that year that a federal judge ruled the racial-identification requirement unconstitutional.

Mr. Evans, an out-of-work Pullman porter from Birmingham, Alabama, soon arrived at the hotel room. He was a *dark, tall Negro with rather straight plastered down hair, parted in the middle*, my father observed. *He has rather long sideburns and a sophisticated-looking mustache which gives him a rather South American appearance.* Mr. Evans recounted the incident that landed the couple in the county jail. Two weeks before, while he and his wife were hosting a party with friends, a police officer pushed open the door and arrested everyone at the apartment, charging them with having a disorderly house. "The copper did not have a search warrant or anything," Mr. Evans reported. At the hearing, under questioning from a judge, the officer conceded that he saw no disorderly conduct, no one was underage or undressed, no one was intoxicated. The judge dismissed the charges, but kept the pair behind bars, pending the results of blood tests, the purpose of which is not explained in the transcript.

The abuse the couple endured at the hands of the judge and police officers reflected a widespread method of punishing interracial marriages in Chicago despite their legality. Government officials often exploited vice laws, which were intended to enforce the city's moral standards, to criminalize interracial relationships. Black-white unions, even when legally recognized, could be redefined as unlawful forms of vice. For instance, in 1918, Chicago police arrested a Black man, Norval Wilburn, in the home he shared with his wife, Mable Fauhl, a white woman, charging him with fornication. Judge Wells Cook, who presided over the Morals Court branch of the municipal court, sentenced Mr. Wilburn to six months in prison. According to the *Chicago Defender*, Judge Cook also ordered Ms. Fauhl to "keep away" from Mr. Wilburn, calling him a racial slur.

Exercising his broad discretion to interpret the vice code, Judge Cook had declared that the legal marriage between a white woman and a Black man constituted "unlawful intimacy" under state law. Large-scale police raids on dance halls, social clubs, and private homes where Black and white residents socialized together reinforced the criminalization of interracial intimacy in the name of cleaning up the city.

The intersection of white supremacy, eugenics, and anti-miscegenation manifested in another alarming power held by the Morals Court. Judges had authority to refer any defendant to the Psychopathic Laboratory, a branch of the court dedicated to the scientific evaluation of defendants, and to commit those diagnosed with irredeemable "mental deficiencies" to state institutions. Legal historian Kate Markey explains that within this eugenics-based program, interracial relationships were viewed as both a symptom and a cause of societal disease. "Being 'mixed stock' was believed to increase the likelihood of degeneracy," she notes, "and one of the symptoms of degeneracy was hypersexuality, often expressed as an attraction to someone of a different race." I was struck by how closely Chicago's legal regime mirrored the framework established by Virginia legislators through their jointly enacted racial integrity and eugenic sterilization laws.

Mrs. Cadwell, a member of the Communist Party in her twenties whose Jewish parents had fled Russia, told my father a similar story. She reported that as recently as 1933, the police used to stop anyone who looked like a communist.

"How could the police tell if you were a communist?" my father asked.

"Any white and Negro man or woman together was a communist," Mrs. Cadwell explained. "Mabel Blake was arrested for walking with a Negro girl. At that time, if two women, white and colored, were found together they were arrested as prostitutes. They would arrest any white woman associating with a Negro man or woman and book her as a prostitute. Only our mass meetings and protests stopped it."

Mr. Cadwell, a leader in Chicago's Communist Party, had been jailed many times for leading protests against unemployment, evictions, discrimination by restaurants, and police brutality. He told my father about narrowly escaping a vicious beating by police when a battalion of officers attacked the demonstration he had addressed. After the police caught and fatally beat a different man, a newspaper headline incorrectly proclaimed "Cadwell Killed Leading Riot against Police." Mr. Cadwell eventually was tried, along with a Negro woman, a white woman, and three other Negro men, for conspiracy with intent to kill, allegedly by throwing a brick. They were convicted and sentenced to one to five years in prison. Represented by the International Labor Defense, the defendants were granted a new trial by the Illinois Supreme Court and sentenced anew to serve only ten days in the county jail.

I find appended to the transcripts of my father's several conversations with the Cadwells an excerpt titled "Some Typical Negro Communists," from Harold F. Gosnell's *Negro Politicians*, which my father had apparently transcribed. The typed excerpt contains interviews of prominent Negro members of the Communist Party. The first person highlighted, identified as "Comrade X," is described as one of the first Negroes in Chicago to join the Party, with a reputation for being a "brave and sensitive leader" and "one of the best-grounded Negroes in the country in the theory of Communism." I realize that Comrade X is Mr. Cadwell when I read that he is married to a young white woman and escaped from the police after a demonstration. As I follow my father's interest in Chicago's communist community as a source of couples for his study, I wonder if he was also attracted to communist organizing and the electrifying activists who were involved in it.

When my father interviewed twenty-two-year-old Mrs. Booth, a white Communist Party member, her husband was locked up in Bridewell—not for activism, but for larceny. The couple lived in a cramped South Side flat with his family, Black migrants from Georgia. Born to Italian immigrants in Iowa, Mrs. Booth moved to Chicago's West Side as a child. In high school, she befriended Black classmates and danced at an interracial boys' club. Her family's struggles during the Depression led her mother to join the Communist Party, and Mrs. Booth soon followed, immersing herself in labor and civil rights activism.

By 1935, she had moved to a Black neighborhood, sharing an apartment with a Party comrade. While protesting an eviction, she was arrested for "having a disorderly house," a common excuse to break up interracial gatherings. A judge warned her to stay out of South Side activism or face jail time. "I still did, but they didn't find me," she told my father. A year after her arrest, she joined efforts to desegregate Jackson Park Beach. "We were trying to break up Jim Crowism," she recalled. When police arrived to enforce segregation, they arrested the white protesters, while ordering Black beachgoers to leave. Apparently, it was an even greater offense, in their eyes, for white residents to defy the racial order than for Black people to cross the color line. The demonstration persisted for three Sundays until the beach was finally open to all.

Mrs. Booth was arrested again while picketing a whites-only restaurant. When fifty protesters, including University of Chicago students, staged a sit-in, police threatened them with arrest. Officers ignored the discrimination, telling Black protesters, "Don't you know not to go where you are not wanted?" The group held firm, spent the night in jail, and eventually won. The restaurant lost its license.

Mrs. Booth had been more committed to the movement than her husband. Fed up with his hanging out with the boys and flirting with girls, she wasn't sure she'd take him back when he was released from jail. She was already considering two potential suitors—one, a well-paid white railroad foreman she didn't love; the other, a Black man she liked, but who struggled financially.

Mrs. Booth stood out among the white wives my father interviewed. Her dedication to racial justice, her deep ties to the Black community, and her willingness to sacrifice for her ideals were remarkable. I wonder if her politics shaped her decision to marry a Black man in the first place. Yet, by the end of the interview, it seemed her next choice in a partner would be determined less by ideology and more by practical concerns. Perhaps marrying across the color line had once been a radical act, but with a child to raise, economic security now took priority.

CHAPTER 8

It Is a Handicap

Bob, right, in the army with his cousin Donald Hollister, England, 1943

Mrs. Tyler
September 29, 1938

When my father rang the doorbell of a brick two-flat on Forty-Sixth Street near Forrestville Avenue, a woman's voice called out, "Who's there?" He asked for Mrs. Tyler. The voice responded, "Wait till I put some clothes on." Within a minute, Mrs. Tyler came to the door, explaining that she had been taking a bath. A thin woman of thirty-one years, she was wearing a light housedress and shoes without stockings, her dark brown hair held up in a net. Born and raised in a Bohemian village in Czechoslovakia, she spoke with an accent. When my father explained that he was studying interracial marriage and was referred to her by Mrs. Haines, another white wife of a colored man, Mrs. Tyler quickly ushered him inside and up the stairs to her second-floor apartment. Turning down my father's offer to return at a more convenient time, she was eager to share her views on the topic. "No, I want to talk to you now that you are here," she said. "I probably will tell you something different than what Mrs. Haines would tell you."

Once seated at the opposite end of a sofa from my father, Mrs. Tyler immediately launched into a tirade against her neighbor and interracial marriage. "As a human being, I think Mrs. Haines has the wrong point of view when she tries to influence others to marry like she did," Mrs. Tyler said. "I suppose Mrs. Haines would tell you she is happy. When they say they are happy that is just a front. Such a marriage can't work."

She reported that Mrs. Haines had to hide her children when she visited the farm where her mother lives. "Is that happiness?" she asked for effect. Mrs. Tyler was especially angry at Mrs. Haines for encouraging young white women to marry colored men, with the promise that a colored man would treat them better than a white husband. Mrs. Haines and her husband had gone so far as to arrange for white girls to meet colored men on the South Side. "She should be put in jail for what she is doing," Mrs. Tyler snorted.

Mrs. Tyler's protest was not exactly against her husband. She complained about his gambling and "ignorant point of view," but quickly added that he had always supported her and their nine-year-old son. "Even when he gambles, he will pawn his coat rather than have us in need." Unlike the Bohemian men she grew up with, who made their wives work hard, her husband owned a garage, didn't smoke or drink in the house, and treated her well. She seemed to have forgiven him for the infidelity that took place four years before. What she could not abide was the way she was treated outside the house when her husband accompanied her. Because of her marriage, she couldn't travel freely, live where she pleased, or visit her relatives.

"I never go anywhere with my husband because it humiliates me," she told my father. "When we ride in the car I sit in the back seat. How can you be happy when people stare at you wherever you go?" Once, she and Mr. Tyler accidentally ran into each other on a streetcar. They didn't speak, pretending not to know each other.

"Not that I don't like my husband," she continued. "I think more of him than I do of anybody else, but still, I'm so sick of that life and I know there's no future in it. No matter how much you love one person, you can't give up the rest of the world."

Mrs. Tyler rehearsed other impediments she had confronted because of her marriage, hardships my father had already heard about from other white wives. She railed against the doubly restrictive mixture of employment discrimination and housing segregation. How she discovered that she and her husband would be forced to live in a colored neighborhood. How she learned that she had to keep her marriage secret if she wanted to earn a living. "A white woman with a colored husband can't hold a job anywhere," she declared.

"If you give a different address and you talk with the girls and they find that you don't live there but in a colored neighborhood you are through," she said. She lost her position managing the dining room at the Chicago Boys' Club when she asked a coworker to mail a letter with a telltale address in the colored section. Another time, a colored maid who cleaned at the nightclub where she waitressed saw her in the neighborhood they shared. Mrs. Tyler didn't bother to return to work the next day. When she was employed as a waitress at the Illinois Central station, she made sure to list her address as located in a white neighborhood. Unfortunately, her boss noticed that she was not riding on the Illinois Central train to and from work, as she should have if she lived at the given address. He conscripted another employee to follow her home and discovered her true residence. "They let me go immediately. They didn't give me ten minutes' notice."

Mrs. Tyler's worst brush with Chicago's racist regime happened in 1934. She had separated from her husband when she found a receipt for rent in his pocket and went to the address it listed, only one block from their house. Her husband was having an affair. Confronting the woman she found there, she told her to vacate the apartment. When the woman brazenly refused, Mrs. Tyler arranged for her to be put in the street. Mrs. Tyler sent her son, five years old at the time, to live with his grandmother, and moved in with her aunt in a rented apartment in the white part of town. On her birthday, she retrieved her son to spend some time together "to make my happiness complete." She found it strange when a man from across the street came to her house that evening to do no more than inspect her son. When she left for work the next day, she noticed that the neighbors she encountered outside were glaring at her.

No sooner had she arrived at work than her aunt called her on the telephone, hysterical, urging her to return home immediately. A crowd of people was surrounding the house, shouting, "We don't want no nigger in our neighborhood," and threatening to break the windows and burn the furniture. Mrs. Tyler grabbed a coworker to take her place and rushed home. A gang of tough-looking men were sitting on the steps of the building where she lived and congregating on the sidewalk in front. The landlord was on the front porch, demanding that she move at once. Mrs. Tyler, her son, and her aunt fled to a hotel. She tried to make ends meet, but within three months she and her son returned to her husband.

"I feel like an innocent criminal" is how she described her marriage. "Like some person arrested for something he has never done and doesn't want anybody to find out."

Mrs. Tyler's anger stemmed from being tricked into marrying a colored man, which explains her accusing Mrs. Haines of leading young white women astray. Growing up in a Bohemian village, Mrs. Tyler was not familiar with colored people when she arrived in America. "The first time I saw a colored man was in Prague in a parade. He scared the life out of me," she recalled. The youngest of seven children, she can remember spending her sixteenth birthday on Ellis Island. When she arrived in Chicago with her mother and brother, the three moved in with a sister and brother who had already settled in the Bohemian community. She didn't get along with her oldest brother, who beat her when she refused to work at a job she hated at Western Electric.

Escaping her family, and barely speaking English, she found a roommate, another Bohemian immigrant, and employment at a lamp factory, where all the girls were colored save her and the foreman was a colored man. To earn extra income, Mrs. Tyler worked for a real estate company on the side. She tried to sell her Black foreman a lot in the white part of the West Side. "I didn't even know that they had a section of the city where colored people live," she said. "Then I found out that there was something wrong because the people there didn't like him." The attempted transaction fell through, but it sparked a romance between the young Bohemian worker and the colored foreman.

When they married, Mrs. Tyler was still learning English as well as the magnitude of white people's animosity toward colored people. At an optometry appointment, the doctor asked her if she had thought carefully about having a baby with a colored man. "Aren't you afraid that you will have a child that is half white and half Black?"

"I thought he meant a child that was Black on one side and white on the other. I said, 'That couldn't happen,'" oblivious to the innuendos in the optician's question.

The racial hierarchy that had eluded Mrs. Tyler became painfully clear soon after her wedding in March 1928. A cabdriver asked if she wasn't afraid to be dropped off in the colored section. She was turned away when she tried to stay at a hotel with her husband. "When I came, I thought it was free for everybody. That's what they said about America in the old country. That isn't true," she said. "I don't think I ever would have married as I did if I knew all this. I wouldn't have the nerve."

Many white immigrant wives like Mrs. Tyler reported a rude awakening when they discovered the dire consequences of marrying a Black man. The unanticipated weight of Chicago's racial order came crashing down on their marriage, like an anvil falling from the sky. In many cases, both the Black husbands and the white wives were migrants to Chicago, the former from the South, the latter from Europe. Yet they couldn't have been further apart in their awareness of racism and what it meant to be a Black person in America. Despite their husbands' citizenship, employment, and love, race made them risky partners. The interviews with these immigrant wives stand out for their condemnation of interracial marriage, accentuated by the feeling of being tricked into a lousy deal. It was as if, unfamiliar with engine mechanics, they didn't realize the car they purchased was a lemon, and once they owned it, they could not easily undo the transaction.

"I was a greenhorn," sighed Mrs. Hanley, a woman who came from Sweden and had married a colored janitor, who was born in Arkansas in 1882. She had never seen a colored person before joining her parents in St. Paul, Minnesota, at seventeen. She met her husband when she worked in the pantry of a hotel, where he was a bellhop. He was the first colored person she got to know. "I was dumb and green," she told my father in November 1938. "Some other women were born in this country and married colored. I don't see how they do it." The unexpected hardships she experienced had turned her completely against unions like hers.

"I don't believe in intermarriage between colored and white," she said. "It is a handicap. You have to go through an awful lot."

If it wasn't for her lovely children, eight boys and a daughter, she would not have stayed with her husband, she declared. She was happy, however, that three of her sons, though able to pass as white, stuck with colored people. Her daughter, who looks Jewish, could have married a well-to-do white man, but chose to wed a nice colored fellow. "She wanted to marry her own race and I believe in that," Mrs. Hanley said. When my father asked his signature final question, if she had her life to live over again, would she repeat her marriage, she was quick with an emphatic "No."

Mrs. Curtis, the white wife living in Morgan Park, felt the same way. Born and raised in Berlin, Germany, she saw a colored person for the first time while riding the train from New York to Chicago. "When I was married, these American ways were foreign to me," she said. "I took my husband everywhere. I didn't know the difference.

"The very first slap I got was I was looking for a flat. I was told that they would rent to me, but 'We can't have a Negro here.'"

Mrs. Curtis could not fathom why a white woman raised in the United States and therefore familiar with its racial inequality would marry a colored man. "They understand conditions and I don't know how they can do it." She refused to entertain a second visit from my father, brusquely giving him an earful of her hostility toward mixed marriages over the telephone.

"The main thing is that I'm bitterly opposed to it," she screeched. "My experience has taught me that it doesn't work and that it is one of the most foolish things a person can do. I think it is a very, very grave mistake to make. If I would ever meet any young person who was contemplating such a thing, I would do my utmost to prevent them. That is my honest conviction, because I haven't met a one yet that worked out well."

When my father later interviewed Mrs. Tilton, a forty-year-old immigrant from Germany, she, too, was exasperated by Chicago's racist ways, disillusioned with the American dream that had lured her across the ocean. Then she made an astute observation that unwittingly contravened a prominent sociological axiom—that marriage to a U.S.-born citizen is a key pathway for immigrant assimilation and therefore upward mobility in U.S. society. She told my father that she was worse off for marrying a U.S.-born Black man than if she had married another white immigrant.

"So what's wrong if a person chooses a colored man for their husband?" she asked. "Had I married a Jew, dago, or any other nationality, not a word would have been said, but as soon as you take on a colored man the world begins to think you're insane or low-class."

Contrary to the "marital assimilation" theory, her acceptance into American society was *hindered* by marrying a native-born citizen of the United States.

Marriage to a Black man may have made white women more attuned to racism, but that didn't mean they were willing to defend interracial marriage. At least, they recognized the cruelty, injustice, and downright absurdity of discrimination against Black people, I thought as I mulled over their stories. But they thought it unfair to suffer for something they hadn't signed up for.

Then there was Mrs. Lang. Mrs. Lang told my father she used to be vice president of the National Interracial League, which reached a membership of sixty couples before disbanding after five years. She boasted that the League was a "higher-class club" than the Manasseh Club. Unlike its rival, the League fought to end discrimination against mixed couples.

"Many mixed couples room in a colored neighborhood. They are afraid they won't be accepted in a white community," she said. "I don't think they should isolate themselves in a colored neighborhood."

When my father asked her for examples of discrimination against interracial couples, she recounted them as a regular aspect of her married life. "I think the only reason they let Harry eat in some of the places we went is because he was with me. They might have thought he was my chauffeur," she said. When they went to the theater, she always bought the tickets. "If my husband bought them, we wouldn't get good seats."

Mrs. Lang even litigated a case of housing discrimination she experienced because of her husband's race. Anticipating her marriage to Mr. Lang, and determined to live in a white neighborhood, she sought the aid of a real estate agent to purchase a house "in the best unrestricted area in Chicago"—in other words, a white neighborhood without restrictive covenants prohibiting sales to colored buyers.

"Many white women marry colored men and move to a colored neighborhood. I think that is a mistake. They associate with the lower class of colored women and are not considered very worthwhile in the estimation of others," she advised, managing to insult colored women in the process. "I was determined to show others that I was different by living in a white neighborhood with my husband and getting people to accept it."

When she arrived at her new home, however, the prior owners refused to leave. "They said they heard that niggers were going to move in," Mrs. Lang recalled. "Do I look colored?" she shot back, and took the offenders to court. She won the case and she and her husband moved into their house. One might view Mrs. Lang as valiantly challenging the restrictions on colored people, but I sense in her remarks more of a desire to maintain her privileges as a white woman despite her marriage to a colored man.

Their neighbors initially resented having a colored man among them, Mrs. Lang said, but they "couldn't help but like him." One neighbor told Mrs. Lang, "It's too bad your husband is colored. He's such a fine man."

"She should have said, 'It's too bad all colored men aren't as nice as your husband,'" she told my father, now managing to insult colored men as well.

She not only made an exception for her husband, but she also improved him, coaching him in the more refined ways of white people. For example, she made him stop saying "the onliest one" instead of "the only one." "That is a common colored expression, but I got him out of the habit of using it," Mrs. Lang said with pride, as if she were Henry Higgins training Eliza Doolittle to speak proper English in *Pygmalion*.

Mrs. Lang described a list of flaws in colored people she attributed to their being "closer to nature" than white people: they were more jealous; they found humor in things that hardly seemed a cause for laughter. She reserved special contempt for colored women. "I do find that where there is a white mother they are brought up differently than if there is a white father," she continued. "The mother is more important in raising children. I've found that the children of mixed marriages who are worthwhile have white mothers." Her words jump out at me, as I detect in them the multitude of stereotypes about Black women's reckless sexuality and depraved maternity, the kind I have spent a career contesting.

Mrs. Lang showed her willingness to extend white privileges to an exclusive group of colored people—those who were light enough to pass as white. "I don't think it's fair to call a very-light-colored person a Negro," she opined. She told my father the story of a light-skinned colored woman married to a white man who had their white-looking baby insured. "I asked her if the insurance man put her child down as colored or Caucasian and she didn't know the answer," Mrs. Lang recollected. At Mrs. Lang's insistence, the insurance agent came to the mother's home to be interrogated. They discovered that the child had been designated colored, not white. Mrs. Lang, indignant, confronted the insurance agent with the injustice of the situation. A doctor was summoned to examine the mother, determining that she was "the last stage of Negro, octoroon, and that the child should be classed as white." The insurance designation was revised to reflect the child's new racial classification. Changing the child's race from colored to white, noted Mrs. Lang, "had done a favor for that child." Mrs. Lang must have been aware of the insurance industry's historic discrimination against Black customers, starting in the nineteenth century, charging them higher premiums while reducing their benefits.

Instead of challenging the racist insurance policies, Mrs. Lang sought to exempt white-looking children from their harm. Instead of wanting to end residential segregation, she wanted her marriage to create an exception to it. She supported the regime that afforded her the best theater tickets, seats at fancy restaurants, and a house in an upscale neighborhood. She would admit only an exclusive class of colored people—those refined men with white wives and their light-skinned children. Mrs. Lang reinforced my sense that, although interracial intimacy has long been condemned by white supremacists, it can be perfectly compatible with white supremacy.

That said, my father also met immigrant women married to Black husbands who embraced their Black neighbors and kinfolk. For example, in August 1938, my father visited Mrs. Carroll, a tall, elderly German widow with thinning gray hair. She lived in a brick two-flat with her son, daughter-in-law, and grandson—she occupied the second floor, while they lived on the first, similar to my father's childhood home. She had met her late husband, a former Civil War water boy for the Confederacy, years earlier while working as a cook for a wealthy Chicago lawyer. At the time, he was employed as the coachman.

"Why are they bothered when colored and white are mixed?" she asked my father, who noted, *Mrs. Carroll was speaking in an excited manner.* "I'm sticking up for the colored. They are all right. I don't have a bit of trouble with my neighbors. I get along fine with the people here. I joined a colored church—what do you think of that?" Yes, she would marry her husband again, she answered my father's final question. "He was a good man and I loved him."

One morning, as I sift through the documents, I make another unexpected discovery. In 1940, my father had submitted a master's thesis titled "Negro-White Intermarriage: A Study of Social Control," based on more than a hundred interviews he had conducted over three years. I hadn't even known he had written a master's thesis, let alone one that explored interracial marriage. I pull the worn manuscript from the box and carry it to the leather armchair in the study, my hands trembling just a little. Settling in, I turn the pages with a mix of awe and curiosity, eager to see how he had interpreted the same stories I had spent the past few weeks immersed in, trying to piece together my own understanding.

At the start of his thesis, he laid out a bold aim: to test whether interracial marriage was shaped by a caste-like social structure found in both the North and the South. By focusing on mixed marriages in Chicago, he sought to understand "under what circumstances they occur and whether or not endogamy is enforced by strong attitudes and sanctions." *Endogamy*, a term used by anthropologists, refers to marrying within a specific group—one's own race, in this case—as opposed to outside it. He was probing the social forces that discouraged or punished interracial unions, as well as what led some people to defy those boundaries.

As I read on, I am struck by the directness and depth of my father's structural examination of Chicago's racial dynamics. His writing feels remarkably contemporary—akin to the introduction of a research paper one of my sociology graduate students might produce today. His analysis begins with a clear presentation of statistical evidence illustrating the societal taboo against interracial marriage in the city. Despite the small proportion of Black residents in Chicago, relatively few were married to white residents. He pointed out that, in a scenario where partner selection was entirely random, "well over ninety percent of Negro brides and grooms throughout the North would marry Whites." Instead, he argued, "a strict set of social sanctions and controls" upheld a system of social separation, effectively preventing interracial marriages and punishing those that took place.

My father went on to describe, in compelling detail, how these social sanctions were enforced by various sectors of society, including families, peers, employers, and government agents. He theorized that this collective effort served to preserve Chicago's racial hierarchy, ensuring the subordination of Negroes and the dominance of the white majority. "Marriage is frequently a ladder to social mobility," he observed, suggesting that unrestricted interracial unions could challenge the status quo by prompting demands for "social equality for their spouses and children." In this statement, I see a kernel of my father's belief that interracial marriages, if allowed to flourish, would foster greater social equality. Ultimately, his thesis concluded that the prohibition of interracial marriage in the North "is probably as effective as the prohibition of intermarriage in other caste systems."

After receiving his master's degree from the University of Chicago, my father decided to continue his graduate studies there, enrolling in the anthropology PhD program the following year. Then World War II interrupted his plans.

In the same box, I stumble across five yellowed and disintegrating pages covered in barely legible pencil handwriting. They appear to be the draft of a letter to the Selective Service. In it, Daddy refers to his petition for a six-month deferment from military training needed to complete his dissertation. He acknowledges that, considering "the unjustifiable attack on the United States by aggressor forces during the past month," his previously held pacifist stance was now indefensible. (This reference, likely to the Japanese attack on Pearl Harbor on December 7, 1941, places the letter in January 1942.)

"While my emotional and temperamental qualities would give me a very poor rating as a prospective soldier," he wrote, "I believe there are other ways that I can be of greater service to the nation." He proposed alternative classifications that would allow him to contribute without engaging in "the aspects of warfare for which I am psychologically unfit." The letter defends his request with surprising passion:

> *I feel that there are two aspects of warfare which I could never face, the business of killing and that of seeing the killed and wounded and listening to the groans, etc. of the dying. Both of these aspects have been part of my personality since childhood. I have hated war, cruelty and even the killing of animals, at least from early childhood. As a naturally timid lad I refused to engage in fistfights although, for a time, this behavior earned me the detested nickname "Percy." I can recall being chased home from school on several occasions by a group of boys anxious to make me fight one of their number. Even today I tolerate incidents which would bring many men of another temperamental background to blows.*

This is the first time I hear of the name Percy being hurled as an epithet and look up its use as a derogatory term. According to *Green's Dictionary of Slang*, "Percy," or "Percy boy," derives from the supposedly effeminate male proper name and denotes a man who is a weakling. The entry cites a quote from *The Girl Proposition*, a collection of satirical short stories published in 1902: "Among the other Things she wore that Evening was a featherweight Escort who had Percy written all over him."

My heart breaks picturing my kindhearted father chased by bullies as a boy. Daddy was always gentle with my sisters and me. He was more likely to share stories with us about his childhood or the customs of people in other parts of the world than to roughhouse with us for fun. I have always thought it fortunate that Daddy had three daughters. I can't imagine him raising a son in America, especially a Black son, with the culture's glorification of tough masculinity.

Another passage from my father's letter stands out to me:

As a youngster in school, I tended to side with the American Indians
who in history lessons were given no peace by the unrelenting advance
of the forces of European civilization. And I wondered what sort
of "civilization" this was that throughout the pages of history so
frequently engaged in the horrible custom of warfare.

I see so much of myself in my father's words—his deep aversion to
violence, his compassion for Native tribes, his condemnation of settler
domination, his fierce opposition to war, and his pain at witnessing any
creature's suffering. These qualities have always felt almost intrinsic to me,
as if they were part of my very being. But I see now that it was my father
who had instilled them in me. The way he treated me and everyone around
him left an indelible mark on my soul. I can't recall a single moment when
he spoke with hatred or cruelty. What I do remember was the message he
returned to over and over—that we share a common humanity and have
a duty to treat everyone with equal respect.

When I reach the end of his letter, I freeze, completely captivated by
his words. "I resolved many years ago that there was nothing decent or
honorable about slaughtering one's fellow men even though the reward
for doing so might be a hero's medal, and the penalty for refusing disgrace
or worse," the letter concluded. "I cannot conceive of myself stabbing
another man with a bayonet or felling him with a machine gun. I am sure
it would be much easier for me to close my eyes and permit him to end
the mental torture that the battle brought." My father believed so strongly
in nonviolence that he would rather surrender his own life than inflict
harm on another person.

When I finish reading my father's letter, I know I have to share it
with my sisters. Of all the hundreds of pages I'd sifted through, this is the
one that will speak to them most. When we gather on Zoom, I read the
letter aloud, word for word. By the time I reach the end, we all have tears
in our eyes. They ask me to transcribe it and send them copies. In those
lines, we each recognize Daddy's gentle spirit and find ourselves reliving
moments his words bring back. My sister Helen recalls him telling her
how, during the war, he had arranged soccer matches for Italian prisoners—
a simple act of humanity amid the fighting. Though miles separate us, we
feel close, bound by our shared love for him and by a deep gratitude for
the kind, principled man we were blessed to call our father.

℘

My father never engaged in combat. Helen recalls him saying he was in a foxhole on D-Day, but that he never picked up a weapon himself. He had successfully convinced army administrators that he'd make a terrible soldier and was not only spared the horrors of battle but was also assigned to what may have been the most pleasant position imaginable: director of recreational activities for soldiers stationed in Europe. "My typewriter was my weapon," he often told my sisters and me when we were growing up. The stories he recounted about the war sounded more like a travelogue to me. He was first deployed to England in 1942. By D-Day in 1944, he was stationed in Normandy, France, and in 1945, he moved to a base in Brussels, Belgium. At the dinner table, he would reminisce about organizing sightseeing tours and excursions for servicemen at each location. When the war ended, he traveled to Germany to visit his ancestral homeland.

Decades later, a Welsh relative who discovered me on Ancestry.com sent photos of Daddy and his father, Alfie, taken during the war. Alfie had traveled to meet my father while he was stationed in England. That must have been the last time Daddy saw his father, who died suddenly in 1944 while my father was still overseas. My father returned to England for his final year of service and took classes on Hindu philosophy, Muhammadan law, and social anthropology at the London School of Economics, I presume taking advantage of a federal military benefit. The following year, he returned to the University of Chicago to work on his PhD. I found a certificate dated 1947 from the grateful citizens of Illinois, signed by Governor Dwight H. Green, recognizing Robert E. T. Roberts for his meritorious service in the armed forces during the war.

While my father was stationed in Europe, his friend St. Clair Drake had completed the book he was writing with Horace R. Cayton Jr., who led the University of Chicago research project with Professor Lloyd Warner. The book, *Black Metropolis: A Study of Negro Life in a Northern City*, was published in 1945 to widespread acclaim with an introduction penned by celebrated novelist Richard Wright, a friend of Cayton. Spanning eight hundred pages, *Black Metropolis* examines the lives of Black residents of Chicago's South Side, from politics to housing, employment, religion, and family life. It was based on the research conducted by the Cayton-Warner team at the University of Chicago.

Growing up, I always knew that Drake had written a celebrated book—spoken of as a classic not only in our household but also in the academic circles I would later move through as an adult. Yet it's not until I begin delving into my father's research that I finally open the worn volume that has been passed down to me—a first printing, its paper jacket torn and frayed with age. As I turn the pages, I am drawn to a chapter titled "Crossing the Color-Line," where Drake and Cayton examine interracial marriage. To my astonishment, I find a footnote crediting my father for providing key research. That brief passage, acknowledging Daddy's interviews, feels monumental. It affirms what I have long believed: that his work offered a rare and powerful window into the lives of the couples who defied Chicago's racial boundaries. Though my father never published a book of his own, seeing his interviews recognized in such a historic text fills me with pride.

Yet I can't help but wonder how Daddy felt, seeing his years of work contributing to his colleague's success while his own life's project remained unfinished. As I read the chapter, I recognize some of the themes I have uncovered in his interviews. But to me, the published version lacks the intimacy and texture of my father's conversations—the back-and-forth that reveal not just his subjects' stories but glimpses of his own thoughts, feelings, and inner life. Without my father's engagement, the stories feel flatter, incomplete, less alive.

In December 1953, my father met up with the Lanes, the couple he interviewed in 1937, who discussed hiding their marriage from employers, along with the work of George S. Schuyler. The Lanes immediately confronted him with an objection to *Black Metropolis*. A friend of theirs told them that their "whole life history" was in the book. "They said, 'Your name is not in it, but anybody who knows you who read it would know it was you,'" Mrs. Lane complained. What upset the Lanes was not the information about their marriage so much as a statement about Baha'i beliefs they said was incorrect and might be attributed to them. *Black Metropolis* states that the Baha'i faith *advocates* interracial marriage, which Mrs. Lane said was "absolutely wrong." "We don't advocate it; we accept it," she clarified. My father tried to redeem himself by telling the couple that he let his friend Drake use some of his interviews, but was an ocean away in Europe serving in the army when the book was written.

When he returned from Europe, my father secured a temporary position as a lecturer in New York University's sociology and anthropology department. In April 1948, he wrote a letter to Drake about his search for a more permanent professorship. He expressed no interest in an opening at a Christian college outside of Chicago. "Despite missionary relatives, I would hardly be at home in Wheaton College," he wrote. Instead, he felt a strong tie to the liberal Roosevelt College, which had the added benefit of being close to the Reinert home on Wrightwood Avenue. "I would prefer Roosevelt College as seven months in a hotel room have convinced me of the advantages of our home in Chicago and Grandma's cooking, and it would be very convenient to take the bus to the college," he explained.

"Robert Roberts Named to Roosevelt Faculty," ran the headline of a tiny article in the *Chicago Tribune* in September 1949. The single paragraph stated that my father had been appointed as a lecturer in sociology in the school of arts and sciences. He was to begin teaching at Roosevelt the following day, at the start of the fall term. My father would remain at Roosevelt for his entire career, promoted to assistant professor when he received his PhD in 1956, and eventually rising to full professor status and chair of the joint anthropology and sociology department. Throughout his nearly four decades at Roosevelt, he continued to conduct his mixed marriage project, interviewing hundreds more interracial couples in Chicago.

June comes to a close, and I am finished working through the interviews from the 1930s. Before reading them, I had often pondered how the Black Belt contained the city's Black residents—how it governed every aspect of their lives, from where they resided to where they could work, travel, and enjoy entertainment. But as I set down the final interview my father conducted in 1939 and reflect on the entirety of the collection, I realize that the color line was not entirely impermeable.

On the streets of the Black Belt, my father—a twenty-one-year-old white student—had ventured into people's homes, asking them about their marriages that breached the geographic and social boundaries. The mixed couples he interviewed navigated this fraught divide in complex ways: some maneuvered within its constraints, others pushed across, around, and through it.

When I close the last box containing the 1930s interviews, I remain unconvinced by my father's belief that interracial intimacy was a cure for America's racial divisions or a barometer of its racial progress. What I can see clearly is how hostility toward interracial marriage in 1930s Chicago was rooted in deeply entrenched racist beliefs and reinforced structural barriers. The hardships the couples described to my father came from defying the city's rigid racial hierarchy. But their marriages didn't necessarily challenge that hierarchy or strike a blow against it.

Still, grappling with what I just read, I can't ignore the husbands and wives in the interviews who actively confronted Chicago's racial caste system. Some challenged its injustices through activism in the Communist Party or conversion to the Baha'i faith; others resisted simply by engaging deeply in the colored communities where they lived. For some of them, their marriages were part of a broader struggle for racial equality. Their stories made me take more seriously the possibility of a radical love—a love that doesn't ignore white supremacy or pretend love alone can overcome it, but wrestles with it head-on.

Their unions could not transcend or destroy the color line, as my father had hoped. But their experiences revealed that the color line was not all-powerful—it could not completely control people's hearts or minds.

I stash the box of the 1930s interviews against the dining room wall, then slice through the tape on the first box containing the 1950s transcripts. As I spread the stacks across the table, I feel a surge of excitement—ready to embark on the next chapter of my father's journey.

Bob in South England, 1944

CHAPTER 9

The Bachelor

White-Negro intermarriage

Interview with
Mr. William Alberti

Chicago
July 31, 1951
by Robert Roberts

I met Bill and Jeanette Alberti the last week-end in July at a
camp in Indiana affiliated with the American Sunbathing Association. On
Saturday, July 28 I had noted Mr. Alberti as he was a very athletic type,
about 5 feet10 inches to six feet tall, and his entire body was well bronzed
by the sun. He has light eyes and light brown hair and his features would
be regarded as fairly handsome. Although his father was Italian and his
mother of Austrian extraction he looks more of North European than of Latin
type. He came without his wife and child on Saturday and I was unaware
that he was married to a Negro. I felt that he was a well-known member
of the nudist camp, as on the basis of my own experiences it appeared that
strangers are not warmly received but I noted that he seemed to be well-
known and participated in volley ball, swimming and other activities with
many others. There were no Negroes present at the camp on Saturday.

Transcript of Mr. Alberti interview, July 31, 1951.

Mr. Alberti
July 31, 1951

I lift the first pile of transcripts from the 1950s to carry to the study. Along
the way, a realization sinks in—I'm stepping into uncharted territory.
This was the decade when my father began his career as an anthropologist. Having returned from army service, he resumed his mixed marriage
project—no longer as a student on a research team, but as the lead in-
vestigator of his own dissertation. More important to me, this was the
decade when he met and married my mother. I can't wait to uncover the
story of how they met and how he reconciled their romantic relationship
with his research. I hope these transcripts will finally unravel the mystery
that had preoccupied me ever since I first discovered them in the boxes
shipped to my office.

On a summer afternoon in 1951, my father arrived at the home of

Jeanette and William Alberti in the Black community of Woodlawn. He found the four-room brick cottage located at the rear of the lot behind another house. At the beginning of the transcript, he noted how he became acquainted with the Albertis. This time, he didn't follow his typical routine for tracking down couples in the 1930s, visiting their homes after being referred by another couple or walking around the neighborhood. Instead, he introduced himself to the white husband and his Black wife in a way that completely catches me off guard.

> *I met Bill and Jeanette Alberti the last weekend in July at a camp in Indiana affiliated with the American Sunbathing Association.*

The location of the meeting rings a bell. I recall my father's casual remark about a camp in Indiana in his notes of an interview with one of the communist wives in January 1939.

> *I happened to mention nudist colonies and Mrs. Frank said that she and Mrs. Cadwell go to a nature club in Indiana where they wear no clothing in the sand pit, and no one thinks anything of being naked.*

The place where my father encountered the Albertis crystallizes in my mind: Daddy first met the couple at a nudist camp. The discovery stuns me. I am feeling lightheaded as I quickly look up the American Sunbathing Association. I learn that the organization was founded in 1931, not long before my father's inquiry about nudist colonies. Now known as the American Association for Nude Recreation, it is the oldest and largest naturalist organization in North America, dedicated to promoting the benefits of nude family recreation and protecting the rights of nudists.

I wonder how often my father brought up nudist colonies in his interviews—and why. Perhaps he mentioned them because he suspected they might serve as meeting places for interracial couples, similar to dances organized by the Communist Party, the Manasseh Club, and colored neighborhood associations. Nudists were already breaking one major taboo; crossing racial boundaries may have seemed like a similar leap. He might have considered their clubs fertile ground for recruiting participants for his study. If so, it seems his instincts were spot-on.

I also wonder whether his curiosity about the nudist camp in Indiana was purely academic. I recall reading an article in the *New York Times Style Magazine* about Germany's strong cultural connection to nudity.

According to the 2019 story, public nakedness has long been common in the former East Germany and is now embraced by 8 to 12 million nudists in Germany, most over fifty years old. A movement, known as FKK, short for *Freikörperkultur*, or "Free Body Culture," began in the late 1800s and evolved into a culturally ingrained national pastime. Perhaps the Reinerts, his grandparents from Germany, were familiar with this tradition and had passed the influence down to my father.

It also occurs to me that Daddy's growing personal fascination with interracial intimacy and Black women may have drawn him to the camp. I suspect that his motivations were all tangled together in a messy knot of curiosity, heritage, and desire.

My father wrote that he noticed Mr. Alberti on Saturday, *as he was a very athletic type, about five feet ten inches to six feet tall, and his entire body was well bronzed by the sun. He has light eyes and light brown hair and his features would be regarded as fairly handsome.* The next day at the camp, he saw *a light to light brown Negro woman pass by wheeling a baby buggy which contained a baby.* When the handsome white man joined her, my father struck up a conversation with the couple, confirming that they were married. The baby, about eight or nine months old, with blond wavy hair and European features, *is lighter than either parent, but would be darker than Mr. Alberti except for the latter's heavy suntan.* My father also noted Mrs. Alberti's shapely figure. Before leaving the camp, he had secured their willingness to participate in his study, their telephone number, and their address in Woodlawn.

I'll never know for certain why my father spent that weekend at the Indiana nudist camp—whether he was looking for interracial couples to interview, curious about nudism himself, attracted by the possibility of meeting Black women—or driven by some mix of all three. Whatever the reason, each possibility points to an intriguing intersection of nudism, Black identity, and race, one I had never come across before. I return to the kitchen for a second cup of tea, then settle into the leather chair in the study, rereading the opening pages of the transcript, reflecting on how these threads might be connected, like pieces of a puzzle whose image is slowly coming into focus.

After the sun set on his first evening at the camp, Daddy sat with other guests around a bonfire. There, he engaged the camp director in conversation, mentioning an article in the latest issue of *Ebony*, the monthly lifestyle magazine for the Negro community founded by John H. Johnson in 1945. My parents subscribed to *Ebony*, and as far back as I can remember, its covers, splashed with sensational headlines and photos of famous Black people, were a mainstay on our living room coffee table, a vivid part of my childhood.

The article in question was titled "Nudism and Negroes." The camp director thought the article was good, but he intended to write a letter to the editor correcting some inaccuracies. He told my father that, at its annual convention, the American Sunbathing Association had adopted a resolution to eliminate discrimination in the nudism movement. The resolution called for clubs to end bias based on religion, political belief, race, color, or ethnic origin and to strive for membership that reflected the diversity of the surrounding community. The predominantly white movement was taking affirmative steps to support racial equality and inclusivity—an ideal that likely helped lead my father to the camp.

The next day, a Penn librarian helps me locate a digitized copy of "Nudism and Negroes," and I eagerly read it, hoping for greater insight into my father's interest. Subtitled "Interracialism Is Introduced in Scattered Camps around the Nation," the article includes several photos of Black and white nudists. One photo features a little Black girl, wearing a striped sundress over a white T-shirt, holding the hand of an unclothed white woman, identified as a nudist elder, with a caption that states "Even youngsters are reluctant to part with clothes after early training in 'getting dressed up.'" The article highlights the growing participation of Black nature lovers in nudist camps, noting that, while many camps claimed they welcomed Black members, few had applied in the past. At a recent American Sunbathing Association convention, apparently the one referred to by the camp director, a Black couple attended as delegates—the first in the organization's history. One of the photos shows a naked white woman welcoming the couple, her outstretched arms covering part of her breasts. The magazine obscured the couple's eyes with white strips—a clumsy attempt to conceal their identities.

What also catches my eye are the advertisements that prominently line the left and right margins. Most promote hair-straightening products aimed at Black women. One ad declares "Your Kinky Hair Worries Are Over," while another promises "Have the longest, silkiest hair you can have to thrill men's hearts, for long hair attracts men." A third sells a cream that eliminates the need for hot combs. The jarring juxtaposition of these ads peddling physical modification with the article on nudism underscores how ideas about race and gender shaped people's views on the body during that time.

Mr. Alberti's first encounter with nudism was in 1933, more than a decade before he met his wife, when an acquaintance introduced him to the naturalist movement and took him and two other young men to the Zoro Nature Park in Indiana. The *Ebony* article also mentions Zoro Nature Park. That must be the name of the camp where my father stayed and met the Albertis. An avid outdoorsman who enjoyed swimming, hiking, and tennis, Bill was enamored with the camp, the closest thing to utopia he had experienced. "One of the outstanding things about Zoro Nature Park is that it's interracial," Bill told my father. "It doesn't have any discrimination." He emphasized Zoro's diversity as a key reason he still belonged to the camp. "It makes me feel like I'm really a part of things and part of a, oh shall we say, cosmopolitan world, a real mixed assemblage," he explained.

My mother—at least the woman I knew growing up—would never approve of going naked in front of strangers. She took meticulous care to present herself with elegance and refinement, always dressed in tasteful outfits that flattered her slender figure while adhering to her impeccable sense of decorum. Mommy insisted that my sisters and I wore undershirts and slips beneath our neatly pressed dresses. My father's habits at home were more unconventional, but never crossed the line. I have amusing memories of Daddy relaxing in our Kenwood house, dressed in nothing but the cloth he had brought back from the village in India wrapped around his waist. It wasn't strange to us, for we were raised on his lessons about non-Western cultures. As children, we often watched films shot during our family's stay in Liberia showing bare-breasted tribal women. Besides, it was no different from seeing him shirtless at the beach or on a hot summer day while he mowed the lawn.

Nudism, however, felt foreign to our family's world, so firmly bounded by my mother's propriety. When I mentioned what I had found to my sisters, Evelyn told me that she had come across documents and photographs related to nudism while packing Daddy's papers and had burned them before sending the boxes to me. "Mommy would have been mortified," she said. And she was likely right. Our mother might have been aware of Daddy's dabbling in nudism, perhaps even before they married, but she would not have wanted her daughters to know about it. She may have been more free-spirited herself when she met him and became more conservative after she became a mother. To Evelyn, the faintest traces of this part of Daddy's past feel like a betrayal of our mother's legacy. She hadn't realized that these traces had already made their way into the transcripts she had packed up and sent to me.

I understand my mother's hypothetical objection to this fascination my father had and my sister's genuine concern. But to me, his visit to the nudist camp reveals something essential about him. It suggests that he saw a deep connection between the unorthodoxy of nudism and the unorthodoxy of interracial marriage. It tells me he believed that embracing interracial intimacy required stripping himself down to his unvarnished self, breaking free from the conventional thinking about race, Black people, and human kinship.

Besides, by the time I had started opening these boxes, my mother had already passed away. If she is watching me now as I read and write about my father's experiences, I imagine her—freed from the weight of earthly shame and enlightened by Heaven's omniscience—finally understanding, maybe even accepting, Daddy's intentions.

During her lifetime, Mommy carefully hid from us anything that might tarnish her image as an upright Christian woman. I think her concealment wasn't rooted in fear of embarrassment so much as her desire to uphold the strict values she instilled in me and my sisters. It was as if she believed that any sordid details about our family's past might rub onto her, staining the pristine version of herself she curated for us, like a smudge transferred from someone else's dirty belongings. She seemed to feel that maintaining a spotless persona was essential to securing our loyalty to her as our preeminent role model.

One year, I traveled to Kingston with my two young sons for the winter holidays. We stayed at the home of my mother's youngest brother, my uncle Bertie, and his wife, Pat. Aunt Pat hailed from Guyana, a nation on the Caribbean coast of South America. Aunt Pat's mother was Black and her father Indian, and she had chestnut skin and straight black hair, with strands of gray. Like Trinidad and Uganda, Guyana had a colonial history of mixing between descendants of enslaved Africans and those of indentured servants shipped from India under British rule.

On Christmas Day, after presents were unwrapped and opened, the family was sitting together in the living room, chatting over slices of delicious black cake, moist and pungent from the generous portion of rum infused inside, my favorite dessert in the whole world. A tall elderly man came into the house and joined us. He looked strikingly like my Jamaican grandmother. Uncle Bertie and Aunt Pat knew him well and he fell easily into the conversation. It was clear to me that he was a member of our family.

When my uncle introduced him as Dudley, I realized that I had overheard that name over the years in hushed conversations between my mother and her siblings. As I ruminated on the name Dudley and the clues from those exchanges, I had another one of those epiphanies about my family. Dudley had to be Mommy's older half brother. I realized that he must have been born to Grandma before she married Grandpa— and that's why Mommy never introduced Dudley to my sisters and me. Decades later, I discovered on Ancestry.com a son born to my grandmother bearing her maiden name, Vincent Dudley Smith. He was born in 1914, when she was twenty years old and still living in St. Elizabeth Parish. My aunt Violet, who I previously thought was my mother's oldest living sibling, was born in 1919 in St. Andrew, after Grandma had married my grandfather.

All these years I had had an uncle I had never met, who had remained in the shadows, like my uncle Edward on my father's side, but for different reasons. I can imagine my mother choosing not to tell us she had a brother born out of wedlock. It was the kind of inconvenient family truth she wouldn't want us to associate with her. Mommy should have known we held her on a pedestal so high that a scandal like that or a visit to a nudist camp wouldn't have shaken our reverence for her. But she seemed unwilling to risk tarnishing the respectable image she upheld for me and my sisters. Or risk that we might take such breaches of propriety as permission.

When I told my sisters about Daddy's exploration of nudism, they agreed that Mommy would have kept it from us—just as she had shielded us from other uncomfortable truths about our family. But they saw her omissions differently than I did. They were less troubled by her desire to protect us from what she considered unpleasant, and more disturbed by the parts of my father she felt compelled to hide. Helen even said she was grateful that our mother raised us to seek out what is good and beautiful. "She told me, 'Don't get used to anything that isn't nice,'" Helen recalled. I understand that instinct. But I see the tension between shielding and confronting as more complicated. I believe in looking squarely at the uncomfortable parts of life, even if I wouldn't choose them for myself. For me, that kind of reckoning is essential to creating what is good and beautiful.

In a later heart-to-heart over Zoom, my sisters and I found more common ground. The tension over shielding and confronting hadn't disappeared but we understood each other better. "You can try to hide the truth," Helen said this time, "but it's still the truth." On that point, we all agreed.

At the Alberti residence, my father connected the wire recorder and handed a microphone to Mr. Alberti, checking first to make sure it was working. I see he had updated his method of documenting the interviews. Fourteen years after his first interview with Mrs. Alberts, he was taping the interviews and getting the recordings transcribed instead of typing up his handwritten notes.

"Howdy. This is Bill Alberti telling about his entire life up to the present; is forty years of age—that's my age—born 1911; and quite a few interesting episodes and incidents in my life," he began.

Mr. Alberti told how he was raised in Chicago by a stepfather, "a type of individual that you wouldn't exactly feel was the type of dad that you would select for yourself," after his Austrian mother divorced his Italian father, a "lark type." Although his stepfather was a first-class cook in a downtown hotel, the family remained in "the poorer class" because he gambled away his earnings. At age five, Bill's family moved into a German neighborhood, and he enrolled in a parochial school, where lessons were taught in German and English. He had inherited his father's last name and olive skin tone and was bullied by the neighborhood children who looked down on Italians.

Not being of "Teutonic strain," "I wasn't exactly wanted or appreciated and quite often made the butt of many gibes and taunts and ridicule," he recalled. "Well, that was my first experience with racial relations, shall we say."

After dropping out of high school to help his family pay the bills, Bill did manual labor for the Hall Printing Company until he learned about the civil service exam, passed it, and began a career for the U.S. Postal Service, a line of work he had maintained at the time of the interview. In 1935, he married a twenty-year-old white woman from the South, a neighbor in the more ethnically diverse section of Chicago he had moved to. It was at his job at the main post office in downtown Chicago that Bill began to meet colored coworkers and made friends with many of them, inviting them to his home after punching out and on weekends. His friendships caused a rift with his bride. She would bolt from the apartment whenever he had colored guests over.

Because of his first wife's southern background, Bill explained, "she could not get herself to, oh, feel natural with people of darker complexion, despite the fact that when I got out there in the summertime and became very dark due to the sun's rays, why I sure used to be very close to colored myself."

I imagine Bill's darker hue and the bullying he experienced because of it as a child may have made it easier for him to "feel natural" around colored people. Maybe he could empathize with his Negro coworkers because they shared experiences of degradation on account of their subordinated status in Chicago's racial hierarchy. The tension between Bill and his southern wife became overwhelming and they divorced after nine years, though it violated the Catholic faith to which both belonged.

Later in his narrative, Bill clarified that his closeness with his colored coworkers at the post office wasn't immediate.

"I was like a lot of Caucasians; I felt rather squeamish," he confessed. "For instance when it came to going to the canteen and seeing various dark-skinned individuals around you and, you know, using the same implements of the table, it probably didn't feel natural at first."

Bill also pointed to using the washroom shared by all the male postal workers regardless of race. "Washing my hands and face in the same washbowls that the colored men had used, it made me feel kind of like, well, a little unclean shall I say," he continued uncomfortably.

"I'm not proud to say anything like that now because as I look back, I realize it was just a foolish, boyish outlook without much analysis to it, because now those things are never thought of by myself."

I wonder why some white people, like Bill, realize the foolishness of their prejudices against Black people, while to this day others hold on to their idiotic beliefs regardless of their maturity. I remember my uncle Edward's birthday card to my father, how he expressed his inability to shake the early associations that turned him against Black people and away from my father—even on his deathbed.

As Bill continued working side by side with the Black staff at the post office, his views gradually changed. Some of his coworkers were distinguished older gentlemen who had been employed by the postal service for many years and gave him much appreciated advice about succeeding on the job. "They could often give me valuable tips, how to do my work better and how to associate myself better with the supervision, how to get along, and so on, and it came in very handy," Bill recalled. He remembered fondly a colored man he met, Joe Gorey, with twenty years seniority, who became his friend. "Joe and I really got along marvelously," Bill said.

"People not being thrown together, not knowing each other, why, that is the biggest barrier to interracial relationships," Bill went on. "That's my main objective in telling this."

Once he was divorced, Bill began dating a Norwegian woman, an avid reader, who was interested in socialism, politics, and social and economic inequality. Bill credited her for influencing his thinking on race. They talked about marriage, but Bill encouraged her to go to college first. Despite her political ideals, once in college, she no longer considered a post office employee to be a suitable husband. They parted ways and she married a man in her graduating class.

For his part, Bill had his eye on a Black woman named Jeanette, who worked alongside him at Chicago's main post office. At the start of World War II, the post office began employing large numbers of women, and they stayed on after the fighting ended. Bill estimated that 25 percent of the twenty thousand or so employees at the post office—carriers, clerks, mail sorters, administrators—were colored women and another 20 to 25 percent were colored men. Of the remaining half, most were white men. Only about 5 percent of the workers were white women, Bill calculated. "The white women don't seem to apply for this position for some reason or other that I have never been able to ascertain," he said, "but it seems to be a better-than-average income position for the colored girls." It also seemed to be an opportune context for white men to get to know colored women, I think. Bill praised the colored female employees as "very, very capable workers, much better than some of the colored men and some of the white men that they work with, around, and past."

Bill recounted how he invited Jeanette to accompany him to a dance sponsored by the Progressive Party at Bacon's Casino at Forty-Seventh and Wabash in the city's main Negro district. It was 1947, a year before the left-leaning political party held its national convention in Philadelphia, launching the presidential campaign of Henry A. Wallace, the former vice president under Roosevelt, on a platform that opposed the Cold War and supported civil rights. They were surprised to encounter several other mixed couples at the dance, allaying Jeanette's initial apprehension about being seen in public together. After going out several times, Jeanette told Bill she was surprised he hadn't pressured her to go with him to a hostelry— a hotel known more for privacy than for comfort—for sex.

"She thought most Caucasian males were very much that way, who insisted on intimate relationships immediately," Bill said.

Bill was aware of surreptitious liaisons between white male supervisors, even married ones, and colored women who worked under their authority.

Some of his white friends bragged about going out with colored girls, but "always in a furtive, underhanded method of meeting and perhaps carrying on an affair." Such clandestine activity had been mentioned in a "grape-vine" article in one of the Negro newspapers, Bill noted. Bill told Jeanette that he wasn't like those disgraceful white men. He had true romantic feelings for her. After seven or eight months of chivalrous courtship, the couple wed in November 1947. Bill moved from his cramped quarters in a rooming house on the white North Side to share the brick cottage with Jeanette on the colored South Side.

My father met with Bill at the nudist camp a second time a month later. Jeanette had to work that week, so Bill brought their infant son to the camp without his wife. Besides, Jeanette didn't enjoy the nudist camp and preferred to stay at home. My father typed a page of observations, which he titled "Notes on Conversation with Bill Alberti, August 25, 1951," but they have little to do with his typical questions about interracial marriage. Instead, they discussed Bill's views about extramarital sex.

My father transcribed only one question:

I asked Bill if he would permit his wife the same freedom he expects, to go out without expecting any questions to be asked as to where she had been or what she had done.

Bill's reply:

He had told her that she could go out if she wanted to, and that he had said, "Only, don't come back with a baby."

At the end of his notes, my father wrote, *I invited Bill to go on a weekend outing next month with an interracial group to which I belong, and he said he would like to go.*

I am beginning to form a clearer picture of my father in his thirties—a lecturer in anthropology at Roosevelt College, surrounded by the mixed circle of friends he had cultivated since his days as a master's student, exploring the nudist camp that had sparked his curiosity. He was entering a new phase of his research on Negro-white marriage in Chicago, the project that would establish him as a scholar in his own right. He seemed more determined than ever to challenge the prevailing belief, both in academia and among the public, that interracial marriage was a threat to society and to the couples themselves.

By the 1950s, biological arguments against "race mixing" were fading, replaced by psychological and sociological theories. Psychologists claimed that marrying across racial lines was a symptom of an underlying mental disorder, while social scientists dismissed interracial unions as being driven by economic motives, warning that couples and their children would face rejection from both Black and white communities. For my father, it was clear, the mixed marriage project wasn't just research—it was a mission to reverse the dominant thinking.

Yet, at the same time, as I continue to read his papers, my understanding of my father's project becomes murkier. I can no longer tell where his research ended and his personal life began. His typewritten notes on a casual conversation with Mr. Alberti at the nudist camp, centered on extramarital affairs, are in the same file as the formal interview he conducted at the Alberti home a month earlier. Both documents bear the same identification number: 206. Do these notes reflect a second interview with a research subject? Or are they more like a private diary entry—a record of a confidential heart-to-heart with a friend? I can't discern the dividing line. As I read through the transcripts of my father's encounters with Bill Alberti, I grow more and more perplexed by their relationship. And intrigued by the handsome, adventurous Italian man my father seemed to be spending more time with than any other of his interviewees—skirting the boundary between research and friendship.

Remarks on Party at Home of Mr. and Mrs. Alberti
April 26, 1952

My father arrived at the Alberti home on an evening in April 1952, this time accompanied by a young Black woman. Two weeks before, Bill had telephoned to invite my father to his birthday party. Bill said that his wife had invited about ten mixed couples in an assortment of combinations—three or four white men with colored girls, one white man with a Filipina girl, another with a girl from Japan, several white girls with colored fellows. The party was for interracial liaisons only. *He said that I could bring a Japanese girl or a colored girl, but that I would be out of place with a Caucasian girl*, my father noted.

At the end of the phone call, my father asked Bill to join him at the

Wesak festival in celebration of the birth of Buddha, an annual event at the University of Chicago he planned to attend the next day. My father took notes on their conversation on the way to the festival, which revolved around Bill's confessions about his marriage and his suspicions about the sex lives of other interracial couples he knew. I had to look up the meaning of *satyriasis* when Bill speculated that a white husband, formerly a musician in Wayne King's orchestra, was suffering from the affliction. According to the Oxford dictionary, *satyriasis* means an uncontrollable or excessive sexual desire in a man. Bill spoke from firsthand experience when he observed that the Black wife in question was normal in her sexual appetite and "very lovely in the boudoir."

As I read my father's notes about the party, one question was foremost on my mind: Is the Black girl who accompanied my father my mother?

Couples streamed into the Alberti house throughout the evening and into the night. My father counted fourteen or fifteen in all, *in addition to the Albertis and myself and two girls I brought.* Two girls! Daddy had made considerable progress in his quest for a Black girlfriend, I think to myself. At 9 p.m., he telephoned the second Black girl and drove to her home to pick her up and bring her to the party.

My father listed the names, descriptions, and estimated ages of the mixed couples he met at the birthday celebration, probably so he could follow up with interviews later.

Edward Kurtz, a white post office employee, and Betty, a Negro neighbor of the Albertis, of medium brown color. Ages about 45 and 38.

Howard and Gertrude Ellis, a medium dark brown Negro and white wife, ages 27, 26?

Charles and Alice Chen, Chinese and light brown Negro wife, ages 40 and 35?

Harvey and Maria Franklin, dark brown Negro and Italian wife, ages 35, 27?

And so on.

My father replaced the music that had been playing when he arrived with a mix of African, Brazilian, East Indian, and Latin American rhythms streaming from his wire recorder. I had never once pictured him as a DJ— let alone as a playboy, showing up at a party for mixed-race couples, first with one Black woman, then later with another. It was hard to reconcile that image with the man I knew growing up: a dedicated professor and devoted family man. Apparently, the first woman who accompanied my father was quite attractive because Howard Ellis took several photos of her in various poses. *He asked me if it was all right with me if he asked my girlfriend to pose for some artistic (nude?) shots on another occasion*, my father wrote. I am increasingly certain that neither woman is my mother.

My father painted more detailed portraits of the guests in his notes—their physical traits, their ancestry, their socioeconomic background, their remarks. He recognized a few couples as participants in his interracial marriage study and pestered them to fill out the questionnaires he had handed them when he had interviewed them. Mr. Alberti offered to distribute blank questionnaires for new recruits, which my father re-trieved from his car. I imagine him carrying a stash of questionnaires in the trunk or a briefcase, ever at the ready to tender them to interracial couples he happened to encounter. My father was no longer asking couples about the defunct Manasseh Club, but about the Cameo Club, a more recently established venue for interracial mingling. I learned in a later interview that the Cameo Club lasted only from 1950 to 1952 and, like the Manasseh Club, had almost exclusively white women and Black men as members.

A buffet supper was served at 11:30 p.m.: an Italian dish prepared by Mrs. Franklin, potato salad, cold turkey, cheese, sausage, beer, and birthday cake. As the guests filled their plates, my father played music by Shan Kar and his Hindu orchestra from his wire recorder. It's likely he meant Ravi Shankar, the famed sitarist who was creating Indian classical ensembles around that time.

After the buffet supper there was more dancing and at about 1 a.m. it was announced that motion pictures would be shown if nobody objected to viewing pornographic pictures.

If it was hard to picture my father conversing at a nudist camp, escorting two Black women to a party for mixed-race couples, or standing at his wire recorder like an avant-garde DJ, what came next leaves me completely flummoxed. How am I supposed to square this version of him with the man who raised me? The one who sat at our dining table every night without fail, sharing the meal my mother had prepared. Who spent long hours in his third-floor study writing his book, and devoted his free time to family outings with Mommy, my sisters, and me. Until now, I had no sense of my father as an adult with a life beyond our family of five. But discovering this other version of him—unexpected and irreverent—feels less like a forbidding contradiction than an irresistible invitation to understand him more fully.

I continue reading, my heart tense with a mix of dread and fascination, like watching a horror film with one eye covered and one eye glued to the screen.

One of Mr. Alberti's post office coworkers, a Black man, operated the motion picture projector, which was set up in a passageway between the living room and the dining room. The guests seated themselves on chairs that had been arranged in front of the screen in the living room or on the sofa or the floor. The first two or three reels of color film portrayed Black girls posing artistically without any nudity or sexual innuendo. *Only a few brief scenes revealed more than is commonly seen on a public beach.* Before proceeding with the next phase of entertainment, there was another warning to those who might object to it and a Black man left the room, *I believe to act as a sentry,* my father surmised. Several reels that were more sexually explicit followed for about two hours, with occasional intermissions for the recitation of erotic poetry. *Nobody appeared to object overtly to the films and both men and women watched quietly and with apparent interest.*

I wonder what kept my father so focused on the screen that night. Was he still observing the party as part of his research project—like an anthropologist studying a ritual in a distant culture? Or was he, too, captivated by the movies with genuine interest? Perhaps he was caught off guard by the turn the evening had taken and felt obliged to stay, either out of loyalty to his friend, discomfort at causing a scene, or the impulse to try on a more transgressive version of himself. I suspect that, as with his visits to the nudist camp, all these motivations were tangled together.

My father departed before the screenings were over, around five in the morning, with one of the Black women he had brought to the party. His notes do not disclose what transpired after that. I am left to wonder how he had met the young women who accompanied him, who they were, and the nature of his relationship with them. I am reminded that my father is the observer in everything he recorded in his notes. For all their revelations, he rarely disclosed his own motivations, responses, or reactions. I must guess how he would answer his own questions, speculate why he asked them in the first place. I must intuit the meaning of his presence at the party, whether to collect more data for his study of interracial marriage or to indulge his seemingly insatiable curiosity about interracial intimacy.

As I think more about the party, I realize that my unease stems not only from the discordant revelations about my father, but also from my aversion to an aspect of interracial intimacy they evoke. I have long felt disturbed by sexual fetishes based on racial preferences, sexual desires evoked by an attraction to individuals based on their race. Americans typically date, fall in love, and marry within their own racialized groups. I suppose we could call being attracted to someone who shares one's racial identity a racial preference. But, to me, the nature of intimacy is different when a person prefers to experience it with someone of another race *because of* the other person's race, when they find their partner's race *itself* the attraction.

I can picture clearly the first time I was unsettled by this type of inter-racial attraction. The moment plays back in my mind now like a haunting scene from a movie.

It is the month before my eighth-grade graduation from my integrated school in Kenwood, as the chilly Chicago spring slowly warms into summer. I am barely thirteen years old. During recess or when school lets out, I notice two white girls in my grade leaning casually against the school wall as Black boys bend toward each one, playfully chatting. The girls pose with an unaccustomed demeanor as they look up at the boys, seeming to hold their attention effortlessly. They are dressed in miniskirts that had become shorter than the year before, knee-high socks, and fitted blouses. I can tell they fancy themselves more mature than our classmates for talking with the boys in this manner. In hindsight, I suspect that the boys were students at the high school, who crossed the park separating our schools for a chance to share this momentary exchange.

That was my first awareness of the dynamic of white girls and Black boys expressing a distinctive attraction toward each other. The sight of those boys and girls interacting was unlike anything I had seen or experienced before. It felt unfamiliar, a sharp contrast to the behavior I was used to from my classmates. In my little autograph book, with a blue cover and multicolored pages, where my classmates wrote playful farewells as we departed for high school, a common inscription from the girls was "2 cool 2 go 4 boys," a phrase that hinted at a collective innocence—

or perhaps a shared resistance to interest in romance. In that moment, I sensed that those white girls and Black boys had crossed a line. And I knew race played a part in what I was seeing.

At that point, the closest I'd gotten to flirting was a phone call from one of the Black boys in my class. He told me he liked me and asked me "to go with" him. Maybe if I had agreed, I might have been one of the girls with her back against the wall, with him smiling down at me that day. But even a second phone call was out of the question. My mother wouldn't allow it. Maybe those white girls were the only ones who were willing, not the only ones who were desired. The Black southern writer Kiese Laymon explains in his memoir, *Heavy*, that the reason the first girl he had sex with was white—even though he was attracted to a Black girl—was because the white girl was the first to ask him. In any case, the dynamic surely would have been radically different if I, a Black girl, were in the scene.

Questions swirled in my mind. Did their flirting extend beyond the schoolyard? I wondered. Was there more to it than the playfulness I was witnessing? My mother had worked hard to shield me from any sexual experience of my own, but I could still detect the charged energy emanating from the scene. I felt a knot form in my stomach. My face burned with intense and confusing emotions I couldn't fully articulate at the time. I resented the girls for the power they held over the boys. I felt disgusted with the boys for being captivated by it. I felt betrayed by all of them.

I never felt similarly offended by my parents' relationship, however. Daddy frequently praised my mother's beauty while I was growing up. He admired my mother's many dazzling traits, her intelligence and grace, along with her appearance, and he made a habit of saying so. Looking back on his attraction to her, I can see that it stemmed at least in part from her African features. As if to leave no doubt, Daddy was fond of repeating the saying "The blacker the berry, the sweeter the juice." I understood perfectly when I was little that he meant that he found Mommy's dark skin—and the charms that went along with it—appealing. I also knew he meant the saying as a rebuke of the white-beauty standard, the dominant societal preference for light skin. Far from hearing anything unseemly in my father's words, I was grateful for his adoration of my mother's Blackness.

At the time, I had no idea that Daddy had pursued Black women long before he met my mother. Still, knowing that now doesn't tarnish my view of their relationship. I concede that I am judging my classmates in my recurring memory more harshly than I am my parents.

The history of sexual violation of Black women and lynching of Black men casts a long shadow over the politics of interracial intimacy. It makes Black women's relationships with white men seem as if the women are capitulating to a white supremacist and patriarchal hierarchy, while Black men's relationships with white women are countering it. But I can also see the opposite. Those exceptional white men who love, admire, and commit to Black women are nothing like exploitative enslavers—and the Black women who love them in return aren't victims of exploitation. By contrast, those Black men who see having romantic relationships with white women as a badge of liberation, a prize that no Black woman can offer, do nothing to oppose the racial hierarchy. In these admittedly skewed scenarios, the white men are contesting white supremacist disparagement of Black women, whereas the Black men are playing into it.

I can't deny my bias—both as a Black woman and as the daughter of a Black woman who married a white man, my father. As I reflect on this, I make a conscious effort not to let that reality completely consume my perspective. Yet, what matters most to me is my fierce loyalty to Black women and my opposition to the stereotypes, policies, dating apps, jokes, social media, TV shows, and movies that demean us. Few things ignite my anger more than the notion that Black women are inherently less attractive, less capable, less nurturing, or less valuable. Everything I have written and worked toward as an adult has been dedicated to celebrating and uplifting Black women's sexuality, childbearing, and motherhood.

I wish I could believe that sexual attraction, desire, and love exist untouched by race. That my feeling of betrayal as a thirteen-year-old was just a fleeting, instinctual reaction. Romantic attraction is supposed to be a magical force, something beyond our control that transcends the influence of society. "Why can't you just be happy for people who love each other?" my husband often insists when I bring up the sociological dimensions of interracial intimacy. "Why does everything have to be political?" I would never discuss these thoughts at the interracial weddings of friends and family—I respect those moments and their marital decisions as deeply personal. I try not to make this about individual choices. But I can't ignore what I've spent years studying: the undeniable ways unequal structures shape our preferences, even the most intimate ones. The evidence is too compelling to pretend otherwise.

Statistics bear out the strong influence race has on intimate relationships. The most obvious impact is that people in the United States tend to marry within their own race. The U.S. Supreme Court struck down bans on interracial marriage in 1967, but no law regulates personal preferences when choosing a partner. While interracial marriages have steadily increased in recent decades—along with popular approval—they remain relatively uncommon. As my father noted in his 1940 master's thesis, mixed-race marriages are far less frequent than we would expect if couples were randomly matched without regard to race. According to a 2008 study, if pairings were random, 44 percent of all U.S. marriages would be interracial. In reality, that number is just about 20 percent—a clear sign that race continues to shape marital choices. For me, interracial intimacy can't be disentangled from the larger forces of race, gender, and power that continue to govern our world.

Even decisions to partner across racial boundaries are governed by a hierarchy of desirability. Soon after I arrived at Penn and opened my father's boxes for the first time, I was introduced to the unsettling world of digital dating research by my sociology PhD student, Sarah Adeyinka-Skold. Her work explores how young women from different racial backgrounds navigate the search for long-term romantic partners. A Black woman of Nigerian descent, Sarah married a white man she had met at church while finishing her dissertation. My husband and I attended her wedding, joined by a joyful interracial gathering of relatives, church members, and fellow graduate students. But the reality she uncovered in her research was far less hopeful. Based on dating app data and interviews with 111 Asian, Black, Latina, and white college-educated women, Sarah found that Black women face the greatest number of barriers in the modern dating landscape.

Most online dating platforms allow users to set racial preferences, including filtering potential matches by race, and the patterns that emerge are striking. While most users, to varying degrees, show a preference to date within their own racial group, what's more telling is who they won't even consider. Black users are ten times more likely to message white users than the reverse. In fact, 80 percent of white users send messages exclusively to other white users, and only 3 percent reach out to Black users. One man, reflecting on these dynamics, described the trend as sexual racism masked as preference. He recalled sending a photo on a dating app and receiving a blunt reply: "I don't like black guys, sorry."

Conversely, whiteness—or even partial European ancestry—provides a noticeable advantage in the dating market. While white people are the least likely to date outside their racial group, non-white people are most likely to choose white people as the group they would date interracially. "Adding 'whiteness' always helps your rating!" observes Christian Rudder, cofounder of the online dating site OkCupid and author of the book *Dataclysm*.

One finding from the dating app data that Sarah shared with me was especially infuriating: Black women are the only group of women frequently excluded as potential dating partners by men of their own race. To put it bluntly, some Black men reject Black women categorically—simply because they are Black.

I was fortunate to have avoided those degrading indignities. In my twenties, while I was in law school at Harvard and he was pursuing a PhD in education, I met my first husband. I was taking an intensive winter course in antitrust with Professor Stephen Breyer—years before he would join the Supreme Court—and each day I walked on the same path from class back to my residence hall. One afternoon, I passed a striking Black man—six foot five, handsome, hard to miss—walking in the opposite direction as I headed back to my dorm during the lunch break. When I left class later that day, I passed him again, at precisely the same spot. We shared a laugh at the coincidence, then exchanged phone numbers. That chance encounter spared me the painful experiences many Black women face in the digital dating world. We told it as a twist of fate, but part of me always suspected he'd planned it all along.

One evening, my current husband, who is also Black, and I were watching the satirical blaxploitation comedy *Undercover Brother*. We had met at a dinner on Penn's campus about a year after my divorce, when he was a senior administrator at a university across the river in New Jersey. In one scene, the main character, played by Eddie Griffin, is exposed while working undercover at the villain's company. Sensing trouble, one of the villain's lackeys, played by Chris Kattan, dramatically announces that it's time to unleash his secret weapon—"the Black Man's Kryptonite!"

The moment is stretched for comedic effect, leaving the audience to speculate what racial stereotype is about to appear. "Probably a tempting plate of fried chicken or ribs," I guessed.

But instead, the camera shifts to a slow-motion reveal: an attractive white woman with long blond hair, played by Denise Richards, struts down the hallway. She moves with exaggerated seduction as she "accidentally" bumps into Undercover Brother. All his training and cool confidence crumble instantly.

"You see?" I exclaimed to my husband, pointing to the screen. He always denies that there's any truth to the notion that some Black men find white women especially appealing.

"That's just a movie," he countered. "It's a joke. Black men don't really think like that."

I tried to explain that the joke wouldn't land if it didn't play on some underlying belief. But my husband wasn't having it. He's often irritated by my habit of dissecting racial themes in every movie we watch and yelling at the screen in frustration. Instead, he offered his own perspective: while Black men might feel the need to keep their white girlfriends hidden at family gatherings or reunions, Black women often openly praise their white partners' qualities. He also pointed out how TV commercials increasingly feature Black women paired with white husbands, but rarely show the reverse.

Still, the comedic trope in *Undercover Brother* bothers me to this day. The film's continued resonance not only reflects harmful myths from the past about Black men's desire for white women, but also says something about interracial intimacy in America today.

While my father was living as a bachelor in Chicago, conducting interviews with interracial couples and launching his career as an anthropologist, my mother began an adventure of her own. At just twenty-five years old, Mommy left Jamaica with her older sister, Violet, to live in Liberia on the coast of West Africa. Having graduated from Wolmer's High School for Girls, she had applied for a Jamaican government scholarship to study medicine, hoping to become a doctor. When the scholarship didn't come through, she worked briefly as a teacher at Happy Grove Secondary School and as a clerk for the Post and Telegraph Department. Then, when the opportunity to teach in Liberia arose, she and her sister seized it.

I have always marveled at my mother's audacity. Where did she find the courage to leave her small island home and cross an ocean to a land as foreign as West Africa? Her journey was bold in every sense. I imagine that in 1948, it was rare for a young woman to leave her homeland to move to another country virtually on her own—a move that would still be extraordinary for many young women today. Even more remarkable, she didn't follow the usual paths of Jamaican migration to Great Britain, Canada, or the United States. My mother's journey to Liberia embodied the contradictions of her personality. She was a woman who defied easy explanation. Regal and proper, yet down-to-earth and fun-loving. Respectable, yet rebellious. Conservative, yet unorthodox. She insisted on strict etiquette and decorum, yet broke every rule that sought to confine how a Black woman of her era should live her life.

As a child, I wondered what had sparked her interest in West Africa and how she managed to make her way there. She was always vague about her motivations. She told my sisters and me that it was our aunt Violet's idea and she didn't want her sister to travel alone. My aunt was a bit more forthcoming. She said that a nurse in Kingston had circulated information about jobs in Liberia, and she and Mommy decided to pursue the prospect. Even so, I found it hard to believe that such an uncertain prospect alone could inspire them to travel such a long distance to such an unfamiliar place. I had always suspected there must have been a deeper connection—perhaps something tied to the Marcus Garvey movement, which had its roots in Jamaica. I knew that Garvey's back-to-Africa campaign had been popular in Jamaica for decades before my mother left for Liberia. My mother had told us that her father's brother, her uncle Eustace, served as a secretary to Garvey, but she never tied that relationship to her moving to Liberia. Might the nurse Aunt Violet mentioned have been the missing link? I wondered.

Marcus Garvey, a Jamaican-born activist and one of the most influential figures of the twentieth century, founded the Universal Negro Improvement Association (UNIA) in Jamaica in 1914. His movement championed the idea of Black self-determination and envisioned a return to Africa for descendants of the African diaspora. Liberia, established in the nineteenth century by freed Black Americans, came to symbolize the homeland where Black people could build a society free from the oppression they faced throughout the Americas, including the Caribbean. Although Garvey himself never traveled to Liberia, his movement inspired many Jamaicans to view the country as a land of opportunity. Mommy and Aunt Violet must have been among them.

My suspicions were confirmed when I read a tribute Uncle Eustace's daughter, Dorothy Whyte, my Jamaican first cousin once removed, wrote after his death in 1967. Dorothy told us that her father changed the spelling of his last name to Whyte to distinguish himself from another Jamaican named Eustace White. I can't recall exactly when or why Dorothy circulated her tribute to family members, but I believe it was after my mother died. To my astonishment, I discovered that Eustace Whyte, born in 1903, was far more involved in the Garvey movement than my mother had let on. Far from being Marcus Garvey's assistant as I had imagined, Uncle Eustace was one of Garvey's most trusted associates and a close friend of

Garvey's wife, Amy Jacques Garvey. A cabinetmaker like my grandfather, he had served as the general secretary for the UNIA's St. Andrew Parish Division and eventually rose to the position of one of the secretaries to the Right Honourable Mr. Garvey.

According to Dorothy's tribute, her father had been struck by a vehicle while riding his bicycle to visit Mrs. Garvey. She wrote that he had founded a branch of the UNIA called the Harmony Division, which held meetings in Kingston on Sunday evenings and hosted events for African visitors to the island. In the 1950s, members of the Harmony Division gathered at George IV Memorial Park (later renamed National Heroes Park) under a bronze bust of Garvey to sing rousing songs and deliver fiery speeches in support of their cause.

One line in the tribute stood out to me: "Miss Iris Patterson, who had been one of the nurses in the Black Cross Nurses Brigade, was always dressed in her white with black trimmed uniform and she would lead the singing of 'Advance, advance to victory, let Africa be free.'" That clinched the connection for me. I suspect that Miss Iris Patterson was the same nurse my aunt Violet had mentioned. She might have been the one who told my mother and aunt about the job openings in Liberia.

Uncle Eustace was one of the pallbearers who lowered Garvey's coffin into George IV Park when his remains were returned to Jamaica in 1964. A year later, during Dr. Martin Luther King Jr.'s official visit to the island, Uncle Eustace had the honor of escorting him to lay a wreath at Garvey's tomb in the presence of the acting prime minister. In the Jamaica *Gleaner* archives there is a photograph of Uncle Eustace standing proudly—erect and beaming, dressed in a pin-striped suit, starched white shirt, and bow tie—beside Dr. King and Mrs. Garvey in the Garvey Mausoleum. Seeing him in that photograph, with his wide smile and military-like posture, I am reminded of my grandfather, Dada, who carried himself in the very same way.

Dorothy's tribute notes that it was Marcus Garvey Jr. who delivered the eulogy at Uncle Eustace's funeral. "For more than forty years, Mr. Whyte had served the UNIA and had developed a large friendship by the life that he lived," he said. "Eustace Whyte was a lover of his race and his people."

Surely, my mother must have known about her uncle Eustace's deep involvement with the UNIA. His close relationship with Garvey and the back-to-Africa movement must have shaped her decision to move to Liberia. But she never shared the full story of her remarkable uncle with my sisters and me. She never once hinted at the important role he played in the movement—or in her own life. Perhaps Dada shielded her from his younger brother's more radical activities. Or perhaps Mommy wanted to shield us. Knowing her, I imagine she wasn't inclined to reveal the militant motivations behind her bold journey, even if they were part of the movement that carried her to Liberia. True to form, she was rebellious yet respectable. Respectably rebellious.

Mommy and her sister became citizens of Liberia soon after they arrived. I know only fragments of what her life there was like in her twenties. Still, I've come to believe that Liberia shaped her worldview just as my father's time in India shaped his. Monrovia, the capital, was relatively modern and bustling, but beyond it lay tribal villages where traditional customs were still part of everyday life. I imagine that her encounters with those cultures awakened a lasting interest in anthropology and belief in our common humanity that she and my father would eventually come to share. In 1949, when a visitor to Monrovia told her about a scholarship at Roosevelt College, she made the bold decision to uproot herself once again, leaving for Chicago to begin the next chapter of her extraordinary life.

Evelyn remembers seeing letters my mother wrote to her parents during her time in Liberia and the long ocean voyage to America. One of the letters she saved in a scrapbook was written on June 4, 1949, from the deck of the ship as Mommy made her way to Galveston, Texas. In it, she recounts a conversation she had with two missionaries returning to Canada.

We discussed all kinds of problems of Western Africa, while we ate apples. It is now 9:05 p.m. and I'm pushing off to my cabin, take a bath and go to bed. So cheerio until tomorrow.

Lots Love,
Iris

Reading those lines, I picture Mommy seated on the deck under the stars, wrapped in a shawl against the sea air, casually eating apples and talking politics. There's something both brave and endearing about her composure, the way she signs off with "cheerio," as if she were on a school trip rather than standing at the edge of a life-changing journey. Her letter makes me feel even closer to—and more curious about—the adventurous version of her I never knew.

Iris White, c. 1950

Over the course of the 1950s, while my mother was a student at Roosevelt and began a relationship with my father, my father stayed in close touch with Bill Alberti, summarizing many of their engagements in a dozen pages of typewritten notes. Bill still worked at the main post office in downtown Chicago, and their phone conversations rarely strayed beyond discussing his extramarital escapades and my father's efforts to track down more interracial couples to interview. Once when he called, in November 1952, my father caught Mrs. Alberti, who confided that Bill had been seeing another woman.

"This is the first time that anything serious has happened since we were married," Jeanette said. "I guess with us working on different shifts he got lonesome. I might have to give up working."

In July 1953, my father invited the Albertis over for dinner and they reciprocated by inviting my father to a birthday party at their home, thrown by a German man for his Negro sweetheart of three years. I'm no longer surprised to read that the party guests consisted of several interracial couples. By now, my father had recruited all of them to his study. He called Bill on December 22, 1954, to make sure he had received the invitation to my parents' wedding, scheduled to take place the next day.

CHAPTER 10

Undesirables

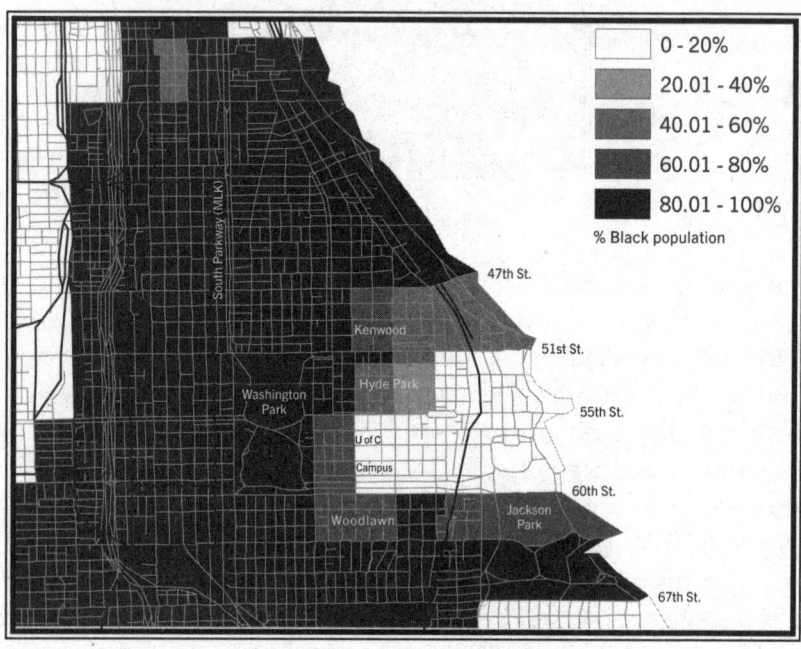

Map of Black Belt, Chicago, 1960

Mr. and Mrs. Alberti
August 7, 1955

On a bright July morning, I return to the stack of transcripts and notes my father had compiled on the Albertis—all marked with the same file number: 206. For the past week, I've been following the thread of his interactions with the couple, uncovering both their story and my father's. This coming weekend, my sister Evelyn and her husband will visit from upstate New York; she wants to walk him through the neighborhood where we grew up. I'm not yet sure how much I will tell her about the surprising discoveries I've made about Daddy's bachelor life. The following weekend, my husband will arrive—our first time together since I came to Chicago to delve into my father's papers. Keen to make progress before my visitors arrive, I reach for the transcript of the final formal interview with Bill and Jeanette, curious to see what more it might reveal.

My father's visit occurred shortly after the family had moved to a brick bungalow in the white section of Chatham, an area on the South Side of Chicago. The saga the couple recounted reminds me of interviews my father conducted in the 1930s. Chicago had retained its residential color line, though the exact perimeters were extending outward, since my father began his study nearly twenty years before. Mr. Alberti was eager to relocate from the colored neighborhood where the couple had resided since their marriage in 1948. Mrs. Alberti, however, was nervous that she would not be accepted by their white neighbors. Nor was she sure how their five-year-old son and the baby she was expecting would fare. Although the little boy could pass as white when in his father's company, his true racial identity would be evident if she were present. Mr. Alberti dismissed his wife's concerns as overblown, a reaction I find surprising given his own experience being bullied as a child on account of his Italian background.

The Albertis had begun negotiating to purchase the house in Chatham six months before. Jeanette had seen its listing in the *Chicago Tribune* and phoned the owner, an Irishman. "The first thing he asked me was whether I was colored," Jeanette recalled. "He only wanted to sell to whites." Jeanette gave a "noncommittal" response, telling the owner that her husband would be in touch with him. Next time, Bill phoned the owner.

"Are you white?" the owner asked.

"Presumably so," Bill answered.

Bill met with the owner at the house, unaccompanied by Jeanette. "When I went to the house, the owner almost got on his knees and asked me to buy this house," Bill reported.

Soon after moving in, Bill and Jeanette decided to attend St. Clotilde, a Catholic church located only a few blocks from their house. On their second visit, the priest urged the mostly Irish parishioners to participate in an important community meeting scheduled for the upcoming Tuesday evening. The Chatham Manor Business Improvement Association called the meeting, the priest explained, "to deal with the problem of undesirables coming into the neighborhood."

"We want to prevent a recurrence of what happened at the eight o'clock service this morning—the two undesirables who came to the service," the priest added.

Jeanette insisted that Bill go to the meeting. She had her suspicions and wanted to confirm whom the priest was calling undesirable. When Bill went to the meeting, held at Golgotha Lutheran Church, also close to their house, he discovered that its purpose was to ward off an influx of colored people into the white section of Chatham.

Bill and my father agreed that the white residents' mission was already futile. My father remarked that he had noticed several ads in the *Chicago Defender* offering houses and two-flat buildings for sale on the white side of Chatham, a telltale sign that Negroes were migrating there. Bill had observed that his white neighbors were racing to sell their homes. For Sale signs were popping up at breakneck speed. A house across the street and another two doors down were up for sale. In the previous few weeks, six men representing real estate companies had called to inquire about his willingness to sell the bungalow he purchased less than a year before. He believed that Chatham would become exclusively Negro within the next five years. Except for, of course, the white spouses of colored residents, like him.

Mr. Alberti's plans to move to a white neighborhood were thwarted by white flight he had not anticipated. After World War II, the boundaries of Chicago's Black Belt that whites violently policed since the start of the Great Migration were beginning to shift. Large numbers of Black southerners continued to pour into Chicago seeking greater equality and better jobs, dwarfing the initial migration in terms of absolute numbers. The city's Black population that stood at 277,731 in 1940 swelled to 812,637 by 1960; while Black residents made up only about 8 percent of the city's population in 1940, they represented nearly one-third in 1960.

The unprecedented growth of the Black population worsened the severe housing shortages that already existed. A parallel migration of affluent and middle-class whites to the suburbs opened the way for Black Chicagoans to breach the Black Belt's borders. Unscrupulous real estate speculators, known as "blockbusters" and "panic peddlers," hastened white flight by spreading fear among white residents of plummeting property values as Black families moved in. As my father continued to locate interracial couples in the 1950s, he began to find them in areas like Kenwood, Hyde Park, Woodlawn, Englewood, and North Lawndale that had been reserved for white residents only in prior decades. The shattered barriers of the Black Belt did not signal an end to racial segregation. Rather, the city was redefining its racial boundaries, and the exclusion of Black residents, and anyone they married, was intensifying.

The Albertis might have considered themselves fortunate to escape the violent backlash that many other Black and interracial couples faced in the 1950s when breaching barriers separating white and Black neighborhoods. As Black migration intensified, white residents became more determined than ever to enforce the city's racial borders, "not flinching at the use of violence to keep the walls in place," writes Isabel Wilkerson.

I had reached for my copy of Wilkerson's *The Warmth of Other Suns* to read its account of the white backlash in 1950s Chicago. There, I discovered the horrifying assault on Harvey Clark, a Black veteran from Mississippi, and his family when, in May 1951, they tried to move from a cramped, overpriced tenement to a modern five-room apartment in Cicero, a white working-class suburb just over the Chicago line. When the Clarks arrived, they were met by a hostile mob and blocked by police officers. Driven from the scene, they later won a lawsuit affirming their legal right to occupy the apartment. That July, despite the presence of an angry crowd, the family managed to move in. But their stay was cut short. A mob soon stormed their home, hurling their furniture from the third-floor windows, ripping out the stove, radiators, and plumbing fixtures, and smashing their belongings, including a cherished piano. By the following day, the violence had escalated into a full-blown riot, prompting Illinois governor Adlai Stevenson to call in the National Guard—the first time the Guard had been deployed to quell a race riot since the Red Summer of 1919.

"All the interracial couples I know, unless the colored person can pass and is not known to be a Negro, live in Negro neighborhoods," Mrs. Hooper, a Negro coworker referred by Mr. Alberti, told my father in February 1953. "The average interracial couple lives in a Negro neighborhood because they're not very welcome anywhere else."

According to his notes, my father found Mrs. Hooper and her husband, the son of Sicilian immigrants, in a run-down three-flat in an equally derelict neighborhood near the Ida B. Wells housing project. *The vestibule was in filthy condition, with chalk marks on the walls. The stairs and walls of the stairway and halls were very dirty, and it appeared that they had not been painted or decorated in many years.* My father noticed that there were two names on the doorbell, Hooper and Tortorello.

Although they met in Chicago, both Mr. and Mrs. Hooper had migrated there from the South. After her family left Richmond, Virginia, Mrs. Hooper had lived as a little girl in Buffalo, New York, before moving to Chicago. Mr. Hooper fled Shreveport, Louisiana, to escape arrest for bootlegging. "I had to come here and wait until the sheriff died," he explained. He told an atypical story of passing. They met when he frequented the candy store where she worked as a clerk, just a block from the bus station where he was employed. His skin was so dark that she mistook him for a colored man.

"I have some relatives about his color back in Virginia and I thought he was colored like them," Mrs. Hooper recalled. "I had no idea he was white until I had been going with him for eight months, and when I did find out I quit him."

"You *tried* to quit me," Mr. Hooper interjected. Before agreeing to marry him, he added, his wife had to overcome her worries about the adversities children born to mixed couples would face.

Mr. Hooper disclosed that he used two names—the name his parents gave him, Tortorello, and Hooper, a name he made up. I can imagine my father's surprise when he learned why there were two names on the doorbell. I had assumed Mr. Hooper changed his name from Tortorello to sound less Italian and more white, but the opposite was true: he changed his name to Hooper to sound less white and more Black. He explained that he adopted Hooper so he could pretend to be colored for the sake of finding work. "Especially during the Depression, I found that I could get a job easier as colored than as white," he said. "Two of the best jobs I had were as colored." One was working as a waiter at the fancy Palmer House Hotel in downtown Chicago, the other as a waiter on railroad cars. All the waiters in those positions were Black.

It occurs to me that the only reason being Black could have proved to be advantageous was because certain jobs were reserved for Black people only, jobs that white people ordinarily didn't want or were considered unsuitable for them. I recall a similar story a Black husband had told my father in 1938. He quipped that there was one place where white men will never replace colored—porters on sleeping cars. "They will never let white men work in Pullman cars where women are undressing and sleeping," he remarked. I had never thought about the contradiction of suspecting Black men of desiring to rape white women while hiring them to guard white women on sleeping cars. Like the contradiction of vilifying Black women as neglectful mothers while hiring them to care for white children. The racist stereotypes that white people circulate to support subjugating Black people are always belied by white people's reliance on Black people's labor.

Those jobs might have been the best Mr. Hooper could find during the Depression—perhaps because of his ethnicity, class status, and skin tone. But most good jobs in Chicago were reserved for white people. That's precisely why some of the Black people my father interviewed passed as white. That's why it was far more likely for Black people to pretend to be white than the other way around.

Mr. Hooper could pass as colored not only because of his appearance but also because he felt comfortable around colored people. He recounted how he grew up in a colored part of Shreveport, where his father owned a grocery market that sold mostly to colored customers. He had more Negro friends than white ones. "As a matter of fact, the white kids called me a 'Black dago' quite often," Mr. Hooper said. When his father died in Shreveport, there were as many Negro as white mourners at the funeral. "I lived in a Negro neighborhood all my life. I'm just one of them, in a way of speaking. I'd be lost if I went on the other side." In a twist of serendipity, Mrs. Hooper said that when her family arrived in Buffalo, they settled in an Italian neighborhood, where she was the only colored student at the Catholic grade school. She became accustomed to living with Italians at an early age. Because of their upbringings, both felt perfectly natural—to use Mr. Alberti's term—relating to someone of the other race.

The Hoopers discovered that landlords routinely refused to rent to white men married to Black women. They had no choice but to live in the colored slum area near a segregated housing project. Like Mr. Alberti, white men with Black wives also were dissuaded from purchasing a home in a white area. Perhaps most surprising, even white men who already owned a home in a white neighborhood encountered trouble living there if they had a Black wife.

When my father interviewed Lloyd Hart, a white man, in November 1952, he and his wife, Geraldine, lived in a nice stone-front house in Lilydale, the colored area on Chicago's South Side my father began traveling to in the 1930s. He noted that the block with attractive cookie-cutter houses and manicured lawns was vacant land when he last interviewed in the neighborhood in 1939. My father had read about the Harts in *Ebony*, a story about a white man and Negro wife who were introducing square dancing to the colored community. He found their number in the telephone directory and arranged a visit.

Lloyd Hart, a stout man of fifty-five or sixty years, raised by German

immigrant parents in St. Paul, Minnesota, said he used to think it was
terrible that a white girl would marry a Negro man, but had changed
his views. Geraldine Hart, forty-seven years old, had hair and features
that *attest to her mixed Negro-White-Amerindian ancestry*. Her father was
Negro; her mother was the child of a Choctaw Indian father and German
mother. His notes don't disclose her birthplace, but my father wrote
that she spoke *with a Negro accent and in a manner of a person who has
not had much formal education*. The couple met in Chicago when Geraldine worked as a cook at Michael Reese Hospital, where Lloyd was the
kitchen manager.

Mr. Hart had been previously married to a white woman and lived in
an apartment at Seventy-Second Street and Yates Boulevard on the white
South Shore in a building that he owned. In June 1947, after his first wife
died, he married Geraldine and moved her into his apartment. The neighbors were curious about rumors circulating about his bride. "One woman
said to me, 'I heard them saying that you married a colored woman,'" he
recalled. "I said, 'Yes, it's so. Why don't you come out and meet her.'" One
of their roomers moved out immediately. Mr. Hart also lost friends. "A
lot of them dropped me like a hot potato. Even my daughter don't write
to me," he said. "She's living the way she wants to live and I'm living the
way I want to live."

Mr. Hart explained why he and Geraldine moved to Lilydale shortly
after their wedding. "In September, a gang stoned the house and broke six
windows in our house. This happened at night; you know they wouldn't
do that during the day. It probably took them that long to investigate and
find out what the situation was," he said. "So, I sold and moved out here.
We moved here the sixteenth of December. That's the reason we moved.
I wasn't going to jeopardize her for these hoodlums."

Mr. Hart was proud of their Lilydale home. "It will be six years in
June, and I don't think I've done too bad," he boasted to my father as he
showed him around the house and backyard carpeted with lush green
grass. *The enclosed rear porch was literally filled with plants of various types and
a large vase of cut flowers. The backyard contained a flower trellis and a small
fishpond which Mr. Hart said is stocked with goldfish in the summer.* When the
tour reached the finished basement, my father spotted about twenty large
goldfish swimming in a bathtub, waiting to be transferred to the pond
when the weather got warmer. There was a den furnished with a card table
and chairs, which Mr. Hart called his gambling room. Mr. Hart showed
my father the issue of *Ebony* with the story about his square-dancing class.

He often invited friends over for square dancing in his large garage that sported a built-in bar or the equally sizable cement-floored barbecue pit in the backyard.

Some of the white spouses my father spoke with resented living in a Black neighborhood and couldn't wait to flee back to the other side, even regretting getting married because of it. But there were others like Mr. Hooper and Mr. Hart who had made peace with being among their wives' people. The only caveat was an understanding between Mr. and Mrs. Hooper during the Cicero riots that if fighting started between Blacks and whites in their neighborhood, "he was to go to Franklin Park and stay with his cousins and not come home."

There is something dissonant about the interviews of these white men married to Black women, something I want to make sense of. I pause and move to the leather armchair in the study, settling into its comfort to think it over. Through the cracked window, I hear the muffled shouts and laughter of children playing baseball in the park below—the same park where I used to play at their age. I reflect on how the discrimination faced by the Albertis, the Hoopers, and the Harts complicates the dominant narrative of the all-powerful white man exploiting Black women. Since the 1930s, my father had heard accounts of despicable white men who sexually assaulted Black women or carried on clandestine affairs with them. Yet these white men who married Black women told a different story.

Despite their status at the top of Chicago's racial hierarchy, white men with Black wives were constrained by the residential color line. Most of the white husbands my father interviewed lived in what he called the "main Negro areas." In the 1950s, some, like Mr. Hart, purchased homes in middle-class Black neighborhoods; others, like Mr. Alberti, moved to neighborhoods that were changing from predominantly white to predominantly Black. Those in the working class, like Mr. Hooper, who couldn't afford such higher-quality housing were stuck in the crowded, dilapidated tenements of Chicago's Black Belt. But regardless of status, nearly all the white men married to Black women, like white women married to Black men, were expelled from the parts of town that were reserved for whites only.

My father theorized in his master's thesis that white wives bore the greatest hardship in interracial marriages. Those who were immigrants had expected that marrying a U.S.-born citizen would help them assimilate more quickly and improve their social standing. Instead, they faced a harsh reality: even newly arrived white immigrant men—doing manual labor and living in ethnic enclaves—held a higher status than any Black husband.

Daddy might have argued that white husbands, in some ways, sacrificed even more. They had more privilege to lose. They chose partners—Black women—who occupied the lowest rungs in the intersecting hierarchies of race and gender. Any hope of gaining political influence in the city, or even securing the freedom to rent or buy property where they pleased, was often dashed. And what of the boldness of marrying women whom society openly disparaged, fully aware of the consequences? Perhaps that deeper sacrifice helps explain why, historically, white women have been more willing to marry Black men than white men have been to marry Black women.

As I sit in the armchair, turning these contradictions over in my mind, I wonder whether my father's views shifted after marrying my mother. Did he ever think about what he gave up by marrying her? If he did, he never said so. On the contrary, his admiration for her revealed that he thought he was the lucky one. If there was any disappointment, it was hers—his failure to finish the book based on these interviews. I sit for a minute longer, awestruck by how my parents defied every expectation.

Considering the sacrifices white husbands made does not discount the privilege and power they still retained. No matter the hardships they faced, white men and women in interracial marriages always had the option to cross back over the color line—to return to the white neighborhoods they came from, so long as they left their Black spouses behind. Their Black partners, however, had no such choice. Regardless of whom they married, Black Chicagoans were confined to the restricted, less desirable areas carved out by the city's white supremacist regime. They were seen as inherently undesirable by the dominant society.

My father's notes on the Albertis skip to September 1962, when Bill stopped by my family's house in Kenwood. *During the interval which has not been recorded, Mrs. Alberti died.* My father wrote that Jeanette's death resulted from a botched abortion. I feel a pang of shock mixed with sadness when I read the news.

During his visit, Bill shared the events that led to Jeanette's untimely death. Several years before, Jeanette had confronted Bill about his affair and he had confessed. "I tried to bluff it off, but she had me up a creek," Bill told my father. Jeanette demanded that he go with her to the other woman's apartment for a showdown, where the two women discussed the situation soberly. In the end, Bill pledged his loyalty to Jeanette and their son. "She gave me no choice," Bill said.

Jeanette never brought up Bill's infidelity again, but it seems she didn't forgive him. "About four years after my indiscretion, she retaliated by having an affair with a Mexican lad about five or six years her junior," he recalled. Jeanette became pregnant by the boyfriend, which is when she had the illegal abortion that killed her. Bill said Jeanette had ended the affair several months before her death. "We settled down to make a better life," but tragedy had cut their reconciliation short. Bill remained in the Chatham house with his son and a daughter who must have been born during the unrecorded interval. A Black woman, whom Bill referred to as a housekeeper, moved in to help care for the children. When Bill said he might marry her, my father mused that she must have been more than a housekeeper. "A matter of convenience," Bill called it.

When my father described a subsequent visit to our house by Bill and his seven-year-old daughter, my jaw drops. It was October 1962. I was six years old. *I know exactly who these people are*, I whisper to myself. *I know their real names*. The man my father called Bill Alberti and his children were close friends of my family. I can see them clearly in my mind's eye. The unforgettably dashing father, his daughter who was around my age and looked white, with wavy blond hair and fair skin, and her older brother, who resembled his father. I never met the woman my father renamed Jeanette, but I recall being told that she was Black and that the couple was somehow related to Daddy's interracial marriage study. I remember playing with the little girl at our house in Kenwood and feeling sad for her because her mother had died.

Frantically, I skim my father's notes to confirm my suspicion. I read that later that month, Mr. Alberti arrived at our house to pick up my sisters and me to go with his children to a birthday party. In May 1964, he stopped by our house to retrieve his daughter, who spent the night with us. He returned in March 1966 with his housekeeper-turned-wife and talked with my father while his daughter played with me at a children's party in our living room. *Mr. Alberti was most effusive and uninhibited in his conversation, as usual, while Mrs. Alberti remained rather quiet*, my father wrote.

Later, I come across several photos of the family my father called the Albertis. One shows my sisters and me seated with the daughter at a birthday party in our backyard. In an earlier photo, a smiling Jeanette holds her barefoot baby girl, while Bill sits with their little boy perched on his lap, gazing up from an open book. It was already obvious to me that my father's scholarly investigation of mixed marriages had become seamlessly interwoven with his personal life. Now it struck me that the couples he interviewed were inseparable from my life as well.

CHAPTER 11

Life Imitates Art

From right, Bob, Iris, St. Clair Drake, possibly Elizabeth Drake, and an unidentified man on a road trip, c. 1952

Mrs. Faulkner
November 19, 1952
by Iris White

I've finished reading my father's file on the Albertis—a thick stack of interviews and notes spanning more than a decade. Now, halfway through my stay in the rented Kenwood apartment, I feel the need for a change of scenery. I carry my laptop and the next interview transcript into the kitchen, setting them down on the small island. On the windowsill, a wooden box holds three small plants my husband had sent to mark the start of my summer project. The early-morning air is still cool and sweet, a brief reprieve from July's usual heat and humidity. I open the back door to let the breeze drift in, joined by a chorus of birds chattering in the trees.

As I settle in, the first thing I notice at the top of the transcript—an interview with Mrs. Eric Faulkner—are the typewritten words: *by Iris White*. It's the first time my mother's name appears in any of my father's interviews. My heart races as I read the opening lines.

> *At about 7:30 p.m. today, Mr. Roberts and I paid a visit to the home of Mr. and Mrs. Eric Faulkner in the sixty-fifth block on Greenwood Ave. in the Woodlawn area. This was my third visit to the Faulkner home. On the first occasion about two weeks ago, I explained, rather briefly, Mr. Roberts's research study in interracial marriages to Mrs. Faulkner, and asked her if she and her husband would be willing to cooperate in making the study a success.*

I had been eager to unearth my mother's first appearance in my father's notes, but expected it would be as a student my father was dating, another Negro woman he brought to a dance or a party. I had no idea Mommy would surface as a research assistant recruiting couples to his study and interviewing them.

Before opening the boxes my sister sent me, I had always thought, as I've said, that he began studying interracial marriage in the 1960s, after marrying my mother—inspired, I assumed, by his love for her. My sisters and I only knew about the interviews he conducted during our childhood. There was never any mention of what came before, so the project seemed born from their marriage itself. Now I realize that misconception obscured two aspects of his research and its connection to my mother—not only that his interest in interracial intimacy far predated his meeting her but also that she had taken part in his research before they were married.

To my eyes as a child, it had been *Daddy's* project. He was the one who had traversed the city interviewing Black-white couples. He was the one who had regaled us at the dining room table about the magnitude of his study. He was the one who was forever urgently writing a book. Mommy stood at the sidelines, cheering him on, preparing to entertain his anthropology colleagues, helping to host the interracial couples he invited to our home, sometimes typing up Daddy's interview notes—but not conducting interviews herself. Like so many wives of that era, my mother had dropped out of my family's story about the work that built my father's career. My mother's visits to the Faulkners' home told a dramatically different one. *It was Mommy's project, too,* I whisper to myself, dazed, as I read on. I won't stop now, but I'm eager to tell my sisters when we catch up in our next Zoom call in a couple days.

My parents were greeted by Mrs. Faulkner, *a dark-skinned, plump Negro woman about thirty-four years old,* my mother wrote. She described the front room of the three-room apartment as "untidy" and listed all the furniture it contained. *Three very healthy-looking children, light brown in complexion, huddled closely to Mrs. Faulkner,* she added. My mother and father both conversed with Mrs. Faulkner, with no indication that one had more authority than the other. Mrs. Faulkner invited them to return when her husband was home to conduct the interview.

"You see, we never do anything unless we agree about it, and I really couldn't do that without my husband's consent," she explained. Besides, she said, they were quite happy after eight years of marriage and didn't care what anyone thought about their relationship.

"My aunt is coming from Mississippi to spend some time with us, she always comes up to Chicago to see us, and she and my husband get along okay. We don't feel that it is anything unusual."

My mother returned to the Faulkner home on her own three days later and found both spouses present. To help win Mr. Faulkner over, she presented him with an article reporting a study of Negro-white couples in Philadelphia *to show Mr. Faulkner just what sort of data was gained from such interviews.*

"Philadelphia of all places! You know, that was the only place where my wife and I had any real trouble," Mr. Faulkner spurted. My mother was probably expecting a more favorable response. He recounted how, after traveling all night, they pulled up to a cabin, where the owner told him there was a vacancy. "I waited and my wife came out of the car," he continued, "but when the owner saw her, she said, 'Oh no, I can't do that. It would be bad for my business.'"

Mr. Faulkner's tale brings to mind a feature of the frequent road trips my family took when I was growing up. When we stopped at a motel for the night, my father would always park the car and walk into the lobby to check in, leaving my mother, my sisters, and me to wait until he returned with the keys to our room. No matter how anxious we were to stretch our legs or dash to the bathroom, the four of us stayed put inside the car. Although my parents never told us why, my sisters and I instinctively knew the reason. Once, when we were reminiscing about our family road trips, we recalled our shared memories about our father's routine. We agreed: he was avoiding being turned away when the clerk saw that we and Mommy were Black.

My mother recorded Mr. Faulkner's outburst with prose that was completely different from my father's, evoking the scene as if in a novel.

> *Mrs. Faulkner, after ushering the children and dog to the other room and appeasing their cries and whining with cookies, busied herself with the television set, trying almost in vain to get good focus of a program in which no one seemed to be interested. Her husband was slowly turning the pages of the article and sipping a glass of beer. After a split second he continued:*

"But all people are not the same," he said. "On that same trip we stopped in Cherry [Valley], New York, and the people received us with open arms as though we were long-lost brothers. As a matter of fact, they told us that if we had any trouble, we could live there."

My mother's writing delights me. She paints vivid scenes, interjecting quirky details about her characters' appearance or mannerisms, and offers tantalizing glimpses of her own emotions. I'd never read her creative work before now, but the voice on the page is unmistakable. It's the same witty, captivating voice I heard throughout my childhood. Yet this is a version of my mother I never fully knew. Each sentence feels like a clue—an invitation to see who she was beyond the role I once assumed she played in our family as I was growing up.

I find especially charming her notes on the visit with my father to the home of Mr. and Mrs. Henry Coleman in October 1953, a year after they visited the Faulkners. The scene opens at three thirty in the afternoon as the professor and his assistant arrive at the stone building in a shabby part of Kenwood where the Colemans rent a third-floor apartment.

> *Mr. Roberts rang the doorbell, and we waited for the buzzer. As we mounted the dimly lighted stairway, a rather gruff voice came from above. I was quite startled at the stern "Who is it? And what do you want?"*
>
> *Q. (I White): "Is Mrs. Coleman at home?"*
>
> *Voice: "No—she isn't. What do you want?"*

Q. (I White): "Is Mr. Coleman at home then?"

Voice: "Yes—this is Mr. Coleman, but what do you want? Perhaps if you tell me what you want, I'll be able to tell you whether we can help you or not. I am in a hurry dressing to go to work and haven't much time to spare."

White: "I am making a survey and thought you would be able to give me some desired information."

Mr. C.: "Well, tell me what it is, and I will tell you if I can help you."

At this point, Mr. Roberts who was standing behind me on the stairway, took over.

My mother records how my father introduced himself, her, and their study of mixed marriages.

Mr. C.: "Mixed—who is mixed?"

Roberts: "You—I think. I interviewed a couple in the neighborhood and was told that your wife isn't Negro. Isn't that so?"

Mr. C.: "Just wait a minute. Right now, I am naked and will have to put on something."

We continued up the last flight of stairs (the entire conversation was carried on while we stood at the top of the second flight of stairs). I was certainly scared out of my wits.

Mr. Coleman, a bespectacled Negro man of medium build, light-brown complexion, and graying hair, greeted them at the door.

He wore an expensive-looking silk red and white polka dot dressing gown and was barefooted.

He was a bit on-edge, and continued to state that he was in a hurry to get dressed, as he usually left for work at about that time.

I was silently amused at the statement, as the apparent lipstick smears on Mr. Coleman's face caused me to feel that he had a woman companion with him in the house at that particular time.

From where I was standing, I could look into the bedroom which opened from the hallway. The bed was quite rumpled, and I thought Mr. Coleman might well have been enjoying a siesta and not a bath.

I contemplate how my mother might have become an accomplished ethnographer had she completed her PhD—or perhaps a journalist, or even a playwright. I think of how she mastered every crossword puzzle and Scrabble game, how she could recite innumerable stanzas of poetry, how easily she lobbed a witty quip at someone's foibles. I feel fortunate to be the beneficiary of her literary gifts as a child, especially during those evenings we spent together while she patiently coached me to be a better writer.

Returning to my mother's earlier conversation alone with both the Faulkners, I learn that Mr. Faulkner had come to Chicago from Massachusetts and his wife from Eudora, Mississippi. They met when both were working at a tractor company in Chicago. When Mr. Faulkner began staying late to keep his future wife company during her night shifts, the foreman transferred him to another department to try to keep them apart. When they got married, Mr. Faulkner was fired. His parents were no more supportive of his marriage to a colored woman. They had refused to meet his wife. Early on, they even tempted him unsuccessfully to return to Massachusetts without her with the promise to set him up in business. "I don't care what people say, my wife comes first, I love her," Mr. Faulkner told my mother in defiance. "Even though my father has never seen her nor the kids, that makes no difference to me, I have to live a life of my own."

My mother arranged for my father to join her the following day, on November 23, so they could interview the Faulkners together. I smile when I realize that this is how Mommy spent her thirtieth birthday, in the field with Daddy, at work on the project that would define the rest of their lives. When they arrived, my mother introduced my father to Mr. Faulkner, whom my father described as *a nonethnic white workingman* who *looked five or ten years older than his thirty-four years partly because of thinning hair.* My father launched into a defense of studying interracial marriage, augmenting my mother's prior attempts to impress Mr. Faulkner. *I spent at least half an hour carefully explaining to Mr. Faulkner (and Mrs. Faulkner also listened to the conversation) the nature and purpose of my research study.* I see that my father has crafted a more sophisticated pitch about his research than when he started out in 1937.

I compared social science research with geologists', physicists', and other scientists' research studies and suggested that it was important that we learn something about society as well as the natural and physical sciences, my father preached, extolling the equal significance of the social sciences, a defense sociologists still find necessary today.

Mr. Faulkner, unpersuaded, asked why there was any more reason to study unions between spouses of different races than those between white people of different ethnicities. "Why does nobody think anything of it if, for example, a Swede marries a Dutchman?" he pressed my father. He said his father's ancestry was Scottish and his mother was born in Holland.

My father had a ready answer. *I then told Mr. Faulkner that relatively little was known about Negro-white intermarriage, but that a number of studies had been made of Jewish-Gentile and interethnic marriages in such places as New Haven, Conn., Pennsylvania, Minnesota, and elsewhere and mentioned some of the studies.*

Then my father turned to his personal motivation for conducting the study, why he was so passionate about recording the narratives of every interracial couple he could locate.

I indicated that in my opinion a study of interracial marriage would be more likely to create favorable than unfavorable public opinion toward mixed couples in that the general impression most people had of such marriages was probably rather negative and that if the facts were known their impressions might be favorably changed.

After some back-and-forth, both spouses agreed to go over the questionnaires my mother had dropped off on her first visit several weeks before. My mother sat beside Mrs. Faulkner on the couch and asked her questions on the schedule for wives. My father moved a chair next to Mr. Faulkner and recorded his answers to the schedule for husbands. I feel like cheering. My father had scored another conquest.

Three years later, one of my parents had slipped a typewritten page in the Faulkners' file, "Information on Mr. and Mrs. Eric Faulkner, S.E. Woodlawn Area, Chicago, from Mrs. V. Flagg." There is no indication of which one authored the note. It stated that on May 10, 1955, Mrs. Flagg and her husband had dinner at my parents' home. By then, my parents were married and living together on Ellis Avenue in the Hyde Park–Kenwood neighborhood. I remember Virginia Flagg as a family friend when I was growing up.

"What became of Mr. and Mrs. Faulkner?" one of them asked.

"They split up," Mrs. Flagg replied. "After she lost her last baby, she left him and took the three children. I heard he treated her terribly. He used to drink a lot. He was only a workingman and she worked to help out. She quit work before she lost her baby.

"I think one trouble was that Mrs. Faulkner's aunt came to live with them," Mrs. Flagg continued, getting to the heart of the matter. "She was supposed to watch the children while Mrs. Faulkner worked. She was a religious fanatic, and he couldn't get along with her."

When the aunt got a job on the white North Side as a maid, she kept her room in the Faulkners' tiny apartment, but paid nothing toward the rent. "Mr. Faulkner didn't like that," Mrs. Flagg added.

I reflect on how Mr. Faulkner had insisted that he loved his wife despite the backlash against their marriage, how Mrs. Faulkner had insisted that she and her husband always acted in agreement, how her colored Mississippi aunt and her white husband were supposed to get along. But I also imagine that the reasons their marriage fell apart had little to do with their racial backgrounds. The Faulkners separated after a decade of matrimony for the typical reasons married couples quarrel—over household finances, over balancing work and childcare, over reactions to a family tragedy, over dealing with difficult in-laws. The page contained no hint of how my parents responded to the news. I wonder if they mourned the interracial marriages that didn't survive.

As I continue to read the 1950s transcripts, I begin to realize that my mother worked with my father, her professor, as a high-level research assistant—more as a coinvestigator, really—who recruited couples to the study and accompanied my father on most of the visits to their homes. In his notes from 1952, my father begins to refer to her as *Miss Iris White, a Jamaican girl who is a senior at Roosevelt College and who has been assisting me with interviews.* Daddy typically interviewed the husbands, whether Black or white; Mommy interviewed their wives. Each wrote a separate set of notes about their respective conversations, observations, and impressions.

Now I find myself questioning my mother's motivations. Why did she take on such an intense role in my father's research project, perhaps even before they were dating? All month, I had followed my father's dual search—for interracial couples to interview and for a Black woman to court—dating back to the 1930s. He must have recognized the advantage of enlisting a charismatic Black woman not only to conduct interviews with the wives but also to locate, persuade, and recruit couples to participate in the first place. I can imagine him captivated by the elegant, dark-skinned young woman he had noticed gliding through the halls of Roosevelt, just as intelligent as she was beautiful. My mother had majored in chemistry as an undergraduate student, still hoping to become a doctor at first, so she may not have taken a class from Daddy. Once, when my sisters and I tried to piece together our parents' connection at Roosevelt, we figured he must have played a role in supervising the international students and that's how they met.

But what about my mother? Was she genuinely fascinated by the study of interracial marriage, or was she just using collaboration with a professor strategically to advance her career? Did she really want to work with my father for his research—or for him? I also wonder how their professional partnership evolved into a romantic one—and whether they worried about the perception of impropriety. Perhaps that's why they waited until she was a rising senior to officially collaborate. I return to the interviews with renewed curiosity, my mind spinning with even more questions about the entanglement of race, research, and romance in my parents' lives.

When I raise these questions with my sisters during our next Zoom call, Evelyn says that among the belongings she inherited from my parents was a book that my father had given to Mommy, *American Daughter*, a memoir by the journalist Era Bell Thompson. Born in 1905 in Des Moines, Iowa, the granddaughter of formerly enslaved people, Thompson had moved to Chicago, where she embarked on a forty-year career as the international editor of *Ebony*. *American Daughter* was published by the University of Chicago Press in 1946. Perhaps my father had met Thompson, for they both lived in Chicago and could possibly have had mutual friends or crossed paths on the university campus.

Inside the book's cover, Daddy had left a handwritten note to my mother, dated August 6, 1952.

Dearest Sweetheart,
Until a month ago the author of this book was my dream girl
whom I admired as a most wonderful person, the type I would be

proud to call a friend. Now you have taken her place. I trust that you
will enjoy reading Era Bell Thompson's life story. Accept it as a slight
token in celebration of one month of happiness and love. May I always
be your

One and only,
Bob

My father had fantasized about a companion like Era Bell Thompson, a fascinating Black woman with extraordinary talent, determination to succeed, and an interest in global affairs. He must have been over the moon at finding this very woman as a student at the college where he taught. His valentine revealed that he and my mother fell in love in the summer of 1952. So, when Mommy accompanied him to interview the Faulkners in November, they were already more than professor and research assistant. They were romantically involved. They had become the kind of couple they were studying.

One of my favorite photos of my parents is from a road trip they went on in the 1950s. They are lined up against a classic bubble-shaped Chevy with St. Clair Drake, a white woman I believe was his wife, Elizabeth, and another Black man, posing for the photo before hitting the road again. My mother, dressed in a blouse and skirt, is leaning back, pressed against my father. Drake, holding a cigarette, is on her other side. Mommy looks sultry, with a subtly mischievous smile on her face. The trip captured in the photo must have happened when my parents were courting, perhaps during that magical first month of happiness and love. At that time, my father and Drake were both junior anthropology professors at Roosevelt, both having worked on the Warner-Cayton study as PhD students at the University of Chicago, and both involved in interracial liaisons. The photographer might be a white woman romantically involved with the other Black man in the photo.

The black-and-white image of the Black-white couples, their pausing for a break on an adventure together, my mother's slyly rebellious stance, evoke for me the essence of my parents' romance. The photo captures the interweaving of my father's academic position, the research they conducted together, their sexual attraction, and their friendships with other mixed couples. It depicts the network of interracial couples my parents were assembling. Their sense of collective sedition against the racial order. Their shared love for travel that would be a mainstay of their marriage and our family life. All of what makes my parents' relationship so fascinating to me is bound up in that single photo.

As I read the 1950s interviews, I notice that my father is making Roosevelt a center of operations for his study. Not only had he conscripted my mother to be his constant companion on the interviews, but he was also assigning other students to make phone calls, conduct follow-up visits, and collect the questionnaires. He was also recruiting research participants from among his students and connecting interracial couples through the university's programs.

"Roosevelt University was created as an act of courage," begins a slim book commemorating the institution's seventieth anniversary in 2014. When I gave a lecture at Roosevelt in March 2013, I met the university librarian and mentioned the boxes of my father's papers. She was excited by the prospect of adding such a rich archive to the university's history. A year later, she sent me a copy of the commemorative book. At the time, I had only flipped through it before setting it aside. Sensing its deeper relevance to my father's project, I return to it and begin to read more carefully.

In 1945, Edward Sparling, president of Central YMCA College in Chicago—where my father had once been a student—had led the charge to establish Roosevelt. Sparling defied a directive from the YMCA board to identify Black and Jewish students, prompting all sixty-eight faculty members to resign en masse. They were soon followed by their students, and together they founded a new college. Named after Franklin and Eleanor Roosevelt, the institution was built on a commitment to equality of opportunity. Eleanor Roosevelt chaired the advisory board, which boasted an impressive roster of left-leaning honorary members, including Marian Anderson, Pearl S. Buck, Ralph Bunche, Albert Einstein, Thomas Mann, Gunnar Myrdal, and Albert Schweitzer.

The college eventually moved into one of Chicago's most iconic buildings—the Auditorium Building, a massive luxury hotel and theater designed by famed architects Dankmar Adler and Louis Sullivan that had fallen into disrepair. At its opening in 1889, it was the tallest building in Chicago. Roosevelt quickly became known for its race, class, gender, and religious diversity among both faculty and students, earning the nickname "Chicago's Equality Lab" from the *Washington Post*. Many of its alumni went on to become civil rights leaders and influential politicians, including Harold Washington, Chicago's first Black mayor; civil rights activist

James Forman; and U.S. congressman and former Black Panther Party leader Bobby Rush.

Clearly, Roosevelt was an ideal place for my father to teach and work on his mixed marriage project.

During the spring semester of 1951, Ed Anderson, a tall, blond, Nordic-looking senior enrolled in my father's ethnology class. My father's ears perked up when he heard that Mr. Anderson was active in the Socialist Club and dated Black girls almost exclusively. One day in March, Mr. Anderson came to my father's office accompanied by an attractive, brown-skinned girl named Rita Lewis, another Roosevelt senior, to explain why his attendance had been so irregular. *He said he would cut my class, as he had no other time to be with Rita because he worked after school.* Leave it to my father to consider romance a legitimate excuse for skipping class, I chuckle to myself. I wonder if Daddy had developed a reputation among his students for being empathetic toward interracial relationships.

I imagine my father was elated when he bumped into Mr. Anderson and Miss Lewis as he was leaving Roosevelt after classes the following week and learned that they planned to be married in a matter of days. He wished them well and told them about his interracial marriage study. Later, Mr. Anderson and his best man notified my father that they would miss the midterm exam because they were busy arranging the wedding. I'm not surprised that my father excused them.

The day of the wedding reception, my father hosted Drake and two Roosevelt sociologists, Harry B. Sell and Rose Hum Lee, for dinner at his house, then drove them to the party at Mr. Anderson's basement apartment in a middle-class white neighborhood. *As I had not been to bed the previous night, I was perhaps less observant than I might have been.* My father gives no clue as to why he stayed up all night. My hunch is that it had something to do with his relentless pursuit of couples to interview. I see that my father was treating his student's wedding in his typical fashion—as a research site.

After the wedding, my father pursued the Andersons as participants in his study. At his Roosevelt office, he handed Mr. Anderson a stack of questionnaires for him and Rita to complete and to distribute to any mixed couples they knew. In June, the Andersons spent an afternoon at my father's house for lunch and a lengthy interview about their life histories and marriage. They were renting an apartment in Hyde Park in an integrated building that housed two other interracial couples.

Mrs. Anderson, the daughter of migrants from Texas, was born in Chicago in 1927. Her family lore included a story about a white man, her great-grandfather on her mother's side, who fell in love with an enslaved woman and purchased her so they could be married. She initially enrolled at Oberlin College, expecting it to be an inclusive place, but ended up joining other students to challenge its discriminatory policies—a dormitory reserved for the colored students, her rejection from the Women's Glee Club on grounds that her voice was not compatible with those of the other (white) singers, and the administration's threat to expel a colored fellow from the conservatory for dating a white student.

Mr. Anderson grew up in a lily-white, well-to-do suburb of Chicago called Park Ridge. He joined the Young People's Socialist League at age seventeen, left the Catholic Church, and applied to Roosevelt for college based on its reputation for being progressive, all three actions to the vehement disapproval of his parents. The biggest blow came when he revealed the race of the man he planned to room with. "Finally, one day just before I moved in, I mentioned that he was colored, and I made the mistake of mentioning it while I was walking down Madison Street with my mother almost at the corner of State Street," Mr. Anderson recalled. "When she heard this, she proceeded to faint." As he helped her up, his mother insisted on going home immediately on a streetcar, without him. His mother's upset continued into the following day, when Mr. Anderson found her at home lying on a couch. "She was going through quite a wild set of convulsions, which seemed to start from the mouth and then carry on through the whole part of her body." From that moment, he vowed to keep secret from his family his activities involving colored people, which included participating in interracial parties and civil rights protests and dating colored girls.

Later that month, my father drove Mr. Anderson to a party in the Negro section of Woodlawn and peppered him with questions on the way there. Mr. Anderson gave him a rundown on interracial dating at the college. About three-quarters involved Negro fellows and white girls and one-quarter involved white fellows and Negro girls, he estimated. He said that he visited his mother a month ago on the North West side of Chicago to tell her he had married a colored girl. *His mother asked, somewhat hopefully, "Is she light?" but when informed that she wasn't, she saw no hope of accepting the marriage*, my father noted.

The Andersons left for New York City that summer so Mr. Anderson could start his PhD coursework in anthropology at Columbia University. When my father caught up with him at the American Anthropological Association meeting in Detroit in December 1954, the month my parents wed, he learned that Rita had annulled their marriage soon after they moved to New York and had already remarried.

My father recorded no explanation for why the couple broke up. Was it the unique pressures of an interracial relationship, or simply the kinds of conflicts any couple might face? In the absence of answers, my mind spins with possibilities. Perhaps his mother's adamant disapproval of his marriage to a Black woman slowly eroded their bond—whether it wore down him, or his wife, or both. Maybe it was their youth; they married while still in college and may not have been ready for the move to New York City or for the relentless demands of Mr. Anderson's PhD program. It even occurs to me that, given how quickly Mrs. Anderson remarried, another man might have entered the picture.

The truth might be any of these theories. I will never know. Still, these unanswered questions draw me deeper into the emotional terrain the interviews bring to the surface. They help me to reflect not only on the couples' stories but also on my parents' own marriage—and how they, too, navigated love, ambition, and social pressure as best they could. And what I find myself returning to, again and again, is how, in the face of all that, they found a way to stay together.

Iris and Bob, Bartlett, Illinois, May 21, 1952

CHAPTER 12

Servicemen and War Brides

Iris, second from right, Negro servicemen, and war brides, Chicago, 1953

Mr. and Mrs. Easton
Mr. and Mrs. Bowen
September 20, 1953

It's nearing the end of July as I pick up a stack of interviews from 1953—about a year after my parents fell in love and began conducting interviews together. What I am most looking forward to is the chance to hear more of my mother's voice in these conversations. I've thought about Mommy every day since she died, and finding traces of her in the transcripts has brought her closer and made me miss her even more. One of them took place on a September evening that year. My parents had gone to dinner at the home of Roy Easton, a Negro part-time postal worker from Kentucky.

He had married an Italian woman named Floria during his overseas deployment, at the end of World War II.

The Eastons lived in a two-story frame house they shared with Mr. Easton's sister in North Lawndale, a neighborhood that had morphed from entirely Jewish a decade before to almost exclusively Black. The reason for the gathering that day was to introduce my parents to another Black serviceman, Mr. Karl Bowen, and his German wife, Matilda. Mr. Easton knew Mr. Bowen from high school, and they were both currently employed by the post office. My mother had brought along her sister, who had recently arrived in Chicago. That must be my aunt Carmen. She was my mother's younger sister, the one who had stayed in Jamaica while my mother and Aunt Violet were living in Liberia. I imagine my mother's move to Chicago had given Carmen the chance she needed to leave Jamaica and join her big sister in America. Aunt Carmen served as maid of honor at my parents' wedding.

My parents had interviewed the Eastons a year before, soon after they met with the Faulkners. It was my mother who had initially interested Mr. Easton in the interracial marriage study, when they took a class together at Roosevelt. During that first visit to the Easton home, Floria recounted how she had met Roy in 1944, after the American army marched into Rome. Roy was assigned as an officer in the Italian regiment, where her brother served as a sergeant. Their romance began when Roy spent his leave at the Italian sergeant's home.

Mrs. Easton had told my parents that she noticed no anti-Negro sentiment there or opposition to their marriage. "Many Italians married Ethiopians," she explained, likely a consequence of Mussolini's occupation of the East African nation prior to World War II. Mr. Easton interjected that they ate at restaurants, attended theater performances, and visited in the homes of Floria's friends without incident. "You can go to restaurants and theaters in Chicago, but here people stare at you as though she was walking with a gorilla," he added.

That September evening, the three interracial couples and my aunt had settled in the stylishly furnished living room to get acquainted as Mr. Easton poured Italian liqueur and played music from his collection of Italian phonograph records. Mr. Bowen was rather handsome, tall and slender with a light-brown complexion, dressed in a double-breasted suit he had specially tailored in Germany. His wife was of average attractiveness, my father wrote, with blond hair and fair skin. She had removed the jacket that matched her red skirt. Shortly, they moved to the kitchen for a sumptuous Italian meal, each served a huge T-bone steak accompanied by spaghetti, mushrooms, and vegetables, washed down with Italian wine.

After dinner, the couples and my aunt retired to the living room so my parents could learn more about the Bowens. Mr. Bowen recalled how he met his wife in 1948, after his discharge, while remaining in Germany as a civilian employee of the army. They happened to be on a bus traveling to the same town and fell into conversation on the way there. The chance encounter quickly led to romance. They married in Frankfurt three years later. Because Mrs. Bowen was classified as an ex-enemy, her husband had been forced to quit his position. A federal regulation required government employees stationed in Europe to cut ties with the U.S. military within three months after marrying a German.

After being relieved of his army post in Germany, the couple decided to move to the United States. They planned to return to Germany after Mrs. Bowen became an American citizen, which would make her husband eligible to reclaim his job with the army. Similarly, Mr. Easton said his wife had given him one more year to finish his classes at Roosevelt before they moved back to Europe together. "We are in one hundred percent agreement, Floria and I," he said. Longing for the greater "psychological freedom" he experienced in Europe, Mr. Easton was even considering becoming an Italian citizen. "With me, there is no sentimentality about my American citizenship," he explained.

Mr. Easton's words reflected the bitter irony faced by the 1 million Black men and women who served in World War II. They fought to defeat fascism abroad, only to return home to a nation that denied them equal rights and opportunities. They were frequently denied access to GI Bill benefits, which provided veterans with aid such as low-interest mortgages and loans. Many Black soldiers encountered outright racist hostility, including shootings, lynchings, and abductions, mostly in the South. Some even refrained from wearing their uniforms to avoid being attacked by white Americans, who deemed them unworthy of respect and saw their military attire as an affront to the racial hierarchy. As the civil rights leader Medgar Evers put it, "We fought during the war for America, Mississippi included. Now, after the Germans and Japanese hadn't killed us, it looked as though the white Mississippians would."

Mrs. Bowen was very talkative despite having difficulty with the English language, which she only started learning when she came to Chicago two years before. Mr. Bowen had taken German lessons when they met so they could converse in German, a practice they had maintained when at home. My father enjoyed the chance to flaunt his fluency in German by speaking with Mrs. Bowen half the time in her native tongue. She told him that she attended a weekly English class for foreigners at a local public school. There were three Japanese women in her class; most of the other students were Jewish. "They accuse me of being a Nazi," Mrs. Bowen said. "I told them my parents and I weren't active in politics. We were ordinary people and should not be blamed for Nazi atrocities."

As it was getting late, my father offered to drive the Bowens home, along with my mother and my aunt. It seems his ulterior motive was to recruit them to his study while captive passengers in his car. *When we were within a few miles of the Bowens' home, I decided to tell them of my study of Negro-white intermarriage and to seek their cooperation*, he wrote. After describing the project, my father handed them the questionnaires in a self-addressed stamped envelope—a new tactic probably meant to save him and my mother a trip to retrieve the completed forms. Still, I could imagine Daddy badgering couples to return the questionnaires, as he had done in the past. He asked if they knew any other Negro ex-soldiers married to European women, so-called war brides. Mrs. Bowen was excited about the chance to meet other mixed couples in Chicago, regardless of their backgrounds. She said when she tried to befriend another German woman in her English class, the woman rebuffed her when she discovered that Mr. Bowen was a Negro. Before dropping them off at midnight on one of the nicer boulevards on the Negro South Side, my father promised the Bowens to arrange a meeting with another German wife and Negro husband.

Once my mother had joined my father on his research expeditions, they began to build their personal coalition of interracial couples together. One hub of their mixed marriage network was a group of couples like the Bowens—Black servicemen who had met their European brides while stationed overseas and had brought the women back with them when they returned home to Chicago. My father coordinated their expanding circle of Black servicemen and European war brides partly from Roosevelt College, as if it were an air traffic control tower from which he orchestrated planes taking off and landing.

The very day after driving the Bowens home from the dinner party, my father phoned Mrs. Bowen to inform her of an American studies program scheduled to start at Roosevelt in ten days, which would include English-language classes as well as special events for foreigners. He sent her a copy of the program, writing his office number at the bottom.

He encouraged several other of the European wives to participate, often greeting them at his faculty office when they came to class. I can't help but wonder how many of the students in the Roosevelt English-language class were also participants in my parents' mixed marriage project and had met each other as a result of my father's orchestration.

Mr. and Mrs. Buckner
October 10, 1953

Within a couple weeks, my father made good on his promise to introduce the Bowens to another Black soldier and his German war bride, James and Gertrude Buckner. He had learned about the Buckners from another couple he interviewed, who told him that a mixed couple that wed in Germany lived next door. My father soon secured the Buckners' agreement to be interviewed. Daddy was on a roll, I think to myself as I dive into the transcript.

My father arrived at the Buckners' apartment in west Hyde Park on a Saturday afternoon in October, accompanied by my mother, whom he now referred to as *my interviewing assistant, Miss Iris White, who is doing graduate work in anthropology at Northwestern University*. Mrs. Buckner proudly took them on a tour of the apartment, which my father described as *attractively furnished, neat, and modern in appearance*. In what had become their routine, my parents split up to interview the couple, my mother and Mrs. Buckner moving to the dining room, while my father and Mr. Buckner remained in the living room.

Settled in the dining room, my mother observed that Mrs. Buckner was very nicely dressed and had a crisp, put-together look. *The general appearance of the home convinced me that she must be a very good housewife.* Mrs. Buckner recalled the day the colored troops arrived in her hometown, Gelnhausen, in 1947. At first, the townspeople were wary of the darker-hued soldiers. "Naturally, they were kind of scared because of the stories Hitler had spread about the cruelty of the Black people," she said. "But there were a lot of people working in the camp who knew some of the colored boys and they felt that nothing was wrong with them." The soldiers greased the wheels of friendship by giving away candy to the German children and soap and chocolate to their mothers.

Mrs. Buckner longed for a job at the segregated army camp, so she took English lessons and was hired to operate the switchboard. Listening in on conversations and talking to lonely soldiers when they called at night worked magic to perfect her proficiency with their language. She met Mr. Buckner when he was repairing the steps to the building where she worked. They exchanged pleasantries when she arrived to find the steps torn up. Months later, they ran into each other at an army football game, and he invited her to celebrate his battalion team's victory at a nightclub in Frankfurt. After dating for several months, she moved out of her family home when her brother reacted violently to her relationship with the Negro serviceman. "Although he had not met James, he said that he had warned me that those colored men were no match for me, and he slapped me down on the floor," she recalled. She rented a kitchenette apartment in a nearby village, where Mr. Buckner soon joined her. They married just before leaving for Chicago in 1952.

Just as Mrs. Buckner neared the end of her story, the doorbell rang and she and my mother returned to the living room to greet the company—Mrs. Bowen and her friend, a German woman named Elsie Ochsner, who was engaged to a Negro soldier still stationed overseas. They planned to wed in November, when the serviceman returned to Chicago. Mrs. Buckner said she knew seven other German war brides with Negro husbands in the city, two of whom had served in the same battalion as her husband.

Two weeks later, my parents returned to the Buckner home to celebrate Mrs. Buckner's birthday. She told my father over the phone that she was planning the sort of party she would have hosted in Germany, one that would begin around five in the afternoon and last until well past midnight. When my parents arrived at the Buckners' apartment, it was approaching 11 p.m. Mrs. Buckner led them to the front room, where they greeted two familiar faces, Mrs. Bowen and her friend Elsie Ochsner. Their host introduced them to four other women seated in the living room, Ursula Elroy, Lena Hairston, Carla Dudley, and Johanna Hobart, all German brides who had recently moved to Chicago with their Negro husbands.

As I sort through my father's papers from the 1950s, I come across a black-and-white photo that I believe was taken at Mrs. Buckner's birthday party. The image shows six white women in dark cocktail dresses standing in front of a square table draped with a white tablecloth, at the center of which sits a large cake covered in white icing and adorned with a dozen candles. Behind each woman stands a Black man in a suit, his arms wrapped around her waist. Two Black women are also in the photo, one of whom appears to be my mother. Everyone is smiling broadly, their expressions reflecting the festive spirit of the moment.

The photo takes on greater poignancy when I recall reading that the federal government censored magazine stories about Black troops dating white women while stationed in Europe, fearing that photos of interracial socializing would spark an uproar back home. Eventually, the soldiers won the right to send such photos to their families—but only if they were stamped "For personal use only—not for publication."

While my mother got acquainted with the German women at the party, my father followed Mr. Buckner into the dining room, where the servicemen, each paired to a German wife, were seated at the table, finishing a supper of potato salad, bread, and cold cuts. The men were discussing the slum area near the county hospital, where alleys were piled high with garbage and disreputable landlords were illegally converting homes into cramped, overcrowded apartments. Mr. Hairston gave the example of a building at Forty-First Street and Lake Park Avenue, where the landlord had previously rented five-room apartments to white tenants for $45 a month. Once Negroes began to move into the area, the landlord cut up the apartments into two-room units and raised the rent to $85 a month.

Around midnight, the husbands joined their wives in the living room. One of the guests produced a portable phonograph and serenaded the group with romantic German records. The German wives and their Negro husbands all sang along to the German lyrics and two or three of the partners danced to the music. Mr. and Mrs. Dudley impressed the party with a perfectly executed waltz, one of the wives commenting that the ex-soldier stepped and swayed just like a German. Another remarked that his German was excellent, as well. Mr. Dudley responded that he adopted these German ways while spending six years in Germany.

The tenor of the evening turned more serious when Mrs. Elroy brought up the culpability of Germans for war crimes. I had pondered whether the group would broach the elephant in the room—the fact that the Negro servicemen had married women who had been on the opposite side of the conflict they went to Germany to fight, the oppressors of the people they liberated. One might say they were sleeping with the enemy in two respects, for their wives were both white and German. How did the husbands reconcile this added complication to their interracial unions? I wondered.

"The so-called German 'war criminals' were criminals only because they lost the war," Mrs. Elroy asserted. "If Germany had won the war, the American and Russian leaders might have been tried as war criminals."

My father took exception to her logic. *I remarked that there had been some inhuman activities such as the use of slave labor and the killing of millions of Jews in concentration camps in Germany during the war which exceeded the worst excesses of the United States.*

"American soldiers were also guilty of war crimes, but went unpunished because they won the war," Mrs. Elroy responded angrily, becoming *quite excited*, my father noted.

"Germany was a dictatorship, but the United States is supposed to be a democracy and yet they treat Negroes the way they do," interjected Mrs. Bowen, coming to Mrs. Elroy's defense.

"When I go out with my husband, people stare at us. They also stare in Germany, but that is only out of curiosity. In the United States, it is out of hate," Mrs. Elroy rejoined.

I recall that several of the husbands had expressed a desire to return to their wives' native soil in part because they experienced less prejudice there than in the United States—supporting their wives' position. Although my father argued that the Germans were guiltier of war crimes than the Americans, he left unspoken his views on how racism in the two countries compared. He had long recognized the connections among racial caste systems—the ones he observed in 1930s Chicago and Natchez, Mississippi, and those he later examined in his PhD dissertation on the United States, India, and South Africa. I'm even less sure how my mother might have responded. She left no written record of her views on global racial hierarchies. But having lived in Kingston, Monrovia, and Chicago, she had the experience to draw such comparisons.

As I set down my father's notes, I find myself hoping that, as the conversation continued in Mrs. Buckner's living room, both my parents went on to condemn the white supremacy of both Nazi Germany and Chicago—refusing to excuse one by setting it against the other. I hold on to that hope as I try to understand who they were, and what they were willing to face and to stand for.

Later that fall, my father arranged for the Bowens to join him, my mother, and some friends on an outing to Starved Rock, a scenic state park on the Illinois River, a hundred-mile drive from the city. They planned to take a boat ride on the river and climb to the top of the mountain. My parents, with my aunt Carmen in tow, picked up Mr. and Mrs. Bowen early in the morning at the elegant two-story stone building owned by Mr. Bowen's aunt, Mrs. Carter, where they resided. My father had observed when he

had driven the Bowens home after they first met that their house sat on
one of the finest boulevards on the Negro South Side. Now he and my
mother could see its grandeur in the daylight. Enclosed by an iron fence,
the building faced a well-maintained lawn on one side and a lovely garden
on the other.

While waiting for her husband to get dressed, Mrs. Bowen escorted
everyone to the living room. My mother seemed mesmerized by the luxurious items that decorated Mrs. Carter's home, and she devoted most
of her notes to describing them. As the couples took off on their journey,
she closely observed the fittings as she exited the house.

> I went to have a look at my hat in a mirror hanging from the western
> wall, next to the front entrance. I then got a glimpse of the dining room,
> which is adjacent to the living room, and separated from it by an archway.
> The highly polished dining table is set off by a bronze fruit bowl and
> bronze candlesticks. From the quick impression gained, I believe that the
> main furnishings of the dining room are of bronze finished material,
> while the furniture is of matching highly polished mahogany or French
> style to match the living room furniture.

In January, my parents returned to attend Mrs. Bowen's birthday party
and my mother gladly accepted the fräulein's offer to give her a tour of the
premises. Maybe Mrs. Bowen had noticed my mother's snooping into the
rooms on the previous visit. My mother commented on the spaciousness
of the kitchen, the glamorous draperies, the fireplace in a dining room
alcove, the French-styled coffee table in front. *The guest room is truly a
picture of middle-class luxury*, my mother wrote. *The bedside and dresser lamps
are hand trimmed, with rich lacy covered shades. A section of one wall has glass
shelves with four china figurines, which are valued at $20–$45 each.* Mrs. Bowen
boasted that her aunt-in-law spent $2,000 on furnishing the room. She
explained that Mrs. Carter could afford such extravagance because she
and her late husband were in the real estate business and owned about
thirty properties on the South Side.

My mother's vivid portrayal of the Bowen residence mirrored in its
precision my father's anthropological accounts of the research participants'
physiques, I think to myself. I am relieved that my father has toned down
his annoying estimates of Negroid and Caucasoid ancestry, turning his
focus more to building a social circle of interracial couples. It seems he
had left the background sketching to my mother, and her eye was drawn

beyond the couples' appearance to their surroundings. I sense there was more behind Mommy's meticulous report than fascination with Mrs. Carter's taste in furniture. I believe she wanted to convey the magnificence of the home Mr. Bowen's aunt, a Negro migrant from the South, had managed to create for herself, her nephew, and his German bride within Chicago's Black Belt.

The other guests arrived around 10 p.m. Most were Negro men accompanied by their European war brides. My father was the only white man at the party. That foreshadowed many occasions during my childhood when my father was the only white person at family gatherings, like when we visited my mother's relatives or when my Jamaican grandparents, my aunt Carmen, and my cousin Edwin lived at our home. Mrs. Buckner shared the good news that she had secured Mrs. Bowen a job where she worked, as a file clerk—my father's introduction already paying off. Mrs. Bowen served punch and highballs until everyone gathered for the buffet supper. The birthday cake didn't make an appearance until 2 a.m. My father had a field day telling the couples he had yet to interview about his study and scheduling times to stop by their homes.

My parents weren't entirely responsible for the friendships that formed among the Black servicemen and their wives who lived on Chicago's South Side. At one point, there even was talk of the German wives establishing a club. But my parents had made initial introductions for many of the couples and facilitated the ties that grew between others. They were the common denominator, having linked disconnected units of friends and neighbors to create a cohesive assemblage, like stitching assorted patches of fabric together to craft a quilt. By the end of the 1950s, my parents had recruited at least a dozen Black servicemen and their European war brides to their intermarriage project and recorded their unique stories of love across the ocean, across enemy lines, and across Chicago's color line.

As I continue to read the transcripts from the 1950s, I begin to wonder whether my parents' community-building efforts had a tangible impact on interracial marriage in the city. Beyond the handful of scholarly articles my father would eventually publish and the lectures he would deliver, did the act itself of conducting the research make a difference? I can't help but think that his recruitment of hundreds of mixed couples—bringing them together through introductions, parties, excursions, programs, and classes—may have increased the prevalence of interracial marriage in

Chicago. Perhaps all his efforts had also helped shift public attitudes after all, as he had hoped. It seems plausible that his proselytizing and match-making had played at least a small role in nudging the numbers upward, like a butterfly's wings setting off an unseen chain of events.

My father may have never finished the book he had planned to write based on his research, but the interactive way my parents conducted their project may have had more influence than any scholarly text could have. They took participant observation to a heightened level—one that may have shaped the very social phenomenon they were studying. The true impact of my father's study of Negro-white intermarriage is impossible to measure. He never became a celebrated intellectual at a prestigious university, and I doubt many scholars in his field had ever heard of him or his hundreds of interviews spanning five decades. But the social gatherings of mixed couples he helped bring together—with my mother's aid—make me believe his work left a mark, if only on the personal network they built together, including the Black servicemen and the war brides who returned with them to Chicago.

As I reflect on the Black soldiers and German wives, a memory comes to mind. When I was growing up, my family was friends with a white mother with a German accent and her two girls around the ages of my sisters and me, with tan-colored skin like ours. Sometimes the mother and her daughters came to our house, other times we visited theirs. My sisters and I had reminisced about playing with those girls with a German mother. I now realize that the girls must have been born to one of the couples that my parents interviewed in the 1950s. I'm not sure which wife became the mother I knew as a child. It could have been Mrs. Buckner or one of the other women my parents befriended at her birthday party. I doubt it was Mrs. Bowen, whose stately stone house, glitzy bronze candlesticks, and French-styled mahogany furniture would surely be imprinted on my memory. Despite the mystery surrounding the family's identity, I feel a deeper connection knowing more of the story behind those two girls I played with when I was little.

CHAPTER 13

Seeking a Haven

My parents' wedding ceremony. From left: my uncle Alfred, Bob, Iris, my aunt Carmen, and Reverend Homer Jack, Evanston, December 23, 1954

Mr. and Mrs. Lund
October 10, 1953

One evening in October 1953, after leaving the attractive Buckner apartment, my parents pulled up to a six-flat in southwest Hyde Park on a block that had gradually converted from predominantly Jewish to one my father estimated was two-thirds Black. *The next block, which is quite close to the University of Chicago, is almost entirely white and includes a number of homes of professors at the university.* That dramatic shift between the demographics of adjacent blocks is reminiscent of Hyde Park when I grew up. My childhood home in Kenwood sat on one of those blocks with magnificent Victorian homes owned mostly by white professors, doctors, lawyers, and other professionals, which butted up against a segregated Black neighborhood.

In his notes, my father reported receiving a list of names, addresses, and telephone numbers of eight couples who met through interracial cooperative housing located near the University of Chicago. The roster was compiled by someone named Lucille, who apparently lived in one of the integrated units and offered to lend a hand in my father's research. He also mentioned an interracial cooperative residence in Kenwood called Howarth House, where he visited his friend Edward Roscoe, a Black student at the University of Chicago who tended to date white women. He and Roscoe frequently went on outings together as members of an interracial club that I suspect was Funference, which our family belonged to when I was growing up.

My father had friends at other residential co-ops, Whitman House at Fifty-Seventh and Kenwood and Concord House nearby, all part of a cooperative housing movement that began in Britain in the nineteenth century and took root in New York City and Chicago, spreading to other parts of the country. By the late 1940s, five co-ops had been established in Chicago's Hyde Park–Kenwood area, which were open to students of all races, making them fertile ground for interracial dating. Alvin and Emily Lund, whom my parents visited that evening, were the sole couple on the list Lucille had gathered that was composed of a white husband and a Negro wife.

As my parents made their way up three flights, Mr. Lund leaned over the banister to greet them. Thirty-three years old, a former long-distance runner of tall, slender build, *he is rather carelessly dressed*, my father wrote. *Unkempt* is how my mother described him. He ushered my parents into the living room of the five-room apartment—*very sparsely furnished, a very marked contrast to the home we had visited earlier in the evening*, my mother noted.

> *The overall disheveled appearance of everything, the low tone of the housekeeping, and the scant furnishing of the apartment led me to believe that the couple was either living under very limited circumstances or saving toward a very bright future.*

Mrs. Lund was sitting at a desk, furiously trying to fill out the questionnaire my father had dropped off a couple weeks before. According to my father, she looked younger than her thirty-one years, short and a bit plump with tan-colored skin, wearing faded blue jeans. The couple had already put their young daughter and son to bed. After discussing the latest sociological research on interracial marriage, my parents paired off with the Lunds, my mother and Mrs. Lund departing for the dining room, my father staying in the living room with her husband.

Mr. Lund grew up in a small industrial city in Massachusetts, where his parents settled after immigrating from Sweden. At twenty, he moved to Chicago to study botany at the University of Chicago. While there, he developed an interest in race relations and other social issues. He joined the Fellowship of Reconciliation (FOR), an interfaith organization dedicated to peace and justice, founded in 1915 at the outbreak of World War I. "Our first project was the founding of an interracial house for young men in an exclusive section of Kenwood to break down the pattern of segregation," he recalled. Committed to FOR's principles, he was a conscientious objector during the war, refusing to register for the draft. As punishment, he spent two days in the county jail.

Mr. Lund told my father that he and several other members of FOR's Chicago cell helped establish the Committee of Racial Equality in 1942, renaming it the Congress of Racial Equality (CORE) within two years. He listed Bernice Fisher, George Houser, and Homer Jack as his cofounders, leaving out the two Black men who were also there from the beginning, James Farmer and James Robinson. There was an additional white member of the founding group from FOR whom he failed to mention: Joe Guinn. Could "Lund" be Daddy's pseudonym for Guinn? I wonder. For reasons I still don't understand, I could find no online records that either confirm or rule out the connection—even though information and photos are readily available for every other founder.

At the time, Mr. Lund explained, there were few restaurants in Chicago where Black patrons could be assured service. CORE launched successful campaigns to integrate these establishments, with interracial protesters entering restaurants and refusing to leave until the Black individuals were served. Others had recounted similar tactics to my father. According to my father's friend Edward Roscoe, who also belonged to CORE, when testing a restaurant for discriminatory practices, they made sure not to seat Black men with white women to avoid "clouding the issue." Otherwise, he explained, "when the reaction is negative, you would not be sure if it was because of the interracial couple or because of the Negro couple coming into the restaurant."

Mrs. Lund had been raised in a racially mixed community of small cottages in Pittsburgh, a neighborhood she described as midway between lower and middle class. Like many areas in Chicago, her childhood neighborhood had gradually become less diverse as she grew up. "When I went back home it was completely Negro," she told my mother.

Her father, a Pullman porter with roots in Virginia, provided the family with a stable income. She attended a Negro college in Richmond before moving to Chicago to pursue a master's degree in educational psychology at the University of Chicago. There, she found housing in one of the co-op houses, designed to bring together students of all races. It was in this environment that she met Mr. Lund.

"When we lived in the co-op, there was seldom the need to go out for entertainment," Mrs. Lund reminisced. "There was always something going on at the co-op. I think almost everyone preferred sitting around discussing all kinds of topics to going to a movie or a party." The residents formed such close bonds that they frequently reunited even after moving away. "The same sort of thing continues—we visit one another and wind up in some lengthy discussion," she said.

Mr. and Mrs. Lund were married in the library of the Theological Seminary on campus by a Unitarian minister—likely Homer Jack, one of CORE's founders, who would later marry my parents. They chose not to inform their families beforehand. "We weren't looking for any trouble," Mrs. Lund explained. Instead, they waited until after the wedding to share the news through letters. The newlyweds lived in one of the co-op houses for two years before moving to an apartment building at the corner of Sixty-First Street and Dorchester Avenue in Hyde Park. They rented a seven-room apartment that had been split in two, sharing a bathroom with another couple. The arrangement fostered a sense of community, with the couples taking turns babysitting each other's children. Their landlord was among the few in the area who welcomed interracial couples.

"The woman who owned it declared that she liked to see the races mix, and was a sort of 'mother to mixed couples,'" Mrs. Lund told my mother. "There were about five interracial couples living in the building while we were there. She also catered to students of all races—especially foreign students."

Mrs. Lund's description reminds me of the role my own mother would later assume while I was growing up, after my parents bought our house on Kenwood Avenue. I can't remember a time when we didn't have a mixed couple or a foreign student living in our guest room, only for them to be replaced by one of my mother's Jamaican relatives who needed a place to stay.

But as I read on, Mrs. Lund quickly dispelled any resemblance between the landlord and my mother. "She knew that interracial couples would have great difficulty in finding apartments, so she gladly rented to them, but charged exorbitant prices," Mrs. Lund continued. "We sued her after we left the building and got back quite a lot of money."

By the time Mrs. Lund gave birth to their second child two years earlier, they had moved to their current apartment. She said they secured it by mistake—she was still in the hospital delivering the baby when her husband signed the lease, and the owner had assumed she was white. Since then, in response to white flight, their landlord had begun renting to Black tenants to fill vacancies—at a premium. Across the street, another six-flat building was cooperatively owned by both Black and white families.

"You need something like that, a controlled interracial situation, to maintain an interracial area," Mr. Lund observed.

"I used to have the idea that if all areas of the city would open to all races at the same time, Negroes would move in inconspicuously," he elaborated. "But Chicago has too strong a pattern of ethnic succession. When Negroes begin to move into a neighborhood, whites begin to think of moving out."

This repeated pattern of white residents fleeing neighborhoods as soon as Black families moved in left little hope for the interracial communities Mr. Lund had envisioned. "A person who wants to have interracial living is forced to keep moving as interracial neighborhoods become all-Negro," he observed.

"Now I feel that for the next two generations in urban areas with a heavy Negro migration from the South, the only way to maintain an interracial neighborhood is through a controlled situation," he concluded.

As an example, Mr. Lund told of a builder constructing 140 houses near Philadelphia with the goal of creating an interracial community. However, to maintain a racial balance, the builder found he had to limit the number of Black buyers. When he initially held an open house on Sunday afternoons, "a hundred Negro families came to look, and white families would drive by, slow down, and then drive away when they saw so many Negroes there," Mr. Lund explained. It seemed that maintaining a so-called "controlled" interracial community required discouraging Black families from moving in to prevent white residents from leaving.

Mr. Lund asked my father if he knew of any interracial neighborhoods like Hyde Park on the Northwest Side, so he and his wife could find a place closer to the lab where he worked as a microbiologist, testing yeast for small breweries. As my parents continued documenting interracial marriages, they had discovered small enclaves of Black-white couples who had settled in rare South Side areas that were beginning to integrate. Like the Lunds, some of these couples were relieved to find a haven where their marriages were more accepted than in the racially polarized communities that made up most of Chicago. But such havens were few and far between, largely confined to Hyde Park and Kenwood—blocks where Black families were moving in, and only the most liberal white residents remained. My father noted that other transitioning neighborhoods seemed to be deteriorating into slums.

Discouraged, Mr. Lund admitted he was considering leaving the United States altogether. He found neighborhoods too segregated, residents too unaccepting of marriages like his, and the mix of racial hostility and indifference too infuriating. He cited an example of violence that occurred nearby at Sixty-Third Street and University Avenue in 1945. A Black friend of his had been walking with a girl of "dubious appearance"—someone who looked as if she might be white or mixed—when they encountered a group of six white soldiers and a sailor.

"Are you colored or are you white?" one of the soldiers demanded of the girl.

"That's none of your business," she replied. The soldier knocked her to the pavement. When the Black man tried to defend her, the group descended on him and beat him severely.

"Of about a hundred people who passed by, nobody interceded," Mr. Lund said. "Only one immigrant who could hardly speak English said anything."

When my father called Mr. Lund in March 1956, he learned that the Lunds were moving to the planned interracial community near Philadelphia Mr. Lund had described. He had found a job as a microbiologist testing the water supply for the Philadelphia suburbs. The builder succeeded in selling all the units and maintaining a 55 percent white to 45 percent Negro ratio, he told my father.

How were you counted with reference to the quota?

"They had a meeting when we applied and they decided to count us as half for the white quota and half for the Negro quota," Mr. Lund replied.

During my mother's conversation with Mrs. Lund in the dining room, a cat had jumped onto the table where they were seated. *As I expressed my dislike for such animals, Mrs. Lund transported him to the back porch,* my mother wrote. I recall Mommy saying that in Jamaica, animals were kept outside. She found the American habit of keeping pets indoors both strange and unsanitary. But I don't remember her having a particular distaste for cats.

In fact, our very first pet in the Kenwood house was a gray cat my sister Evelyn named Diamond. She chose the name because, to her, the cat's green eyes sparkled like gems. Diamonds were the only jewels she knew. For some reason, Evelyn claimed Diamond as her own. During a later interview with the Lunds, when their cat approached my father, he remarked, "I have a cat that looks just like that one almost. My little girl has it—but it's almost the same color, and the most gentle little thing you can imagine." Diamond was part of the family. We kept her inside our home throughout my childhood until we were forced to give her away when we moved to Egypt when I was thirteen.

Later, we took in another kitten from a litter my best friend Lisa had at her house. We named him Apache because the colors of his silky fur reminded us of a Native American blanket. But we might as well have named him for the tribe's reputation as fierce warriors. He and Diamond never got along, and Apache holed up in the basement, keeping Grandpa company in the carpentry workshop my parents had set up for him down there. Unlike Diamond, Apache wasn't gentle. If anyone other than Grandpa tried to pick him up, they risked being mauled.

In one of our home movies Helen desperately tries to hold Apache as the family poses for the camera. When he starts wriggling to escape, clawing her in the process, my cousin Edwin reaches in to help—only to be attacked himself. The fiasco is forever preserved on film, becoming a source of endless laughter at the expense of the hapless cat wranglers.

As I read about how quickly Mommy had Mrs. Lund's cat removed, I marvel at how she put up with our cats for so long. Even as a guest in someone else's home, she hadn't hesitated to banish the Lunds' pet. Yet she helped us care for sweet Diamond—and even unruly Apache—throughout our childhoods.

While going through my father's papers from the 1950s, I come across a newspaper clipping that sheds light on my mother's years as a student. On October 26, 1954, the *Chicago Sun-Times* reported on the state visit to Chicago by President William V. S. Tubman of Liberia. The longest-serving president of the West African nation, whose tenure lasted from his election in 1944 until his death in 1971, Tubman was known as the "father of modern Liberia" for expanding the nation's infrastructure with funds from Western investments and the rubber industry. At the same time, his leadership was often described as autocratic, marked by tight political control and deepening economic inequities that many believe helped sow the seeds of Liberia's later civil conflicts. This visit helped solidify Liberia's friendly relations with the United States during the Cold War, when America was competing with the Soviets for influence in Africa.

Under the headline "Swift Visit Here Impresses but Tires Liberian President," the article quotes President Tubman, clearly worn-out after five relentless days—two major speeches, city tours, a round trip to the state capital, and several receptions packed into his schedule. The visit also included a stop at Roosevelt, newly renamed a university that same year. "In my own country we have at least a two-hour siesta every day," he told students there. "Here I have had no siesta, and I need one."

The *Sun-Times* article displays one photograph from President Tubman's visit. It shows the Liberian leader presenting Roosevelt's president, Edward Sparling, with the first volume of the university's Tubman Collection of African research materials. The caption says "With them is Iris White, a Roosevelt graduate from Liberia." My mother stands next to Sparling dressed stylishly with a striking striped cape draped around her shoulders and small matching hat on her head, beaming. The Tubman Collection, the article explains, will consist of books, pamphlets, and official papers from Liberia. I wonder if subsequent volumes of the Tubman Collection contain materials donated by my parents, though I could find no evidence that Roosevelt continued to maintain the archive.

Another photograph memorializes the Liberian president's time at Northwestern. Some years ago, I received an email from a librarian at Indiana University attaching the photo he discovered in the university's Liberian Collections. There is a yellowed note tacked onto the photo: "At Northwestern University, shakes the hand of Liberian student Iris White Roberts, the President of the University at right, others looking on." The note must have been added after my parents wed in December, two months later. Reading the note was the first time it sank in that my mother was a Liberian citizen when she gave birth to me. I have a dim memory of when Mommy became a U.S. citizen in 1961, when I was five years old, just a sensation of excitement surrounding the event. At the time, I thought of Mommy only as Jamaican, but she had already given up her British citizenship (Jamaica didn't gain its independence until 1962) to become a Liberian.

In the photo, my mother is proudly grasping the hand of President Tubman, their eyes locked, both with polite smiles on their faces. She is wearing the same striped cape, now without the matching hat. On her outstretched wrist is a bracelet I recognize from my childhood—a wide band

Iris greeting Liberian president William V. S. Tubman at Northwestern, with Melville Herskovits, far left, and Northwestern president J. Roscoe Miller, far right, looking on, 1954

with long ivory beads linked together, probably a keepsake she brought back with her from Liberia. To my mother's left looking on is a short bespectacled man wearing a dark bow tie with what look like white polka dots. I recognize him as Melville Herskovits, chairman of the anthropology department. His mouth is agape, as if in awe of this moment uniting my mother and the Liberian president on the university campus. I imagine this must have been a momentous occasion for the Program of African Studies he founded at Northwestern six years before. The appearance of my mother in both photographs tells me she was an important part of President Tubman's stopover at Roosevelt and Northwestern during his whirlwind U.S. tour.

At the time of the presidential visit, Mommy had graduated from Roosevelt and was pursuing her PhD in anthropology at Northwestern. Professor Herskovits was her dissertation adviser. As I ponder my mother's ambition to earn a PhD, I'm ashamed to realize I have no idea what her research was about. The main thing she had told me about her dissertation project was that she didn't complete it. She gave up her fieldwork when she gave birth to me and then to my sisters a year and three months later.

Herskovits was a familiar name in our household when I was growing up. My mother impressed upon my sisters and me that she had been working on a dissertation under the mentorship of the preeminent anthropologist when she abandoned it to raise us. "Herskovits told me I should finish my dissertation and do the fieldwork later," I recall Mommy saying more than once. She said that she couldn't follow her mentor's advice. It would violate her work ethic to submit such a shoddy product—implying that her standard of excellence was even higher than that of the esteemed

Professor Herskovits. Her words were meant as two life lessons. First, *age quod agis*—do your work well or don't do it at all. Second, don't let marriage interfere with your ability to do your work.

I hadn't known much about Mommy's years as a graduate student until I received an email out of the blue from an unfamiliar anthropologist in February 2023.

> Dear Professor Roberts,
> I have been for a long while doing research for a (critical/evaluative) book on the Northwestern University anthropologist Melville J. Herskovits (1895–1963). I think I have come across photos of your parents (and perhaps one of you) that I thought you might like to have.

The email was signed by Kevin A. Yelvington, Professor, Department of Anthropology, University of South Florida. He explained that he had conducted interviews with fifteen of Herskovits's former students and postdoctoral fellows. One of the interviews was with a man named Warren d'Azevedo, who died in 2014 at age ninety-three.

I immediately recognized d'Azevedo as another name I had heard my parents mention frequently at our Kenwood house. Mr. d'Azevedo had told the professor that he and his wife lived in "Anthro House" within a block from the Northwestern campus in Evanston, Illinois. Anthro House was a large private residence on Chicago Avenue where rooms were rented out to graduate students who tended to be in the anthropology department. I pinpointed its location immediately, for I had an office in a house like it a few blocks away when I was a faculty fellow at the Institute for Policy Research on the Evanston campus. Anthro House had been demolished at some point to make room for a university dorm. My mother had been one of the graduate students who rented a room there.

Professor Yelvington attached five photos that included my mother. In each photo, Mommy is posing with other students, always garbed elegantly in a dress, a sweater or coat, and a small hat atop her head. She stands out, drawing the viewer's eyes to her. It is not only her dark skin. It is her self-assured posture, her lovely smile, her mysterious aura.

In one photo, Mommy is sitting on the steps of Anthro House next to a white woman, Warren d'Azevedo's wife, Kathleen. A Black man named George Brooks and an Indian man named Surajit Sinha are standing behind them, denoting the diversity of my mother's housemates. In another, she is sitting on the lawn with Kathleen and another white woman, Paula Hirsh. Kathleen is grinning at my mother, who is sitting up tall, her legs bent demurely to the side under her carefully spread-out dress, looking completely sure of herself.

My favorite photo captures d'Azevedo squatting between his wife and my mother, who are seated on the lawn. His hands rest gently on their shoulders, creating a sense of connection. My mother's legs remain poised to the side, but now she leans in slightly, resting her elbow on Warren's thigh and her hand on her cheek, displaying absolute ease. What strikes me most is that her posture conveys a deeper familiarity with Warren than even his own wife's does. I had never seen my mother pose like this, so alluring, like in the photo of her leaning against my father on the road trip. I try to imagine this woman I never knew, this sensual siren whom my father fell hopelessly in love with and married.

Iris, right, with Warren and Kathleen d'Azevedo at Anthro House, c. 1953

"Your father waited until his mother died to marry me. He didn't want to upset her," my mother once told me. These were the only words with which she disclosed that my grandmother was opposed to her son marrying a Black woman. She said them with a disapproving tone that indicated it was cowardly of my father to delay the wedding. My mother thought he should have had the guts to stand up to his mother and marry her sooner. I later discovered that my father's mother died in July 1954, just five months before my parents wed in December. The timing supports my mother's view of my father's timidity.

My parents were considered old for newlyweds in their time—Daddy was thirty-nine, and Mommy was thirty-two when they married. My father still lived in the Wrightwood Avenue home where he had grown up, a place he once told Drake he longed to return to after the war, craving his grandmother's cooking. Though he rarely spoke to my sisters and me about his mother and never mentioned her in his field notes, looking back, I get the distinct impression that he was a mama's boy.

I imagine my father at his mother's bedside as she lay dying—the once chubby woman from the photos now likely emaciated by cancer. He must have wrestled with the agony of whether to reveal a distressing truth, knowing it would burden her in her final days. I've heard of people who shield their loved ones from unsettling realities when the end is near. I wonder if my father did the same. I'm not sure if it was a cowardly deception or a forgivable act of mercy.

It was no secret what kind of men my mother found attractive. She often extolled the charms of tall, slim, and debonair celebrities, with Harry Belafonte at the top of her list. He was a celebrated actor and civil rights activist, but in our house, he was, above all, the voice behind the Jamaican songs that played habitually on our family's stereo. I can still see the striking red cover of his *Calypso* album—Belafonte in a crisp green shirt, smiling, eyes lifted, hands open in invitation. My sisters and I knew every lyric by heart, our voices rising in unison with the stereo. Even now, the words return effortlessly, carrying me straight back to those Saturday mornings in the Kenwood house. Those were the first songs my sisters and I learned—alongside the German tunes Daddy taught us.

My mother also swooned over the silky-smooth jazz and pop vocalist Nat King Cole. She had one of his albums, too, though I don't remember the music as well. But his handsome face on the cover comes back to me—his dark brown skin, his straightened wavy black hair parted to the side, his enchanting smile. His untimely death from lung cancer in 1965 brought a hush of sadness over our house. And it became an opportunity for Mommy to remind us why we should never smoke cigarettes. Another favorite was the Welsh-born singer Tom Jones, whose voice and swagger she enjoyed. Though she didn't watch much television, she always made sure to catch *This Is Tom Jones* when it began airing in 1969. My mother's

other heartthrobs were Omar Sharif and Gregory Peck, actors who shared
that same suave demeanor. I remember one time my mother praising my
father's looks. We were standing together at the kitchen screen door on a
hot summer day, looking out at Daddy cutting the backyard grass, shirtless.
Mommy whispered to me, "Doesn't your father look handsome?"

I have a faint memory of Mommy mentioning a tall, dashing Jamaican
man she had admired. I sensed that she left him behind when she set sail
for Liberia and sometimes wondered what might have been. When I asked
my mother why she married a white man, she replied that when she was
attending Northwestern, the Black male students were only interested
in dating women with fair skin. They applied the paper bag test: women
had to be lighter than a brown paper bag to be considered attractive.
Mommy's luminous dark brown hue failed the test. I never had the impression that Mommy had excluded Black men and married my father
because he was white. It was social status, not necessarily race, that was
important to her. I believe she wanted a husband from within the lofty
academic circle she had entered. As if miraculously, she encountered a
professor, a white professor, who had been searching his entire adult life
for someone just like her.

I realize now that this whole time, I have granted my parents a mercy I
have denied to the interracial couples they studied. I have not examined
the role race played in their marriage with the same scrutiny I have applied
to interracial relationships more broadly. I have barely questioned the
ethics of my father pursuing a romance with my mother when she was a
student. My reluctance comes from knowing the depth of their love for
each other—and from my love for both of them.

Perhaps this is how most people feel about their own mixed-race
families. It explains why so many couples told my father that race didn't
matter in their relationships, that they were just like any other couple in
love. It is one thing to analyze interracial intimacy in the abstract, with
the politics of racial hierarchy always in focus. It is quite another to be
personally bound up in it.

My parents were married on the twenty-third day of December 1954,
the year the Supreme Court decided *Brown v. Board of Education*, its first
blow against the Jim Crow regime's separate but equal doctrine. It would
take more than a decade of further civil rights activism before the Court
was prepared to overturn bans on interracial marriage in *Loving v. Virginia*.

The minister of the United Methodist church my mother attended in Evanston refused to marry her and my father. He personally had no issue with her marrying a white man, he told her, but members of his congregation were less tolerant.

My parents turned instead to Homer Jack, the well-known Unitarian Universalist minister and activist who helped found CORE and National Committee for a Sane Nuclear Policy (SANE). Reverend Jack performed their wedding ceremony at the Unitarian Church of Evanston. There's a photo from the wedding: the minister holding an open book as my parents look on, Uncle Alfred beside my father, Aunt Carmen beside my mother, gazing straight into the camera. My mother has a slightly quizzical look in her eyes. Afterward, my parents held a reception at Anthro House. "A splendid multitude thronged about the premises for what I believe was the first public inter-racial wedding reception in the area," d'Azevedo would later recall in an unpublished memoir.

In a formal wedding photo, my mother is wearing a fitted but tasteful lace dress, which she dyed a very pale shade of blue. She has a simple strand of pearls around her neck and pale blue gloves that go up to her elbows. A small matching hat sits atop her hair worn short and pressed. My father is dressed in a dark three-piece suit, white shirt, and dark necktie. His jacket and vest are buttoned to the top. A white carnation garnishes his lapel, a white handkerchief peaks from his breast pocket. They both look solemn with only a hint of a smile on their faces, but not unhappy or afraid. They look dedicated to each other.

My favorite wedding photo captures them in a more candid moment, likely after the reception at Anthro House. My mother has removed her hat and gloves. My father is sitting on an upholstered chair, my mother snuggled close on his lap. One of her hands is clasped in his, the other reaches up to grasp the top of his lapel. Their foreheads are touching. He is whispering something to her. She is smiling, eyes downcast. They look deeply in love.

After they were married, my parents purchased a two-flat at 5325 South Ellis Avenue in Hyde Park, near the University of Chicago. They managed to afford it with income from renting out one floor of the house, along with the proceeds Daddy had shared with his brothers from the sale of their childhood home. While Mommy was pregnant with me, Daddy had returned to writing his PhD dissertation, a project interrupted first by his stint in the army, then by his devotion to interviewing additional interracial couples. From what I can tell, my father was more dedicated to tracking down every Black-white couple in the city than to finishing the dissertation project he had started more than a decade before. The year of my birth finally marked the completion of his PhD in anthropology.

My father's dissertation was titled "A Comparative Study of Social Stratification and Intermarriage in Multi-Racial Societies." He examined caste as a type of social hierarchy, which he defined as "the division of a society into hereditary groups ranked with respect to rights, privileges and status, and between which social intercourse is ordinarily much restricted and little or no vertical social mobility and intermarriage are sanctioned." Noting that the classic, nonracial caste system existed in India, he identified racial caste systems in South Africa, the United States, Guatemala, and the West Indies. He compared these five caste systems, paying special attention to endogamy, or the practice of marrying only within caste boundaries, and concluded that "the frequency of intermarriage and social controls governing such marriages shows considerable variation." Reading my father's dissertation, I was struck by how it presaged Isabel Wilkerson's 2020 bestseller, *Caste: The Origins of Our Discontents*, which compares racism in America to the caste systems of India and Nazi Germany.

I was born Dorothy Elizabeth Aileen Roberts on March 8, 1956, at Lying-in Hospital on the University of Chicago campus, my parents' first child. The identifying features of my parents on my birth certificate are their ages, their birthplaces, my father's occupation (there is no space for mother's occupation), and their races: father white; mother Negro. My parents brought me home to their two-flat on Ellis Avenue.

My birth and my father's PhD paved the way to another academic venture my parents embarked on together. When I was three months old, my parents moved to Liberia, where my father served as a visiting professor at the University of Liberia in the nation's capital, Monrovia. The university dates back to 1851, when the legislature of the newly independent nation chartered Liberia College. The Liberian government provided a seven-room concrete house on two acres of land that stretched to the ocean and was lush with banana, pineapple, and coconut trees. At that time, a Vai tribal village bordered the edge of the expanding capital. We lived in Liberia for two years. My father engaged with the cultures of Indigenous tribes in the nation's interior and consulted with the Liberian government to document its traditional heritage. My mother reconnected with friends she had made during her stay there in the 1940s. Daddy preserved our time in Liberia with hundreds of slides and film reels of our family's activities at home and his interactions with tribal people in the Liberian hinterland.

The home movies from Liberia start with a scene that marked the beginning of the journey. Mommy is standing at the top of the steps in front of the opened door of a small plane emblazoned with the words "Capital Airlines," about to board. Dressed stylishly in a crisp light blue dress, she is holding me wrapped in a baby blanket. We are taking off for Washington, D.C., to pick up my first passport. I have retained that passport, issued on May 1, 1956, with a dark green cover and my photo as a newborn. My first international trip was to Jamaica a month later to meet my grandparents before my mother departed her island home a second time for West Africa. As a child, I looked at that image of Mommy and me on the airplane steps countless times. I can remember sensing that we were joint pioneers, staking out the voyage to Liberia that would create the foundation for our family. It imprinted on my soul the faith that I was destined from birth to traverse the world.

Later, I would discover on Ancestry.com the list of outward-bound passengers on the SS *African Pilgrim*, sailing from New York City on June 22, 1956, bound for the ports of Monrovia, Liberia, Lagos, Nigeria, and Lobito, Angola. When my eyes scroll down to the bottom of the list, I see *ROBERTS, Dorothy, 5325 Ellis Ave., Chicago, Ill., 3 mos.*

My sisters, twins, were born in Liberia a year later. "Irish twins" is a term for siblings born a year apart. We were Irish triplets. My parents had three daughters in diapers while living in West Africa. The fact that my American sisters were born in Liberia to a Jamaican mother who was a Liberian citizen cemented our family as a band of nomads, citizens of the world. Since we were kids, Helen longed to return to the land of her birth, a dream made unrealistic by two devastating civil wars that raged from 1989 until 2003, when the factions signed a Comprehensive Peace Agreement. The election of Ellen Johnson Sirleaf as president three years later signaled the safety Helen needed for her move. She lived in Liberia for more than a decade helping to reconstruct the education system that was ruined by war.

Professor Yelvington also sent me the unpublished memoir titled *Rebel Destinies: Remembering Herskovits* that Mr. d'Azevedo wrote about his time at Northwestern and the early years of the Program of African Studies. At the end of the memoir is a series of photos, many of which were taken during d'Azevedo's fieldwork in Liberia and a visit Herskovits and his wife made there in 1957. Their stays in Liberia coincided with the years my family was living there. One stunning color photo shows my mother, pregnant with my sisters, at the front of a band of twenty or so people hiking down a dirt road in the interior with lush vegetation as the backdrop. The caption reads "Frances Herskovits, Iris White and friend, Warren d'Azevedo and Melville Herskovits on procession into host village." Of course, my mother was Iris Roberts by then.

Mommy is wearing a green smock that covers her protruding belly over orange culottes. She sports a large straw-colored sun hat on her head. She is holding hands with a young Liberian woman, barefoot and dressed in a traditional skirt that goes down to her ankles. To their left is Herskovits, a few steps away, looking at them. He is using a large umbrella as a walking stick. On the other side of my mother is his wife, Frances, and a barefoot Liberian man in shorts. D'Azevedo, donning a black hat and sunglasses, walks directly behind my mother and her Liberian friend. A barefoot Liberian boy can be seen at the end of the row, behind Mrs. Herskovits. Marching behind the first two rows is a coterie of at least a dozen Liberian men, whose fuzzy images merge and are hard to distinguish.

From right: Melville Herskovits; Warren d'Azevedo; Iris and her friend; and Frances Herskovits, on procession into the host village, Liberia, 1957

My mother's position in the middle of the first row of the corps of anthropologists and Liberians gives the appearance that she is helping to lead them. What was Mommy's role in this expedition to a Liberian village? I wonder. Did Mommy facilitate the villagers' agreement to host the white American researchers? Was it sheer coincidence that d'Azevedo and Herskovits decided to venture to Liberia, where my mother, a citizen, was now living with her anthropologist husband? Whatever her importance to their investigation of Liberian tribal culture, I doubt she ever got credit for it.

In his memoir, D'Azevedo mentions my mother only once in connection with their time in Liberia, when recounting a picnic with Mel and Frances Herskovits on a palm-lined beach on the Atlantic shore.

> *We were accompanied by Iris White, a vivacious and lovely Jamaican student of Herskovits who was married to the sociologist Robert Roberts currently teaching as a visiting professor at the University of Liberia. She had lived at Anthropology House in Evanston where their memorable wedding reception took place. Now pregnant with a second child, she presided over this small and cheerful reunion on the Monrovian seaside.*

Professor Yelvington continued to send me discoveries about my family he made while researching Herskovits. He wrote to me from the Schomburg Center for Research in Black Culture in Harlem, where he was digging through the Melville J. and Frances S. Herskovits Photo Collection. Among the gems he found were a photo of my mother and Herskovits sitting casually together in Liberia, my mother wearing the sun hat and smiling, Herskovits holding a cigarette between his fingers and speaking to someone off camera. On the back of the photo, my mother wrote, "Hope your reception is just as grand throughout your trip. Iris R. Roberts." The photo must have been taken in the village after the procession arrived.

Later, Professor Yelvington sent me a letter, dated July 21, 1965, that d'Azevedo wrote to my parents. It is on his letterhead from the University of Nevada, where he was chair of the Department of Sociology and Anthropology. He thanks my parents for a pleasant two-day visit at our home on Kenwood Avenue. "I still remember the faces of your three lovely daughters," he writes, "and Cathy and I are eagerly awaiting the snapshots you promised." He says that he especially enjoyed reuniting with my mother, and adds, curiously, "It was a delight to see you as marvelous as ever and, particularly, to learn that you are going on with your work." Was he referring to the dissertation my mother had begun when they were graduate students at Northwestern? I have no recollection of Mommy ever returning to her academic work. It must have been disappointing to host her former classmate who was now the chair of a department in their field when she had failed to complete the path they embarked on together. I wonder if she tried to save face by inventing a story about resuming her graduate work. Or perhaps she had been secretly attempting to resuscitate her dissertation while raising my sisters and me, failing a second time to fulfill her mission.

My aunt Violet remained in Liberia after my mother had left for Roosevelt, becoming an attorney there. She was a stunner with the looks and glamour that reminded me of Diana Ross. In her middle age, Aunt Violet had also married a white man, my uncle Basil, a Jewish geologist from Belfast, fifteen years her junior, who had traveled to Liberia on a work assignment. Neither having children, they lived an exciting life together, moving to Brazil, France, and Zambia for Uncle Basil's job. My sisters and I relished our glitzy aunt's visits to Chicago. She always arrived with tantalizing tales of her travels all over the world and gifts for us from her latest journey. One year, each of us got a beautiful silk kimono she had picked up while visiting Japan. The kimonos replaced the cotton housecoats Mommy had us wear over our pajamas if we ventured out of our rooms at bedtime. I remember lounging in mine all day long when I had the mumps and stayed home from school.

Aunt Violet was an excellent seamstress, taking after my grandmother. She fashioned all her clothes, fancy suits and dresses made from luxurious satins and tweeds. Among her gifts to me and my sisters were remarkable handmade garments—a brown tweed skirt encircled in pleats for me, a long velvet skirt for Evelyn to wear during her cello recitals, a winter coat of black and tan plaid wool for Helen. Her most distinctive creations were her hats. They came in a variety of fabrics and shapes and were decorated with grosgrain ribbons and silk flowers. One made of purple felt was especially striking with its tall crown and flat top, resembling a Pilgrim's capotain, but fashionable when she sported it. Aunt Violet and Uncle Basil would retire to a country home in France and remain married until her death at age ninety-seven in 2015, Uncle Basil joining her a year later.

Mommy and her sister were reunited when my parents and I arrived in Liberia. When I was growing up in Chicago, Aunt Violet loved to re-count the banter between my father and me as a toddler back in Liberia. "Dorothy, stop being so recalcitrant!" he would plead with me when I was engaged in some mischief. "Daddy, Daddy, stop aaaaaggravating me!" my aunt would mimic me, parroting my two-year-old drawl.

According to Aunt Violet, I could be a brazen little girl. She frequently recalled the day I strayed out of the house, provoking her and my mother to look frantically all over the property for me. As they were searching outside, I approached them with an air of defiance, coming from where a group of Liberian men who tended the yard were eating lunch. When they reached me, I opened my mouth wide and declared, "Look! I eat rice!" They realized that I had joined the Liberian laborers to partake in their afternoon meal. All of Aunt Violet's recollections about me in Liberia, which she recapped every time she visited, had a common theme. They were early signs of the rebellious streak I had already evidenced as a toddler, my eagerness to break social rules and cross forbidden boundaries.

In a scene in one of our home movies from Liberia, Daddy is sitting outside at a table and holding me on his lap when I am about six months old. He tries over and over to feed me from a bottle, but I refuse to take it, stubbornly moving my tiny head away each time he brings it to my lips. Then he picks up a bottle of rum that was sitting on the table and holds it just beyond my grasp. My infant hands eagerly reach for it. He pours a glass of rum, takes a sip, and then pretends to let me drink from it as I try to draw the glass closer. I remember thinking when I was little that he actually let me taste a little of it. But it was a ruse, a cinematic trompe l'oeil my father directed for our family's amusement. We laughed together every time we watched the scene. Despite the film's implication, my mother forbade my sisters and me to touch alcohol while we were growing up, and we dutifully obeyed her. I recall nearly fainting the first time I drank a rum and Coke at a party during my first year of college.

Aunt Violet's stories also foreshadowed my relationship with my father. His "stop being so recalcitrant" and my "stop aggravating me" would come to symbolize his efforts to get me to adopt his perspective and my resistance to it. Our early repartee signified mutual respect more than antagonism, a closeness even in our disagreements, a liberty to lovingly spar. In hindsight, as I reflect on stories I have heard about domineering fathers, who force their will on their cowering children, or aloof fathers who ignore their children altogether, I appreciate how fortunate I was to have a father who respected me enough to try to persuade me of his views while encouraging me to think for myself.

In 1958, when Daddy's two-year professorship at the University of Liberia came to a close, my family that had mushroomed to five prepared to return to the South Side of Chicago. Aunt Violet, who delighted in quoting my two-year-old proclamations, liked to recall how I would proudly tell every visitor about my upcoming journey across the ocean. "I'm going on a big ship," I'd announce—except it came out as "I'm going on a big tip."

CHAPTER 14

Kenwood

Clockwise from top left: Bob, Iris, Dorothy, Helen, and Evelyn, Kenwood, 1959

Mrs. Wolff
February 24, 1966

As August approaches, I enter the final stretch of my summer in Kenwood. The heat has intensified, making the study unbearable by midday. I've never liked air-conditioning, but now I switch on the window unit first thing in the morning and slide the heavy wooden doors shut to trap the cool air. After breakfast, I return to the study with the next stack of transcripts and rely on the ceiling fan to carry me through the morning. I'll cool the room again when I break for lunch. With the weekend visits from my sister and husband behind me, I return to the interviews with uninterrupted focus.

I'm eager to dive into this new phase of my parents' mixed marriage project—the interviews from the 1960s. This era holds special weight for me: it overlaps with my childhood in Chicago. After two years in Liberia, my parents chose to settle in what they believed was the most welcoming neighborhood for interracial families—Hyde Park–Kenwood on the city's South Side. When I was three, they moved us into a sprawling Victorian house on Kenwood Avenue, where I spent my school years from kindergarten through eighth grade.

As I open the boxes now, I feel a tug of curiosity, part joy, part trepidation. I sense what I'm stepping into. These interviews will bring back memories of my parents: the sound of their voices, the belonging I felt with them, the lessons they taught me—and the constant presence of my father's book and interracial relationships in our home. They'll return me to the world my parents built together and ask me to reckon with how their research, their marriage, and the upheavals of that decade shaped not just their story but my own unfolding sense of identity as a Black girl with a white father.

In the early 1960s, one of the interviewees, a white husband with a Negro wife, told my father about Paul Wolff, an editor of the *Chicago Maroon*, the University of Chicago student newspaper, whom he met at a left-wing youth conference in East Berlin. Mr. Wolff was Jewish and married to a Negro woman named Ethel, so the couple could potentially contribute to my father's research project. It wasn't until August 1964 that my father dispatched one of his students to the Wolffs to hand them a set of questionnaires and arrange an interview to discuss their answers. More months elapsed before another student, in the spring of 1965, spoke with Mrs. Wolff, hoping to pin down a meeting. The timing could not have been worse. Mrs. Wolff informed the student that, after twelve years of marriage, she had gotten divorced the week before. She was in no mood to discuss her failed relationship. Not one to be deterred, my father phoned Mrs. Wolff himself in February 1966, making one more attempt to secure an interview. After apologizing for his student's inopportune intrusion, he persuaded Mrs. Wolff to agree to a conversation at her home the following day.

At about 1:05 p.m., my wife and I arrived at Mrs. Wolff's home which is located in a rather rundown area just east of the Illinois Central Railroad Tracks at the northwest corner of the South Shore area and just south of the East Woodlawn area. The block contains a mixture of apartment buildings, two-flat buildings and small frame single-family houses. The Wolff house is a two-story frame house with inexpensive siding. The wooden steps, door, windows, etc., were in poor condition and in need of paint.

My eyes focus on the words "my wife and I arrived at Mrs. Wolff's home." Once again my childhood understanding of my father's research—and my mother's role in it—is thrown off balance. I had already discovered from the 1950s interviews that my mother had joined my father as his research assistant during the period leading up to their marriage and my birth. But I imagined that her participation in the mixed marriage project had ended there. Growing up, I wasn't aware of my mother helping with the study beyond occasionally typing up transcripts of interviews my father conducted. I have no image of my mother as an ethnographer, no recollection of her accompanying my father on his research expeditions. Nor do I recall her taking any credit for the book he was writing. Helen says she remembers once accompanying our parents to the home of an interracial couple. But did she know then that the visit was part of their research—or did that realization come later? In any case, all three of us agree: it was always Daddy's project. As I delve further into the 1960s interviews, my mother's story alters yet again, as if I've shaken a kaleidoscope and see the patterns of colors rearranging one more time.

Mrs. Wolff, a tall, slim woman with a brown complexion and short, natural hair, took my parents' coats and escorted them into the living room. The furniture—a sofa, two chairs, and a broken coffee table—was shabby. A Black man who appeared to room in the house was speaking on the telephone. My father recognized him as a former student at Roosevelt whom he had interviewed with his white wife during the summer of 1964. When the man got off the phone, he told my father that he had divorced, and that his former wife had reverted to using her maiden name.

Before the formal interview began, my father spent twenty minutes discussing his reasons for studying Negro-white marriages with Mrs. Wolff. She seemed jaded about the topic. She and her husband had first met as teenagers in Chicago when she was friends with his younger sister. They got to know each other through their involvement in a civil rights organization and closely knit group of left-leaning college students. She was twenty, he was three years her senior, when they wed in 1953. She said that since they married, they had come to know thirty or forty other interracial couples. "We had a party attended by many of them," she recalled. "It was sort of a United Nations." At first, married life was glamorous, sparkling with parties with their liberal friends. But she and the interracial couples she knew were burdened with insurmountable difficulties beyond those experienced by same-race couples.

"The problems society creates for any male-female relationship are great and the added problems of white male and Negro female or Negro male and white female are so great that most of them have dissolved," Mrs. Wolff said.

She estimated that only six or seven of the dozens of mixed couples she knew were still together. Chief among the problems dooming interracial couples was a paradoxical frustration, one resulting from a false hope in interracial intimacy.

"For many of these mixed couples their religion was we've got to integrate to prove to the world that integration will work," she explained. "It was almost impossible to find a Negro marrying a Negro."

Given what I know about the rarity of interracial marriages at the time, I'm certain Mrs. Wolff was exaggerating. But perhaps, like my parents, her social circle was deceptively skewed toward interracial relationships.

The glitch, she went on, arose "when we become confronted with the fact that by integration, we weren't solving any problem."

I believe Mrs. Wolff was using "integration" in two senses, one personal, one societal. I hear her saying that interracial couples felt they needed to integrate their own marriages as a way of demonstrating that integration could succeed in the broader society. If white people could share married life with Black spouses, they reasoned, it would prove that white Americans could also work, attend school, live in neighborhoods, ride buses, and eat in restaurants alongside Black Americans. Their disillusionment, when marriage failed to fulfill that promise, only deepened the burdens they already faced. In other words, interracial couples had to contend not only with the external challenges of racism but also with the painful realization that marrying across racial lines wouldn't solve them.

By this point in the interview, Mrs. Wolff was expressing doubts about continuing. She questioned the purpose of the study.

"If it is only to say integration is lovely, then no," she insisted. "We've been talking and talking about this for years and all we see is relationships deteriorating. I don't want to see people go into marriage on that weakened basis."

My father must have been deeply disappointed by Mrs. Wolff's diatribe. If there were a religion devoted to interracial marriage, he would have been its most faithful follower—even its most devoted minister and missionary. Since the age of twenty-one, he had preached the virtues of mixed marriages, proselytized the uninitiated, and built a network of believers who he hoped would spread the message forward. By the 1960s, he was convinced that increasing the number of mixed-race couples and their children was the most powerful way to refute false notions about racial difference and to populate the nation with people who rejected and disrupted the hierarchy of white supremacy.

At the time, Daddy was spreading his message around Chicago. A member of the Roosevelt Speakers Bureau, he gave talks about interracial marriage, as well as other aspects of current race relations, at various academic and public forums. An advertisement in the *Hyde Park Herald* from February 1968 promoted his public presentation at the Chicago Ethical Society on "Negro-White Marriage in Chicago and America—the Background Facts and Social Consequences." Everyone invited.

Perhaps it was his passionate conviction that persuaded Mrs. Wolff to proceed with the interview. My parents talked through Mrs. Wolff's experiences with her circle of liberal interracial couples. The transcript of their tape-recorded conversation doesn't distinguish whether my mother or father asked the next question, but I suspect it was my father.

Would you say therefore that the marriages that were made were sort of built upon sociopolitical orientations rather than just plain social connections?

"We were all intellectual or pseudo-intellectual," Mrs. Wolff replied. "We went camping and hiking; we discussed every issue. We did all these things, but they were all because we were interested in the, as you say, sociopolitical aspects of our lives. I don't think we would have done much of the dating that was done or much of the marrying that was done if we had just seen somebody on a bus and decided to say, 'Gee, I like the way you look. May I get your home number?'"

I am struck by the difference between the reasons for marrying that my father had heard in the 1930s and 1950s and Mrs. Wolff's account in the 1960s. In prior decades, most of the couples were quick to say that they married for love, that race played no part in their decision. Mrs. Wolff was describing a very different motivation—one that hinged precisely on racial politics. It raises again for me the question of my father's own reasons for wanting to marry a Black woman. Whether he married my mother because he fell in love with her, because of his attraction to Black women in general, or because of his beliefs about interracial marriage, it had to do with race.

I continue to ponder what it means to choose a partner of another race *because of their race*. Is it morally any different from choosing to marry someone of your own race—as most white and Black people do—because of their race? I think about why I married Black men and how much that choice had to do with their race. What moved me most about my first husband was his passionate devotion to Black liberation—something I can't separate from his being Black. Maybe that kind of attraction isn't so different from the interracial couples Mrs. Wolff described, who married with the explicit aim of advancing racial equality. It's hard to tell where love and politics blend into something more complicated. My father, I think, didn't experience the intertwining of love and race as complicated. For him, loving my mother and believing in interracial connection seemed perfectly aligned.

"I didn't like the reasons they were together at all," Mrs. Wolff went on. She said that Negro husbands would come and go as they pleased, while their white wives countenanced their inconsiderate behavior.

"Or it was the other way, where the white wife was the boss," Mrs. Wolff continued.

"She had a chauffeur," my mother interjected, I imagine with a twinkle in her eye.

Mrs. Wolff said that the problems in her marriage stemmed more from her husband being white than his being Jewish. My father pressed Mrs. Wolff to identify the difficulties caused by racial as opposed to cultural differences, as if daring an adversary to a duel, confident in winning the battle of wits.

"If you had married, say, a student from West Africa who was the same age as your husband, whose cultural background would have been different, too, except that he would have been a Negro, I'm sure that the cultural differences may have been even greater than you experienced," my father elaborated. "Would this have made a different marriage? In other words, would the problems have been as great or less, or different?"

Mrs. Wolff was insistent. She pointed out that casual comments made, or slang terms used, around family members or friends could feel like a slap in the face to a partner who was of a different race.

"Going to see a show at a nightclub was all right if we go downtown," Mrs. Wolff said, giving another example. "But just to go to some other place that I might like to go because of the life that's going on there, this became a very difficult chore for my husband."

I smile at my father's familiar reference to a West African student to illustrate his point. Many of my father's lessons while I was growing up would inevitably include one of his PhD students from Liberia, Ghana, or Nigeria. Surely, he implied, people raised in America—regardless of race—have more in common with each other than with someone raised in West Africa. Compared to traditional West African culture, the cultures of Black and white Americans appeared strikingly similar. Yet, my father conveniently overlooked the shared experience of Black Americans being treated as inferior by white Americans, regardless of their place of birth— and how that might impact their marriage to a white person. I think of the European immigrant wives in the 1930s who regretted marrying a Black man when they discovered the stark difference that race made in America.

One unforgettable image stands out from the photos from Liberia my father frequently showed us: a slide of two Liberian men standing side by side. One was a laborer at the Firestone rubber plantation, dressed in a soiled shirt and shorts, balancing a heavy bucket on his head with one hand. The other was one of my father's students at the University of Liberia, dressed sharply in a suit, tie, and glasses. Daddy told us that the student once worked as a rubber tapper when he was young. The contrast was jarring. For my sisters and me, the image was meant to deliver a message we heard over and over from Daddy: social barriers, not inherent ability, kept people from reaching their potential. The plantation laborer could become a university student like the man posing beside him. He wanted us to see that all human beings—regardless of race, birthplace, or humble origins—have the capacity to thrive when given the chance, and that our shared humanity can transcend the false ideas that divide us.

One day, when I was around eight years old, my father and one of the African graduate students who lived with us were painting the trim on the outside of our home in Kenwood. My father called me over from playing in the backyard. "Do you see Charles?" he asked me, pointing to the man on a ladder leaning against the house. I nodded. "He was born in a village in Nigeria where everyone lived in thatched-roof huts and spoke a tribal language," my father said. "Now he's working on his PhD in anthropology at Roosevelt." I nodded again, committing my father's lesson to memory.

As an adult, I now wince at the complexities I had failed to grasp as a child. Back then, I didn't know how Liberia's political and economic systems were shaped by the dominance of the Firestone Tire and Rubber Company and the Americo-Liberian elite, descendants of freed enslaved Americans. I didn't realize that a legacy of domination and exploitation had separated the plantation laborer from the university student and shaped Charles's journey from an African village to America. I was eager to understand my father's perspective. Now I see his oversight: his failure to reckon fully with how colonialism and white supremacy erased cultural bonds between Black and white people, obliterating even the kinship ties that might have connected them.

Yet, amid it all, there was a golden nugget my father planted deep in my heart: a belief in our shared humanity, in the human capacity for love, and in the hope for a transcendent unity that could overcome division. I don't think my father was oblivious to the barriers erected by white supremacy. After all, his academic work focused on the idea that prohibitions against interracial marriage were tools of social control, designed to uphold America's racial caste system. But, unlike me, he believed— fiercely—that those barriers could be dismantled through marriage.

When I return to the transcript, Mrs. Wolff had moved beyond cultural conflicts to the real nub of the problem. The difficulties in interracial marriages stemmed from the differences in political status between white people and Black people, when "you throw together one person who has been raised as a superior and one person who has been raised as an inferior." Besides, she added, these unions created pockets of integration amid a wider terrain of segregation and inequality.

"It's denying that ninety-five percent of the rest of the Chicago community is completely segregated. It leads to exceptionalism," she explained. "But it's much easier to fight for interracial living than it is to fight for strengthening Negro organizations and the Negro family as a whole.

"The problem doesn't lie in integration," she concluded emphatically. "The problem lies in opportunities and advancement and respect. Once these things are obtained, then it will be nothing in the world to live where you want to live. Then you will date who you want to date."

In response, my father asked Mrs. Wolff to explain why some mixed couples were able to stay together while, according to her, most failed. She observed that the 25 percent of couples who survived were composed of a Negro man and white wife. I am certain that her description of one of the resilient husbands did little to console my father's dashed expectations.

"He became less and less Negro as the years have gone by—to such an extent that most of us, even the Negro friends, just have very little to do with him," Mrs. Wolff recounted. "It's as though they completely went to another side. They developed and acquired all the habits and characteristics of the majority society."

My father's tug-of-war with Mrs. Wolff reminds me of his relentless efforts to persuade me of his beliefs about interracial marriage throughout my childhood. It wasn't enough that he and my mother were living proof of its success. Nor was it enough that they had surrounded my sisters and me with other mixed couples and their children, not so subtly reinforcing the idea. No—Daddy was determined to win me over. Ever the professor, he took every opportunity to lecture me about his research. He spoke as if unveiling a well-guarded secret, as if guiding me to a hidden treasure on a map, or hawking a gold watch pulled from the depths of his coat. When I think back on those lessons, I don't just hear his words—I see him at a whiteboard, pointer in hand, tapping at graphs and charts he'd drawn to bolster his claims. We were at home, not in a classroom, but the nature of his instruction blurred those lines in my memory.

My father would refer me to the latest studies on interracial marriage and recite various statistics he culled from them. I recall him saying that Vermont had the highest rate of Black-white marriages because there were so few Black people there. He stressed that when people of different races are forced to interact, as when there is little chance of finding a mate of one's own race, they would intermarry. My father was illustrating for me that the decision about whom to date and marry was influenced by social circumstances, and that we could adjust the social circumstances to encourage more interracial relationships. I was a diligent student in elementary school and at home. I listened carefully to my father's lessons, weighed the evidence he presented, and contemplated my own position.

Most of these conversations took place in my magical childhood home in Kenwood. My parents had bought an enormous fourteen-room house on Kenwood Avenue, a wide street lined with majestic maple, elm, and oak trees, surrounded by other Victorian homes owned by doctors, lawyers, entrepreneurs, artists, and professors. At the end of our block stood two houses that were built in 1892—around the same time as ours—and designed by Frank Lloyd Wright, the most celebrated architect of the era, at the start of his career. He became familiar with the neighborhood while courting his first wife, Catherine Tobin, who lived at Forty-Seventh and Kimbark, three blocks away. Wright recalled admiring the Kenwood houses as he strolled through the neighborhood, which he wrote was "in the process of becoming the most fashionable of Chicago's residence suburbs." Despite my father's modest salary as a junior professor, my parents were able to buy such a magnificent house thanks to the sale of their two-flat on Ellis Avenue.

The years we spent in the Kenwood house dominate my childhood memories. I recall it in slow motion, while everything that followed races by in a blur. It lasted only ten years, yet it feels like half my life. Throughout that time, my father worked on his project, and it touched every part of those years. My father's book—*the book*—had a palpable presence in my family's life. It centered in my father's study on the third floor, where he did all his writing, and spread throughout the Kenwood house, as if a specter with the otherworldly power to transport itself. The book made its way into our conversations around the dining room table, into the backyard parties my parents threw for my father's colleagues, into visits from people my parents befriended on their interviews.

Our house at 4830 South Kenwood was a grand three-story gray frame with a wraparound spindle porch, four stately columns, and elegant bay windows. With its whimsical Queen Anne style—an asymmetrical facade, front corner tower, conical roof, and turrets—it resembled a castle from a storybook. Inside, it was our enchanted playground. A winding staircase spiraled through all three floors, letting you peer from the top all the way down to the large first-floor foyer. We turned that space into our stage, using the coat closet as our theatrical backdrop. With a dramatic flourish, we would emerge from the curtain covering its entrance to perform for whomever was seated on the staircase landing.

A narrow back staircase snaked from the basement to the second floor, a perfect escape route in our frequent games of hide-and-seek. My parents' dressing room held a row of tall, mirrored closets that stretched to the ceiling. If you stood in front of a middle door and opened the ones on either side, your reflection echoed endlessly, like a carnival fun house. One of those closets even had a secret exit into the hallway, so you could disappear from one room and reappear in another hiding spot—vanishing into the third-floor playroom, stealing down the back stairs to the kitchen or basement, or slipping under a bed in any of the six bedrooms.

The living room and dining room, separated from the foyer by beautiful French doors made of leaded glass panes, had a stately ambience with high ceilings and ornate moldings. The living room was filled with artifacts my parents brought back from Liberia. On one of the bookcases stood a colossal mask carved from wood and festooned with a cascade of straw, a gift from a tribal chief. The mantel over the fireplace was decked on either side with tall lamps crafted from elephant tusks, each intricately engraved with images of beautiful Liberian women. A stand showcased the gigantic real horns of a water buffalo.

Above the piano, a reproduction of a painting by Paul Gauguin hung on the wall. The painting depicted two brown-skinned Tahitian women bathing in the teal ocean. Their backs were turned to the viewer, with one woman, naked, poised to dive into the water, while the other woman sat on the flower-laced shore, observing. Dressed in an indigo and gold wrap, her bare back and the tip of her breast were visible. At the time, I thought my parents chose the painting not only for its vibrant colors but also as a reflection of their curiosity about other cultures. To me, it echoed the values that were the backbone of our family—the belief that we were connected to people from around the world through our common humanity. What I didn't see then is the complexity behind that image: Gauguin's exploitation of the young women he portrayed, shaped by a colonial gaze that denied the very humanity my parents meant to honor. I still see the beauty my parents wanted to display in our living room, but I can't ignore the weight of history it, along with all the other intriguing objects, now carries.

The kitchen was appended by a spacious butler's pantry, lined with wooden counters and cabinets. The floor was covered in black and white linoleum squares arranged in a checkerboard pattern. The refrigerator was in the butler's pantry instead of in the kitchen. Whenever I reached for something from the refrigerator, I played a game where I had to skip across a certain number of squares before the door closed behind me. Above the cabinets was a set of bells that chimed from various rooms in the house, a remnant of an era when servants were summoned to attend promptly to family members' wishes.

Hand-painted jungle murals from the previous owners—African safari enthusiasts named the Sergels—still adorned some of the walls. In the TV room, monkeys swung from trees; elephants, antelopes, and giraffes strolled leisurely across one side of the bedroom that my sisters shared. As a child, I marveled that my parents preserved the unconventional decor. Back then, the scenes were reminders of our connection to Africa. Now, with my mind focused on their marriage and research, I see them as reflecting their unconventional lives. I had a bedroom all to myself on the second floor, next to my sisters' room. Located at the back of the house with a sunporch overlooking the yard, it felt like my private sanctuary. My mother hung green curtains across the porch, patterned with twisted branches, and I would lie in bed gazing at them, searching for—or fabricating—animal shapes hidden among the leaves.

On the third floor, my parents turned the ballroom into our playroom, with closets filled with games and books. We inherited the prior owners' eccentric library—James Thurber's fantasy novel *The 13 Clocks*, collections of ghost stories, and grisly Hans Christian Andersen fairy tales. They bequeathed us several original editions of L. Frank Baum's Oz books, each featuring stunning illustration plates in vibrant colors, glossy and smooth to the touch. Running your finger over them would mesmerize you with the enchanted images.

Across the hall from the playroom stood my father's study, closed to us by lock and key. This is where he worked on his book. His departure to teach at Roosevelt or conduct an interview was my chance to climb the stairs to the third floor and sneak into his private sanctum. He kept the door locked with a fancy old-fashioned key with a long ornate stem and circle at the end, from which it hung on a nail at the top of the door. When I was little, I would drag a chair from the playroom and push it against the door, climb up on the chair, and stretch on my tiptoes to grasp the key. Stepping down off the chair, I turned the key in the lock and creeped into the mysterious chamber. Inside was a long wall completely lined with books. The books were about the cultures of people all over the globe, arranged by continent. Books about Africa and India took up most of the shelves.

Among my earliest memories is sitting cross-legged on the floor in front of the bookshelves, captivated by anthropologists' accounts of life in far-flung corners of the world. It is my earliest recollection of reading books to myself. I remember two books vividly: Margaret Mead's 1928 classic, *Coming of Age in Samoa* (my first introduction to sex), and a book with a yellow cloth cover by an author from India (my first introduction to yoga). The yellow book had drawn figures of people in various yoga poses. The author wrote that he had traveled to the United States and observed sleeping children who were breathing the wrong way—their chests falling as they drew in air and rising when they exhaled. I remember pausing to test how I was breathing and taking pains to breathe the right way. What the author wrote made sense to me. Of course it's better to fill your lungs and belly with oxygen as you breathe in and to contract them as you breathe out.

From that day on, I breathed the right way and have turned to breathing deeply many times throughout my life. Before I give a major speech, when I get blood drawn, when worries keep me up at night. Breathing allowed me to birth three babies at home, enduring labor without the need for any pain relief. The yellow book was also pivotal to my views about the mainstream. I mark it as the first time I started to question dominant thinking, and Western thinking, in particular. I distinctly recall realizing at that early age that just because most people believe something doesn't make it true.

Outside, our backyard also had plenty of room for us to play. My parents installed a swing set and, in the summer, my father would put up a net for badminton and fill a small plastic pool from a garden hose. We also played croquet, using mallets to knock wooden balls through the metal wickets we had stuck into the grass. Sometimes, Daddy lined up my sisters and me in front of him, letting us hold the long metal handle of the manual grass cutter so we could pretend we were helping him mow the lawn.

Home movies captured these backyard scenes. Daddy's good friend Vernon, a travel agent and amateur filmmaker, often staged our family antics as if we were actors. In one scene, my parents ride the twins' tricycles, laughing as they struggle to push forward with their feet, the pedals spinning uselessly beneath them. In another, Evelyn dramatically falls off her trike, her little foot flexing for effect, only to be scooped up by Daddy and returned to her seat. According to family lore, Evelyn, born fifteen minutes after Helen, had been squished by her twin in the womb. I remember thinking that Mommy had to take special care of Evelyn because she was extra delicate. She remained the smallest sister when we were very young. By high school, however, she had grown to be the tallest and Helen the shortest, with me in between, no longer in need of rescue.

Chicago was no less segregated when I was growing up in the 1960s than when my father conducted his interviews in the decades before. But my Hyde Park–Kenwood neighborhood was an exception. It had become the haven that many interracial couples had told my father they longed for. I picture my childhood as taking place on an integrated street.

Most of our neighbors were white, but two Black couples lived on our block—our next-door neighbors, the Clayters, and an older couple across the street whose names I don't recall. Richard Clayter was a prominent trial attorney who represented the Charles S. Jackson Company, the first Negro funeral home business in the United States, originally established in Philadelphia, in a landmark case. In 1958, he brought a lawsuit against a funeral association that had refused to cremate several Black individuals whose bodies had been transported there by the Jackson Company. His victory integrated the association's crematorium.

Near the end of our years in Kenwood, another Black family, the Underwoods, moved in down the street. Most of the families we were close to, whose children I played with on our block—the Baums, the Engels, the Fertigs, the Rothblatts, the Wolfsons—were Jewish. Cathy Jones, whose mother was a busy lawyer and whose father may have been a surgeon, is the only playmate I can recall on Kenwood who wasn't Jewish. While we lived on Kenwood, the Nation of Islam began buying properties in the neighborhood. Elijah Muhammad built a brick mansion that stood out from the Victorian houses that characterized its surroundings. At one point, I'm told on good authority, three heavyweight boxers lived in the neighborhood—Joe Louis, Sonny Liston, and Muhammad Ali. Now Barack and Michelle Obama own a house in Kenwood, on Greenwood Avenue, five blocks from my childhood home.

Heading north from our block, you hit Forty-Seventh Street, a bustling commercial strip. In summer, horse-drawn carts clopped down the road, the vendors shouting, "Watermelons, watermelons!" Forty-Seventh Street was more than a thoroughfare. It marked an entirely separate region. In my father's files, I came across a glossy 1959 brochure calling Kenwood one of Chicago's most beautiful neighborhoods—then drawing a hard line: "a shambles of stores, taverns, rooming-houses along 47th Street form the northern boundary of this 'suburb in the city.'" My sisters and I roamed our neighborhood freely—on foot or by bike—to friends' houses, the YMCA, Girl Scout meetings, stores. Yet for all that freedom, the area beyond Forty-Seventh Street was forbidden to us.

But Forty-Seventh Street beckoned me. Its draw was Woolworth's, a direct shot down Kenwood Avenue. Inside, I made a beeline for the section that displayed porcelain animal figurines—horses, cows, birds, cats, and dogs. I'd sit cross-legged on the chilly floor, carefully selecting which one to buy with my coins. My favorite was a proud caramel-colored boxer with a broad chest and square-shaped muzzle. I vividly remember the satisfaction I felt admiring my growing collection, the pleasure of running my fingers over the cool, smooth surfaces of their tiny bodies.

Once, on my way home from Woolworth's, I decided to explore the world on the other side of Forty-Seventh Street and got hopelessly lost. Panicked, I stopped a teenage girl from the neighborhood and asked for help and she walked me home. My mother was so grateful she welcomed her into our lives. She bought her clothes and school supplies, and, I think, kept in touch with her through letters for years.

Walking south toward Forty-Ninth Street, past the Frank Lloyd Wright houses, led to Beulah Shoesmith Elementary School, which I attended from first through eighth grade. The school opened in 1961, when I was five, just a block from our house—close enough that my sisters and I could walk there on our own, crossing only one street. It felt perfectly safe. But in my first year making that walk alone, a car turning off Kenwood struck me in the crosswalk. I was knocked to the ground, briefly unconscious. I can still see my mother flying down the sidewalk after someone banged on our door to tell her. I wasn't hurt badly; the accident left just a faint scar on my left thigh—and a story we would tell for years. I kept walking to school after that.

Shoesmith stood out for its diversity in a city marked by segregation. Affluent Black families, low-income and working-class residents, and white professionals all sent their kids there. In those days, even wealthy white parents in Kenwood often chose it over private schools—except the Lab School, where University of Chicago faculty sent their children.

Though a public school, Shoesmith had more than its share of prominent families—and visits from celebrated Black figures associated with them. Civil rights activists, business leaders, celebrated artists, and prize-winning athletes spoke at school-wide assemblies. One day, the entire school buzzed with anticipation as Muhammad Ali—still Cassius Clay—arrived. The daughter of his business manager was in my sisters' class. I remember lining up outside with my classmates, clutching a piece of notebook paper for an autograph. He took my hand as he signed it. My sisters were even luckier: he visited their classroom.

Another unforgettable moment came when Jesse Owens, the Olympic hero, whose grandchildren attended Shoesmith, spoke to us. We watched a film of his four gold medal wins at the 1936 Berlin Olympics, where he defeated Hitler's claim of Aryan athletic superiority. Students erupted in cheers as he crossed the finish line. His visit underscored Shoesmith's message: Black children could accomplish anything.

Oscar Brown Jr., the legendary writer and performer, a regular at our assemblies, was known for permeating his songs, plays, and poetry with Black culture and civil rights activism. His performances deepened the meaning behind the freedom songs we sang at school—"We Shall Overcome," "If I Had a Hammer," "We Shall Not Be Moved," and the one I associate most with Shoesmith, "No Man Is an Island," with its message of sharing each human being's joy and grief as our own.

I admired how Brown reached out to local street gangs, including the Blackstone Rangers, from nearby Woodlawn. I remember attending meetings at a neighborhood church around that time, wanting to hear the gang members' side of the story. Soon after Martin Luther King's assassination, Shoesmith held a memorial assembly. Students were asked to write poems for Coretta Scott King. Mine and one by Brown's son, Oscar Brown III, who was a grade behind me, were selected to be read aloud. Standing beside Oscar on that stage in front of the entire school felt both solemn because of Dr. King's death and special because I was chosen to perform alongside a student as artistically talented as Oscar.

In eighth grade, I was appointed as coeditor of the school paper, the *Shoesmith Crusader*, with Janet deGrazia. With encouragement from our assistant principal, a Black woman with bluish-gray hair, we wrote to John Johnson, the renowned publisher of *Ebony* and *Jet*—whose niece was in our class—asking to meet with him. To our amazement, he invited us to his downtown office. He treated us like real journalists and gave us advice on running a paper. Our meeting left me feeling that the *Crusader* wasn't just a school paper; it was a noble calling.

There was a strange familiarity and division among students at Shoesmith. In our grade, we were all close classmates, some of us spending nearly a decade together in the same classroom with the same teachers every day. Yet the difference of one block created an unfathomable distance between us. When class ended each day, streams of children headed down Kenwood Avenue toward Forty-Seventh Street. I turned into my house in the middle of the block and the kids from Forty-Seventh Street kept running past. It was as if there were an iron gate that let the children out in the morning for school, then slammed shut behind them when they returned home. None of my close friends—the girls I invited to my house for birthday parties and sleepovers and whose homes I spent the night at—hailed from Forty-Seventh Street. I got along with the Forty-Seventh Street girls. But we moved in different circles after school with boundaries even Shoesmith's kumbaya ethos didn't transcend.

The boy who asked me to go with him in eighth grade was from Forty-Seventh Street. I thought he was attractive—taller, darker, and more mature than the other boys in our class. When he asked for my phone number, I gave it to him without hesitation. I don't remember what we talked about, but I still recall the thrill of hearing his voice on the line. My mother would never have approved our after-school connection—not just because he was from Forty-Seventh Street, but mainly because I wasn't supposed to be interested in any boy. So I told him not to call me again. Whatever spark there was between us went unignited, leaving me wondering what might have come of it.

The Forty-Seventh Street girls were whizzes at double Dutch, two girls swinging a rope in each hand in perfect rhythm as they chanted with the beat. The girls who jumped in added challenging moves to their skipping—jumping up and down on two feet, on one foot, spinning around and back again, springing out of the ropes as another girl jumped in or skipping two at a time. I watched them during recess, mesmerized, until one day I joined in—and they welcomed me. From then on, I took turns at swinging the ropes and trying my hand at their fancy footwork. While we jumped rope, the social lines that separated our neighborhoods seemed to vanish. We were a group of Black girls having fun together.

One year, I joined several of the Forty-Seventh Street girls in a talent competition. We choreographed a routine combining the latest dance moves and performed it to the music of James Brown on a stage at Ray School. I don't remember if we won, but we brought down the house. That feeling of ease and joy in a shared Black space is one I've returned to throughout my life. I sometimes wonder why I didn't grow closer to those girls while I was at Shoesmith. Perhaps the Forty-Seventh Street boundary ran so deep, crossing it fully felt forbidden. I raised my own children not to let borders like Forty-Seventh Street interfere with their friendships.

All the teachers I remember at Shoesmith were Black. My favorite teacher was Mrs. McCoo—thin and tan-skinned like me, cat-eye glasses matching mine. She kept us up-to-date on civil rights marches, the war in Vietnam, and elections. We called her Cool McCoo. When Dr. King was assassinated, she came to class in a black dress and made sure we all wrote poems to Mrs. King.

Mrs. McCoo nurtured my writing and entered me in citywide contests. One honored Jean Baptiste Point du Sable, the Black trader credited for founding Chicago in the 1780s. I made the finals and traveled downtown with her to read my essay onstage. Next came a small Black boy in a suit and tie, who stepped up and declared with theatrical flair, "I am Jean Baptiste Point du Sable." He recited his entire essay in character, as if he were du Sable himself, and I knew instantly that no one could top his performance. Afterward, Mrs. McCoo took me to lunch and reminded me I still had something to be proud of: "You had a chance to perform on the Chicago stage."

Eighth grade brought a different kind of teacher. Mrs. Browne wasn't hip like Cool McCoo. She was a disciplinarian who demanded order, which only tempted some students to test her patience. She revered Ralph Bunche, the esteemed political scientist and diplomat, and often praised his accomplishments in the global arena. Her high standards were frequently met with mockery. Whenever she extolled her idol, the class would chant, "Ralph Bunche is all bunched up! Ralph Bunche is all bunched up!"

One day, after scolding the back of the room for making too much noise, a bold girl named Angelique shot back, "I wasn't talking."

"I didn't say your name," Mrs. Browne snapped. "Does the shoe fit?"

"No, it's too small," Angelique quipped, not missing a beat.

The class roared. Mrs. Browne sent her to the principal's office, but we crowned her the victor.

I had my own test with Mrs. Browne. Early in the year, she wrongly accused me of talking. Not wanting to snitch on the true culprit, it was useless trying to defend myself. But I was determined to change her impression. Not long after, I was named coeditor of the *Shoesmith Crusader*, and by year's end, she announced I'd been chosen valedictorian of my graduating eighth-grade class. My mother bought me a beautiful white lace dress with bell sleeves for the ceremony. I started my speech declaring, "We are an enigma!"—though I've forgotten why. The whole class sang "No Man Is an Island," perhaps at my suggestion.

When Mrs. Browne passed away at 103, I read her obituary in the *Hyde Park Herald* with affection. Looking back, I see how deeply she cared for us, how hard she tried to instill her high standards despite our taunts. Though I once joined in the snickers, I now count myself among her grateful protégées.

On her naturalization petition filed in 1961, my mother lists her occupation as housewife. At some point after that, she was employed as a social worker for the Cook County Department of Public Welfare. Years later, she received her teacher's certificate and became a Chicago public school teacher. For some of those years, as I discovered, she was helping my father with his project. Growing up, I thought that her job involved helping less fortunate people.

Mommy sometimes brought home people who needed a place to stay for a few days or weeks. Looking back, I believe some were her clients and others interracial couples she interviewed. There was a young Black man named Anthony, who slept in a basement bedroom for a while. He once remarked that our living room was intelligent because it had a piano, a story my mother would repeat with a laugh in her voice for years afterward. For all her kindness, Mommy had a biting wit that she often deployed to make fun of others' social blunders.

My mother bought a stuffed toy dog for each of my sisters and me. We adored those toys almost as much as our cat, Diamond. I named mine, something like a miniature poodle, Coffee, after its brown, curly coat. Evelyn's was a bloodhound with long droopy ears and big sad eyes she called Troubles. Once, two little girls stayed with us and slept in the guest room on the second floor after their mother attempted suicide. They left with Troubles. My mother must have given them the toy without seeking Evelyn's permission. We woke up another morning to find that a couple Mommy had taken in, a Black man and a white woman, had flown the coop along with all of my mother's swanky coats that had been hanging in the front closet.

I can't remember any time at the Kenwood house when we didn't have guests or relatives living with us. My mother said she had been a foreign student needing a place to stay, so it was her duty to invite students arriving from overseas to stay with us. I have vivid memories of two Haitian students, Claude and Serge, and two students from the Middle East, Haroushi and Ahmed, living at our house. I can also picture a woman from India we called by her last name, Mrs. Singh, who wore saris and drew a red dot on her forehead. The foreign students regularly ate dinner with us in the evenings and went with us on outings, so my sisters and I were privy to their conversations with my parents and got to know them.

We also provided a home for two years for Grandma and Grandpa and Aunt Carmen and her son, my cousin Edwin. Grandma and Grandpa occupied the guest room on the second floor. Aunt Carmen and Edwin moved into the third floor, my aunt staying in the guest room and my cousin taking over the playroom. Edwin was my age, so he, my sisters, and I all played together, except that Aunt Carmen was even stricter than Mommy and kept a tighter rein on him. One summer day, when I was eleven, Edwin was hit by a car while riding his bike near our house. Thrown hard to the ground, he broke his femur. He returned from the hospital in a cast that enclosed half of his body. He was bedridden on the third floor for weeks. I spent many hours at his bedside during his convalescence, and our long conversations and card games drew us closer to each other. "Today I taught him how to make a Jacob's ladder with string," I wrote in my diary that August. "He is like a brother to me now." Years later, when Edwin left his mother without warning as soon as he graduated from high school, he showed up one day at my college dorm to let me know he was safe.

Then there was the day I opened a closet in the butler's pantry to find it filled from top to bottom with white jars labeled as a hairdressing I did not recognize. Mommy said she was helping a woman named Mrs. Shinn, who was trying to start a business selling her special hair pomade for Black women. I recall Mrs. Shinn coming to the house and having the impression that she was a mixture of Black and Chinese. I suspected that she had developed a secret formula that combined African and Chinese folk wisdom about taming hair. Mrs. Shinn couldn't afford to rent enough space for her merchandise, my mother explained, so we were making our butler's pantry available to her. For many months thereafter, Mommy grabbed a jar from our unlimited supply of Mrs. Shinn's pomade to use on our hair instead of our regular VO5 in the black and gold tube. That must have been the deal she negotiated with Mrs. Shinn in exchange for the storage space in our house.

While I remember my father's lessons about interracial connection and human equality as lectures, my mother's came through acts of generosity— a shared bedroom, a gifted toy, a closet full of someone else's jars. Both kinds of lessons left their mark on me during my years in Kenwood. Looking back, as I immerse myself in their research project, I realize how deeply they shaped the way I conduct my own work for racial justice. From the beginning of my career, I've felt it essential to pair rigorous empirical and theoretical inquiry with genuine human engagement. I didn't learn that in college or law school. I learned it from my parents, growing up in our magical Kenwood home.

CHAPTER 15

Raising Children

Iris (pregnant with Evelyn and Helen) and Dorothy, Monrovia, Liberia, 1957

Mr. and Mrs. Marcel
March 24, 1966

Evening is approaching as I pick up the next transcript from the pile I've transported from the dining room table to the desk in my study. Fatigue is setting in as I sink into the comfort of the leather chair, determined to soldier on. But as I begin reading, a surge of energy overtakes me—I am overjoyed to find pages and pages filled with my mother's voice.

In the first week of March 1966, an acquaintance of my father told him about Roger and Ella Marcel, a Black Haitian man and white American woman, who had married in 1957 after they met as students at Moody Bible Institute, an evangelical Christian college in Chicago. My father arranged for him and my mother to interview the couple at their home a few weeks later. The Marcels lived on the first floor of a well-kept brick six-flat in the northeast South Shore area. The once mostly white neighborhood had recently transitioned to being mostly Black. They had four young children, two girls and two boys. My mother interviewed Mrs. Marcel in the living room, while my father spoke with Mr. Marcel in the sun parlor, which doubled as a study. What stands out to me is the attention my mother paid to the children in her notes.

The boys were at it again. Henri and Jacques were still fussing about a toy. Mrs. M. got Jacques to give in and he went to the kitchen only to return with a slice of bread and a slice of salami. He was whining and Mrs. M. thought he wanted her to make a sandwich for him.

Mrs. M.: "Yvonne, will you fix a sandwich for Jacques please?"

Jacques: "Ah-h-h-h- (whining) I don't want it that way."

Mrs. M.: "Now, what does he want with it?" (Quite disgustedly, and looking at me.) "What do you want if you don't want this?" (Almost ready to give Jacques a good bang.)

Q.: "Maybe I could stop for a little while and let you take care of him."

Mrs. M.: "Just let me put some mayonnaise and maybe he'll take it." (She left for the kitchen with Jacques in tow whining.)

Q. (Mrs. M. returned looking rather annoyed): "Now, let's see, where were we?"

I talked with Mrs. M. for a few minutes about the setup of Moody, and wound up mentioning my children. When I mentioned the birthdate of my twins, Yvonne who was sitting on her mother's knee said, "My birthday is in June, and I'll be five."

I wonder if my father brought Mommy with him to interview the Marcels because Mr. Marcel was Haitian and he thought that Mommy's Jamaican background would make him more comfortable. Or perhaps it was simply to divide the work between them. But it may have been because Daddy anticipated the presence of four little kids who threatened to interrupt any engagement with Mrs. Marcel.

Mrs. Marcel told my mother that after her husband received a certificate from Moody for his three years of study there, he attended Wheaton College, another evangelical Christian institution twenty-five miles from Chicago with more of a liberal arts focus. Ella and Roger had kept their relationship secret while at Moody, but word got out at Wheaton. A Wheaton dean wrote a letter to the dean of education at Moody, where Ella was still a music student, informing him that Roger had been seen in the company of a white woman, requesting that Moody please check into it.

"I was wondering how long it would take them to find out," Mrs. Marcel remarked. "Here it was going on for three years, and actually we had more or less taken this as a token of the Lord's guiding."

The dean of women at Moody had called Ella into her office and told her not to meet with Roger in public if she wanted to tour England with the choral group. It was against Moody rules for a person of one race to do more than greet a person of the opposite sex of another race. "You could be roommates with a Negro girl, but you didn't dare speak to a Negro boy other than just to say 'Hello' and go on," Mrs. Marcel clarified.

"I told the dean of women if it came to a choice between the school and Roger, I would take Roger because I felt that this was the Lord's leading and there was no talking me out of it," Mrs. Marcel continued. "And she just sat there with her mouth hanging open. It was so much fun to get her on the carpet for a change instead of the other way around." She laughed as she remembered the scene. Mrs. Marcel's defense of her serious relationship with a Negro man impresses me. How could the administration of the most evangelical school in Chicago quarrel with the Lord's will?

Mrs. Marcel told my mother that the Wheaton administration refused to give Roger permission to marry her, despite his being a senior honors student and president of the foreign students' club.

"We figured since they refused us permission anyway, what difference does it make, so we got married anyway," Mrs. Marcel said, noting that she hadn't sought her parents' approval, either.

In response, Wheaton refused to let Mr. Marcel continue to attend classes, just five weeks short of graduation, denying him the opportunity to earn his college degree. The couple moved to Haiti, where Mr. Marcel worked as a translator for the American Bible Society. "All the foreign students were up in arms about it," Mrs. Marcel recalled. Wheaton eventually relented and the administration allowed Mr. Marcel to take his final exams and mailed him his diploma.

Here we were interrupted by Yvonne who wanted to know if we would make the recorder "talk again." Mrs. M. told her to take her crayons and doll and slate and get to playing with them.

Yvonne: "Where's my sponge and my chalk?" (Dashing back into the living room.)

Mrs. M.: "I don't know where your sponge is but go into the bedroom, your chalk is on the dresser. You can use any little cloth or toilet paper, or something to wipe it."

Yvonne: "Where's my chalk again?"

Mrs. M.: "Chalk is on your dresser" (Back to me.) "So" (Heavy sigh).

Yvonne, the four-and-a-half-year-old, is following the conversation very thoughtfully. She breaks in with: "What color am I, Mommy?"

Mrs. M.: "What color are you? You're kind of a light tan. Taffy color, I suppose."

Yvonne was not satisfied with this reply. She stood with her head leaned to one side and her brows furrowed.

Yvonne: "I'm not Negro. I'm peach."

It was obvious that Mrs. M. was becoming tired of the children's interruptions and, I am sure, of the interview session. About ten minutes before we got to this point, Yvonne was so overbearing that her mother called out to Roger to come and get Yvonne. Mr. M. spent a few minutes trying to determine what the child really wanted but was unsuccessful. The impression I gained from the incident was that Mrs. M. felt it was high time that her husband had his share of interruptions. Her "Roger, will you come and get this child and find out what she wants" was rife with the thought—you are not around here enough to help with the children. Here's your big chance to face the battle.

I wonder whether Mommy had been projecting her own feelings about Daddy's relinquishment of most of the childcare to her. Here she was, helping him once again with his research, while he participated little in the day-to-day work of raising my sisters and me. Daddy was very involved in our lives, but he never did any cooking or housework, combed our hair, helped us get dressed, or disciplined us. Apart from on the weekends or summer vacations, my father was at Roosevelt or up in his third-floor study until Mommy rang the little bell signaling it was time to enjoy the dinner she had prepared.

Mommy was the consummate homemaker, keeping our Kenwood house in impeccable order—at the expense of her own academic ambitions. Yet, despite the exasperation she expressed on Mrs. Marcel's behalf, I never heard her voice such feelings to Daddy. She orchestrated the caregiving and household tasks with such skill, grace, and apparent joy that, as a child, it never occurred to me she might have resented any of it. Now, as I search my memory for any sign of frustration, a faint recollection emerges: sitting beside her on the edge of her bed, trying to comfort her as she murmured something about exhaustion.

Still, when I was growing up, I had the impression that I had a closer relationship with my father than my friends had with theirs. In a letter Daddy wrote to Drake dated June 20, 1956, when I was three months old, he complained of having difficulty concentrating on revisions of his dissertation. "Whenever Iris goes out for lunch or shopping, I'm kept busy by the baby, who doesn't want to be left alone. She insists that Daddy hold her." I was glad to see that Mommy occasionally handed me over to him, though I wondered if her shopping was for herself or for groceries.

I do think that Yvonne's tantrum had thrown the interview session off its track. My sixth sense told me that Mrs. M. was becoming very tense and I decided to terminate the interview. Mr. Roberts then took the tape recorder to complete his session with Mr. M. Mrs. M. and I continued talking for about fifteen minutes about the future of race relations in the United States.

Mrs. Marcel seemed to be a believer, like my parents, in the power of interracial marriage to heal America's racial wounds. "If relationships continue to move in the direction they are going today, I believe in the next twenty years or so the problem won't be half as great as it is now," she told my mother. "Really, I'm not worried about our children, and I don't know of any other interracial couple who is. There are quite a few at our church and I am sure they live normal lives."

My mother, as always, ended the interview by asking Mrs. Marcel for the names of the interracial couples at her church. The Marcels attended the First Baptist Church in Hyde Park, on Fiftieth Street, between Ellis and Drexel. Mrs. Marcel retrieved the church directory and thumbed through it slowly, coming up with six more couples to add to what I now see was still my parents' joint mixed marriage project.

Mommy didn't manage the Kenwood house on her own. I vaguely remember that for some time during my childhood she employed housekeepers, though I don't recall them being very involved with my sisters and me. More vivid is how she enlisted us in her elaborate housekeeping, cooking, and entertaining rituals. We were a dutiful staff of three who were always at the ready to assist her. She had a strict regimen of household procedures that we obediently followed. When she arrived home from work, she took her place in a chair in the living room. One of us immediately fetched her slippers so she could get out of her high-heeled shoes. On occasion, she would drink a small glass of sherry before heading to the kitchen to cook dinner. We were at her side in the kitchen and had assigned tasks for getting dinner on the table and for cleaning up afterward.

On weekends, we had even more regular chores. All the rooms in the house had to be tidied, all the furniture dusted and rubbed with Pledge, any soiled tablecloths or lace doilies replaced. We stripped our beds and put on clean sheets every Saturday morning. My mother had a complete set of cutlery made of silver. In preparation for dinner parties, she would take out the wooden box that held them and place it on the kitchen table before the three of us. We would remove the knives, forks, and spoons from their velvet pouches and polish each one with a special cream, all three daughters laboring like workers on an assembly line.

When I was around ten years old, a classmate named Amy invited me to her house for dinner. Amy was a white girl with slight stature and long brown hair. She was very artistic, and her creative projects surpassed those of all the other students in our class. Her family lived in one of the single-story tan brick homes that sat in a long row on Dorchester Avenue next to Madison Park. Doors marked the distinction between each separate home, but there were no dividing lines or windows facing the street. You couldn't tell from the outside, but each home faced an interior atrium that let in the sunlight. In any other context, such a windowless edifice would seem more like a prison, but Amy's house looked ultra avant-garde.

During dinner, without warning, Amy reached for the butter sitting at the middle of the table, pulling the entire stick out of its dish. To my utter astonishment, she began molding the butter into a horse with her bare hands as if it were a block of clay. Her parents were delighted. I couldn't believe my eyes. There was no way on earth my mother would let me reach for the butter without asking politely for someone to please pass it, let alone treat it as a plaything. I remember thinking how starkly different my mother was and wishing she wasn't so strict.

Some of my mother's rules seemed nonsensical to me, and I chafed against her sense of decorum. Once, when we were walking home from running an errand, I sprung onto a stone border that ran along a building, arms spread out for balance. "Get down from there," my mother hissed sternly. "Why? It's fun." I didn't see how I was bothering anyone but her. "It doesn't look right," she shot back. "Now get down from there right this instant." My mother's British Jamaican accent lent her commands an air of extra gravity. I hopped down, begrudgingly, inevitably complying with my mother's edicts. Inside, at least for that moment, I yearned for the day I could break free of my mother's unreasonable restraints. Such an innocuous incident among millions like it, but it left a lasting impression on me.

My mother never resorted to cruelty to commandeer our obedience. She miraculously instilled in me a desire to please her, never to disappoint her. She was strict, but never abusive.

I don't recall her ever using physical force to make me comply. Once, when I was in elementary school, a classmate reported that her mother had chased her around the apartment with a hairbrush the night before. I distinctly remember thinking that Mommy would never do something like that. I couldn't imagine her acting in such an undignified way. Nor could I imagine me being so disobedient as to incite such a reaction.

The concept of spanking loomed as a potential punishment in our house. I remember my mother using the term "a pants down," which meant getting spanked on your naked behind. But I have no memory of ever receiving one. Helen remembers Mommy lining up all three of us on the second-floor landing and spanking us for some misdeed we conspired to do collectively. Maybe it was the time we hawked her dinnerware set when she was away on a trip to Jamaica with Aunt Violet. We took down the plates, cups, and saucers from the butler's pantry cabinets, loaded them onto our red wagon, and pulled the contraband down the block, offering it to our neighbors for sale. We didn't make a single sale, and one of the parents ratted us out. Helen says that while she and her twin bawled, I laughed in defiance. "You just stood there laughing, Dorothy," Helen recalls. "As if to say it didn't hurt you, you didn't care." Although I was typically as respectful as my sisters, it seems spanking me crossed a line. It must have been a mild punishment intended to express disappointment more than anger.

The prohibition my mother enforced most vehemently was getting involved with boys. Dating was simply out of the question. Interest in boys would interfere with our schoolwork, which had to be the number one priority. Mommy admonished us repeatedly, "Don't get married until you get your PhD!" I'm not sure which came first: avoiding men to get an education or getting an education to never be dependent on men. My mother seemed to be encouraging us both to be independent of men altogether and to be married before we got pregnant, another example of her rebellious and conservative nature. Whatever her chief motivation, the message was clear: stay away from boys and men until you have your graduate degree. Her mandate worked for as long as I lived in my mother's house. I had close male friends in high school, but I didn't have a boyfriend.

Growing up, I considered myself lucky to have a father who was so easygoing. He would let me do whatever I wanted. While my mother was stricter than my friends' mothers, my father was far more permissive than their fathers. I thought I had the coolest father because he talked to me as if I were an adult. Once, when a group of friends were at my house, I deliberately acted up in front of my father, talking to him as if we were on the same level, to show them how laid-back he was.

I can recall only three times over the course of my entire childhood that my father showed anger toward me. When I was very little, I would cuddle up to my father's side while he was reading and engage in a particularly comforting routine. I would suck the thumb on my left hand while simultaneously rubbing Daddy's elbow with the other hand. I suppose after months of this self-soothing, my father was fed up, for I recollect clearly the moment he put a stop to it. "Look at my elbow," he snapped at me as he broke away and pointed his sore elbow in my face. "It's turning red!" I remember feeling bad that I'd caused the injury to my father, but much more miffed that I'd have to abandon my beloved ritual. I can't say how long I kept up the habit of sucking my thumb and rubbing Daddy's elbow, but I remember how safe it made me feel. I can still see his elbow held in front of my face, all blotchy and beet red. Given how young I must have been, it stands as one of my earliest memories—not just of childhood, but of closeness to my father, of being known by him.

Another outburst occurred on a rare occasion when my father was responsible for feeding me dinner. He had cooked hot dogs—a culinary travesty far beneath the caliber of my mother's gourmet meals—and I refused to eat them. After pleading with me to consume one frank, Daddy's frustration flared. "You are going to eat this hot dog," he barked. He tried to drive the hot dog into my mouth, but I clamped my lips shut. The standoff lasted only about a minute before my father gave up. I did not eat the hot dog. The battle was a later rendition of his "Dorothy, stop being so recalcitrant," followed by my "Daddy, stop aggravating me" that Aunt Violet recalled from our time in Liberia.

The third instance had to do with my grades. Both my parents expected their daughters to excel in school. Our report cards consisted of sheets of blue paper with grades for each subject—English, math, social studies, PE—marked by hand. E for excellent, G for good. I don't remember what fell below those. At my house, nothing less than straight Es was acceptable. So, when I brought home an aberrational E– in English on my report card, my father was vexed. "I have a graduate student from West Africa who grew up speaking a tribal language and he now writes beautifully in English," Daddy scolded me. "You have no excuse."

In February of 1964, a month before I turned ten, the Beatles were scheduled to appear on *The Ed Sullivan Show*. I was excited to view the once-in-a-lifetime event. Despite his usual easygoingness, my father said I wasn't allowed to watch the show. "Why not?" I demanded to know. "That music isn't good for your mind," Daddy tried to persuade me. I suspected Mommy put him up to it. My mother disapproved of rock and roll. She disparagingly called it "bowsey rouse music." I argued back, "All my friends are going to be watching. *Everyone* is going to watch it." As was our pattern, I resisted, and Daddy relented. I saw the Beatles on Ed Sullivan that night.

Later, I had a mad crush on the soul singer Al Green and had bought one of his albums, which I played in my bedroom incessantly. When I learned that Al Green was scheduled to perform in Chicago, I begged my parents to let me go. He was going to appear at the Auditorium Theater, in the same building as Roosevelt. It hosted all the most popular musicians at the time. The university also held its annual commencement ceremony there. My parents agreed on the condition that Daddy chaperone me.

I recalled the concert taking place when we were still at the Kenwood house, but I could find no record of Al Green performing in Chicago in the late 1960s. In those years, the Auditorium Theater hosted such musical luminaries as Jimi Hendrix, Aretha Franklin, Diana Ross and the Supremes, James Brown, the Doors, Ravi Shankar, Joan Baez, and my mother's heart throb Harry Belafonte, but Al Green was not on the roster. The concert we attended must have been the one that took place on April 29, 1972. I had turned sixteen the month before and was completing my junior year in high school. The album I bought was *Let's Stay Together*, released in January of that year.

Daddy and I went to the concert together—just the two of us. Sometimes, when I think back on moments alone with one of my parents, I later realize my sisters must have been there, too, even if I don't remember it that way. But the Al Green concert was different; I know it was just the two of us.

We stood out among the throngs of hysterical Black teenage girls in the audience. My father was out of place, a middle-aged white man wearing a suit and horn-rimmed glasses. Dozens of the girls rushed up to the stage screaming as the silky-smooth star crooned his greatest hits. Some of them threw their panties at him. Daddy restrained me from leaping from my seat and racing to join them. On that occasion, I wasn't embarrassed to be seen with my father. Or at least it was worth the embarrassment to be in the presence of Al Green. I felt like the luckiest girl in the world. I used to wonder if my father had felt terribly uncomfortable surrounded by hundreds of frenetic Black girls, soul music blaring, Al Green gyrating onstage. But now, knowing more about my father's life as a bachelor, I wonder if the concert might have been fun for him, too.

My father's bookshelves symbolized his inexhaustible knowledge about world cultures. Daddy seemed to know everything about the diverse and fascinating human beings who inhabited the earth. You could spin a globe, plunk your finger down anywhere, and Daddy would hold forth on a tribal or ethnic group who lived there—their language, their customs, their colonial history, their current political situation. When my sisters and I were little, we would test his anthropological proficiency as if it were a circus act. I was awestruck by his erudition.

Sometimes listening to my father was like being a student at a college lecture. Hardly a day would go by that Daddy did not explain some anthropological insight about a ritual in one of the movies from Liberia or a local or foreign crisis Walter Cronkite reported on the evening news or an interesting narrative one of his research participants told him during an interview.

But my mother was the one who helped me with my homework and writing projects at the Kenwood house. I sat beside her in her bed on many evenings after dinner, notebook and pen in hand, as we talked through my ideas for a book report or essay. Mommy never told me what to write; she helped me think through what I wanted to say. We toiled sentence by sentence until every word was just right. Her vocabulary seemed endless, as if she were a living thesaurus, revealing words that made writing feel like stepping through a secret door into a world with no limits.

Yet it was only when I read her interview notes buried in my father's papers, her witty interjections and vivid descriptions of the participants' homes, appearance, and mannerisms, that I thought of Mommy as a writer in her own right. While Daddy described couples in anthropological detail, Mommy added a literary flair.

One night, when I was around ten years old, Mommy said, "That's the last essay I'll help you with. You have to figure it out by yourself from now on." She must have known she'd already given me the tools I needed to write well for the rest of my life. Others would later nurture my love and skill for writing—Mrs. McCoo, my seventh-grade teacher who enrolled me in competitions; Mr. Crotty, my AP English teacher, who knelt by my desk in class to help perfect every line of an essay or poem; and the demanding litigation partners I worked for as an associate in Manhattan, one of whom insisted that even a complaint "should sing." But Mommy was my first and most important writing coach.

My mother called me "gift of God" because that's what Dorothy means, "Firstie" because I was her firstborn child, and "my PhD" because she abandoned her graduate studies when I was born. She made me feel beautiful and capable. Mommy told me stories that emphasized my kindness and my loyalty to her. When she was pregnant with my sisters, she felt faint and fell to the floor. Little more than a year old, I toddled to her side. Realizing that she couldn't get up, I found a pillow, dragged it across the floor, and placed it by her so she could rest her head on it. Mommy repeated this story to me many times, meant as a testament to the loving bond we shared from the very beginning. Another oft-repeated account: "When you were in third grade, your teacher, Mrs. Hunter, told me that every morning when you arrived at school, you were like a ray of sunshine entering the classroom." When Mommy reminded me of my teacher's words, she would add tenderly, "You are my ray of sunshine."

Mommy had three beloved sayings, which she learned as a child in Jamaica, and she recited over and over to me as a child. One was "Power corrupts, and absolute power corrupts absolutely." She would repeat it whenever there were news reports of a foreign dictator's imprisonment of political rivals, the arrest of a politician for bribery or fraud, or government abuse of U.S. citizens. I'm not sure of its origin, but my mother didn't trust the government. When I was in high school, I subscribed to the Black Panther newspaper, and had it delivered to our house. One day, my mother intercepted it before I had a chance to retrieve it from the mailbox. "Don't you know the FBI is following the Black Panthers and tracks everyone who supports them?" she asked me, that ominous tone in her voice. She made me cancel my subscription, for I was putting our family in jeopardy. It wasn't because she thought the Black Panthers were dangerous; it was because she thought they—and their supporters— were in danger from the government.

The second was "Oh what a tangled web we weave when first we practice to deceive." My uncle Bertie recalled my grandmother saying it to Mommy when she tried to evade a chore in the garden at their childhood home. Mommy passed down her mother's admonition of obedient honesty to me.

My mother's favorite saying, or at least the one I remember her rehearsing most, carried multiple lessons: "There are three things in life you can never get back: the spoken word, the spent arrow, and the lost opportunity." Pay attention, she was saying, to the consequences of your actions and inactions. The phrase is seared into me because it so perfectly reflects the fusion of principles Mommy instilled. On the one hand, she taught me to be exceedingly conscientious—to speak and act with care, to never do anything reckless that might put me to shame or hurt another's feelings. On the other, she urged me to seize every opportunity to achieve my goals, even when it required risk, sacrifice, or taking the harder path.

Mommy was discreet and cared about how she was perceived, but she never compromised her principles to win approval.

She passed those values on to me, and they continue to shape the way I move through the world, for better, and at times, with regret. Once, in a Bible study class, we completed a questionnaire designed to help us discern what spiritual gift God had given each of us. Mine was mercy. That felt right. I do tend to forgive easily, and empathize even with those who have caused harm, and seek healing. But mercy also compels me to speak out against cruelty when I see it. Mommy laid the groundwork for the rebellious scholarship and activism I would eventually pursue—work that pushed far beyond the political boundaries she had drawn for herself and for me.

But her lessons also mean that I sometimes worry too much about disappointing others or hurting someone's feelings. And when it comes to opportunities, I rarely let one pass. No matter how many scholarly or activist projects I have already taken on, I tend to say yes to the next urgent one that lands at my feet. That mix of conviction and compulsion drives me forward—at a pace even my mother might have found exhausting. Evelyn recalls Mommy once boasting that in college I stayed up all night writing a paper in the library, eating nothing but an apple I'd slipped inside.

I have heard it said that in interracial couples, the white spouse is always more radical than their non-white partner. The white wife or husband is the one who shows greater willingness to lower their status for the sake of the marriage, who goes to greater lengths to break with the dominant societal norms. I'm not sure if that is empirically true, but in some ways that describes my parents' relationship. My mother restrained my father's free spirit just as she restrained her daughters. I imagine that Daddy would have led a more bohemian life if he weren't married to my mother. I wonder if he would have continued to explore nudism or adopted more radical politics, perhaps joining the Communist Party members he fraternized with in the 1930s when he returned from the army. But then I remember that my father seemed perfectly content with our family life. With my mother, he became a devoted father. She ensured he came home every night to a carefully prepared dinner, an orderly house, and three well-behaved daughters.

For as far back as I can remember, my father was writing his book. I couldn't possibly count how many times Daddy excused himself from the dining table to return to his study to work on the book. Or I overheard my mother tell someone on the phone that Bob was away conducting more interviews for the book. Or my father was leaving for an anthropology conference or lecture to present some aspect of his research for the book. Or he built up anticipation over an editor who expressed interest in publishing the book.

Daddy began his book project soon after our family moved into the Kenwood house. In 1959, he applied to Roosevelt's Committee on Faculty Research for a grant to be relieved from teaching duties, allowing him to focus entirely on writing his manuscript. His proposed project was based on interviews with two hundred Negro-white couples whose marriages spanned nearly seventy-five years, from 1882 to 1954. Unlike existing studies of interracial marriage, which relied on data from marriage license bureaus or far fewer face-to-face interviews, his project aimed to provide the first comprehensive sociological analysis of Negro-white intermarriage. University of Chicago professor Sol Tax, who had advised my father on his dissertation research, wrote a letter of support, describing the data as "important and probably unique" and emphasizing that it had "already gone too long unpublished." My father's book on interracial marriage promised to be pathbreaking.

As the years on Kenwood Avenue stretched on, my mother relentlessly pressured my father to finish his book. She saw its publication as his ticket to a faculty appointment at a more prestigious university. Her haranguing intensified dramatically when my father's colleague Drake was recruited by Stanford University and left Roosevelt to establish its African studies program. As early as 1951, my father had collaborated with Drake, linguist Lorenzo Dow Turner, and political scientist Frank Untermyer—all household names during my childhood—to launch an African studies program at Roosevelt. Drake's departure was a major event in our Kenwood house, as if an earthquake had shaken its foundations. I can hear Mommy's shrill scolding, made more stinging by her British intonation. "Bob, Drake has gone to Stanford," she would remind my father repeatedly. "Finish the book so you can follow suit and leave Roosevelt as well!"

My sisters and I thought that my mother was mean to Daddy. Her recurrent reprimand of "Finish the book!" seemed a merciless assault on our mild-mannered father, who never uttered a harsh word to her. Why wouldn't she leave him alone? What was wrong with his being satisfied with teaching at Roosevelt, content with our happy family life?

It is only now that I grasp the reason for my mother's frustration. The blood, sweat, and tears that had gone into my father's book were mingled with her blood, sweat, and tears. The interviews that were the meat and bones of the interracial marriage study were also her interviews. She had helped to recruit the mixed couples and interviewed a large share of them. She had given up her PhD to raise his three children. She had kept an immaculate house, served him dinner every night, and entertained his academic colleagues. She had put her hopes, her ambitions in my father's ascension in academia. No wonder she pressured him to attain the professional status she would have achieved had she not sacrificed so many opportunities to support him. As a child, I never understood what was behind my mother's aggravation. Now I see it clearly.

I also understand better how my mother's unfulfilled ambitions were redirected toward me. You can never get back a lost opportunity, but you can drill into your daughter—whom you call "my PhD"—that she must never let one escape her grasp. My mother wanted to make sure that I never suffered the frustration that she experienced with my father. Hence, her repeated admonitions to finish my education before I got married, to have my own goals in life, and never to rely on a husband to achieve them. That lesson well-learned has its innate challenges. It's meant finding a partner who is not threatened by my ambition. Not an easy task in a world still permeated with sexist assumptions about male and female achievement. But it has also meant that I can appreciate my partner for his own virtues, not for what virtue I expect him to possess on my behalf.

Mr. and Mrs. Sussex
March 30, 1966

It's time for bed when I put back the interview with the Marcels. But I decide to read one more transcript, hoping to see more of my mother. The week after meeting with the Marcels, my parents ventured to a block in Hyde Park where my father had heard there were several Black-white couples living in two six-flat buildings recently purchased by a cooperative housing project. Before my parents' visit, my father had gone to the location and tracked down one of the husbands, Clifford Sussex, a Black man who lived with his wife, Jean.

My father described Mr. Sussex as a "medium to dark-skinned" man with "long semi-Negroid hair" dressed in a long-sleeved sport shirt and slacks. He worked as a caseworker with the Department of Public Aid while taking courses toward a master's degree in musicology at Roosevelt. He listened briefly to my father's description of the interracial marriage study, then summoned his wife from the kitchen to hear the full spiel. Impressed, both agreed to welcome my father back in a week's time to be interviewed.

My father noted that, despite their courtesy, the couple had been inconvenienced by his visit. His unannounced arrival interrupted the piano lesson that Mr. Sussex was giving an eight-year-old white child in the living room. I ponder this aside for a while. Could Mr. Sussex be my piano teacher? I wonder. I would have been about ten years old when I started taking piano lessons from one of the Black husbands my father recruited to his study—corresponding to the year my father met Mr. Sussex. My father dropped me off on Saturday mornings at the man's apartment, where my teacher valiantly nurtured my mediocre talents at the piano. I got as far as playing Beethoven's "Für Elise" perfectly, but never beyond that rudimentary level. I can imagine my parents getting to know the Sussexes and suggesting that Mr. Sussex start giving me piano lessons, likely at my mother's urging.

My father's never-ending study of Black-white couples shaped every experience I had growing up in our Kenwood house. Not only were my parents a mixed pair, but so were most of their friends. They forged close ties with many of the couples they interviewed, creating a network of interracial relationships across the city. Our house was a way station for the couples most everyone else viewed as weird, but whose unions seemed completely normal to me. My piano teacher, our babysitters, my father's best friends Drake, Vernon, and the man he called Bill Alberti, the plumber, the desperate young couple my mother invited to stay at our house, the German wife and her daughters, the white priest with a Black female companion—all were in mixed-race relationships.

As promised, my father returned to the Sussex home, this time with my mother, so the two of them could properly interview the couple. As was their familiar pattern, my mother and Mrs. Sussex stayed in the living room, where my father set up a tape recorder. Mr. Sussex led my father to the dining room and sat down in a large wooden rocking chair, while my father stationed himself at the table to facilitate taking notes.

Mr. Sussex told my father that his mother was very light, and he remembered telling her, "When I grow up, I want to marry someone like you." All his secret infatuations when he was a little boy were of white girls or Negro girls who had skin closest to white. He escaped the slum conditions of the West Side when he went to college, finishing at a junior college followed by attending the Illinois Institute of Technology for two years, and entering the Chicago Conservatory College when his brother's purchase of a piano unfurled his musical talents.

It was then, at twenty-two or twenty-three, that Mr. Sussex realized he could date white women. I wonder if my father noticed the coincidence—he was about the same age when he, too, discovered he could date women of another race.

Mr. Sussex had moved to Hyde Park, in a building at Fifty-Third and Drexel, to room with another Black man, whose very reason for selecting that neighborhood was the potential for interracial dating. "There were white girls to go around with," was how Mr. Sussex put it.

Did his [the roommate's] going with white girls make an impression on you?

"Yes," Mr. Sussex readily responded. "Because I never had any idea of sexual relationships or friendship with white girls. I guess I knew my place. Then I began to realize 'what an ideal situation this was!' Those were his words."

Before that point, Mr. Sussex had gone out only with Black girls, even contemplating marrying one of them, an attractive, slightly lighter woman who was three years his senior. That relationship ended because, as Mr. Sussex told it, she was too pushy, pressuring him to get a job and make money. When he stalled at a proposal, she married someone else. Mr. Sussex recounted how, once he realized this newfound permission to date white girls, he began to develop an appetite for them. Those were his words.

"There was a sexual appetite," he went on. "I see it as happening that the floodgates were opening. I would no longer look at advertisements and say, 'That isn't mine.' I began to see I was attractive and was attractive to them. At the moment I began realistically to have an idea of having relationships with white girls, I cut off having relationships with Negro girls."

My delight at possibly finding my childhood piano teacher evaporates instantly, like a drop of water hitting a red-hot skillet. Mr. Sussex spoke about dating white girls as if he had achieved a priceless trophy he always thought was beyond his reach, all the more precious for its unattainability. That meant that Black girls turned unappealing by comparison, too ordinary to find attractive. The memory of the Black high school boys leaning over the white eighth-grade girls rushes into my head, extinguishing the sentimental feelings I had for the man who gave me piano lessons as a child. I try not to feel this way, but I can't help but take it as a personal insult, a slight against me and all Black girls, whom Black men like him categorically deem unworthy of desire.

It's not that we are entitled to be appealing to all Black men. It's that we shouldn't be considered subpar because we are Black. Mr. Sussex didn't see the floodgates opening more options to date freely; he saw them as closing the option of dating Black women, drowning out the desire for a relationship with any Black girl. He viewed his relationships with white women as rebellion against the white supremacist prohibition of interracial intimacy, breaking the shackles of "that isn't mine" that constrained him before. I see the opposite: in his rejection of Black girls, he is upholding the white supremacist stereotype that white girls are inherently more desirable.

His words suggested that realizing that white girls found him attractive boosted his ego. As a result, being attractive to white girls made them more attractive than Black girls. To him, dating white girls was better than dating Black girls because it defied two taboos—the taboo against Black men desiring white women and against white women desiring Black men. Black women lost out on both counts. I hate every aspect of his logic.

Can you recall your first date with a white girl?

"I was on cloud nine—exhilarated," Mr. Sussex replied. "This was the sort of thing where you wake up and think about it, go to work and think about it, want to talk about it, and can't because people wouldn't understand."

When my father asked Mr. Sussex to compare his feelings toward the white girls he dated to those with Negro girls, Mr. Sussex conceded that his exhilaration stemmed from his "lust for forbidden fruit," though he was too shy to always act on his internal longings. He admitted that latent biases against Blackness and preferences for whiteness he had since a child were coming to the fore.

"I became prejudiced toward Negroes. My standards of beauty came out in the open. Light skin was more beautiful and white skin best. Straight hair was better than Negro hair," he confessed.

When my father asked him for his current attitude about race, Mr. Sussex expressed a modified stance.

"I did reject Negro women," he replied, then seemingly reflected on the implications of his statement. "My attitude has changed. I am a Negro. I can't reject myself, and this is what I'm doing when I reject Negroes." It is hard to tell whether Mr. Sussex had genuinely changed his views about

Black women or if my father's questions merely prompted a temporary shift in perspective.

Meanwhile, in the living room, my mother had been interviewing Mrs. Sussex, visibly pregnant, dressed in a maternity smock and skirt. I recall that my piano teacher had had a new baby, adding evidence to my suspicion that he was Mr. Sussex. When Mrs. Sussex mentioned that she had been seeing Dr. Bild, my heart warms because Dr. Bild was my friend Diane's father. Diane, who we called Didi, was in my class and lived around the corner from me in a big redbrick house on Kimbark Avenue. "I think he's interested in his patients at heart, especially the ones that don't have very much money," she said, mirroring my impression of him as a kind man, the kind of doctor I had come to expect in Kenwood.

My mother's doctor was also well-known as a champion for social justice in health care. Quentin Young, whose son Michael was also my classmate and friend, was national chairman of the Medical Committee for Human Rights, which was formed in the 1960s to provide medical care to civil rights activists. It later gave volunteer assistance to the Black Panthers when they established free medical clinics. I crossed paths with Dr. Young as an adult when I spoke at medical conferences in support of single-payer health care, for which he was one of the nation's leading advocates.

Mrs. Sussex recalled how she had met her husband at a weekly folk-dancing program sponsored by a club at the University of Chicago. They were both there seeking a romantic partner, she confided, and both were good dancers. The participants were mostly white, she said. I suspect that this racial composition was a key draw for Mr. Sussex. My mother wanted to know if her husband was dating other women when he encountered her on the dance floor. He was dating two or three girls, Mrs. Sussex replied.

Were these Negro or white girls?

"White, I think," Mrs. Sussex recalled. "I'm not so sure he was dating any Negro girls. I think he was living in Hyde Park about four years. So this was new and exciting, and try everything; and try something different!" (Laughter.)

It seems that Mrs. Sussex was aware of her husband's exhilaration over his newfound access to "forbidden fruit." Did it bother her that his attraction to her was tied to her race? Her laughter suggested it didn't—

or perhaps she was simply reminiscing about a youthful infatuation that had long faded. She mentioned that Mr. Sussex was the only Black man she ever dated. Their marriage led to her brother and sister cutting off communication with her.

Mrs. Sussex spoke fondly about their neighborhood—my neighborhood—echoing what others said about the haven it had created for mixed couples. "We have our own group here at the co-op, which is integrated," she said. "We have our own little world in Hyde Park."

From left: Evelyn, Helen, and Dorothy in our Kenwood backyard, July 29, 1961

CHAPTER 16

Symbol of Racial Harmony

From right, Iris, Bob, Janheinz Jahn, Dorothy, and St. Clair Drake in our
Kenwood backyard, Chicago, c. 1964

Mrs. Wexler
February 3, 1969

It's well into August and I've made steady progress reading through the
1960s transcripts—despite pausing often to reminisce about my childhood
in Kenwood. On another steamy morning, I'm reading an interview with
Mrs. Charlotte Wexler, a white woman married to Bill, the son of an interracial couple Daddy had previously interviewed—a Black woman and
white man who had met as volunteers in leftist organizations in New York

City and later moved to Hyde Park when he was hired as a professor at
the University of Chicago. My father interviewed Charlotte at her home
in February 1969, while Bill was stationed at an army base.

In reviewing the full set of 1960s interviews, I noticed that Mommy
only accompanied Daddy on interviews in 1966 and 1967. Perhaps those
were years when she had more free time, after she trusted my sisters and
me to manage after school without her, and before she became a Chicago
public school teacher, when evenings filled with lesson plans and stacks
of homework to grade left little time for fieldwork.

Mrs. Wexler grew up in a small farming town near Omaha, Nebraska,
with parents of German and Swedish descent. The entire population was
white, Protestant, and "hickish." "Everybody was either Methodist or
Lutheran, and that's as far as you divided it up," is how she described the
town's scant diversity.

"You mean they didn't even have any Czechs or Poles or Italians or
anything like that?" my father asked.

"No."

Like most of the people in the town, her father, a computer program-
mer who worked for the telephone company in Omaha, was a staunch
conservative with backward ideas about society, including the inferiority
of Black people. Her mother, whose father had been a dentist, was the
opposite. She cared about social equality, even becoming a dues-paying
member of the NAACP and working as an editor of a Nebraska civil
liberties newspaper. Unsurprisingly, Mrs. Wexler reported that her father
had disowned her over her marriage to a Black man and refused to attend
the wedding, while her mother and sisters were fond of her husband and
celebrated their nuptials.

Growing up, the only Black person Mrs. Wexler had contact with
was the lady who occasionally cleaned her family's house. Her first real
engagement with Black people took place during the summer of 1966,
after her freshman year at a small Nebraska college. She had volunteered
with the Unitarian Universalist Service Committee (UUSC) to work as a
day camp counselor for "welfare kids" who lived in a housing project on
the Southwest Side of Chicago. My father seemed amazed when she told
him that she resided in the housing project along with the Black children.

"Right in the middle of the poor neighborhood?" he asked.

"Uh-huh. It's on Forty-Fourth and Cicero, right south of where the
Cicero city ends, where they had that march," she replied, referring to the
protest by hundreds of Black Chicagoans and their allies in September

of 1966 as part of the Chicago Freedom Movement, led by Dr. Martin Luther King Jr.

"4400 South? That area is mainly white except for the project then, isn't it?"

"Yeah, there's a project like a black spot in the middle of a . . ."

"You lived in the little dot, then?"

"Yeah."

"How did you feel, after coming from Nebraska?"

"Well, I felt conspicuous."

Mrs. Wexler described the reaction of the Black children as she and the other volunteers explored the vicinity on the day they arrived. "We slowly got like pied pipers—more and more Black children following us," she recalled. "And they were feeling my hair. I had never had anybody so fascinated with straight hair before."

Mrs. Wexler said she had felt uncomfortable about the way her new neighbors interacted with her. Most of the adult residents had migrated from the South and treated her with special deference because she was white, what she labeled "an inverse type of prejudice."

"I felt like there was a kind of phoniness to the relationships this way, because I didn't really feel like I was being liked because of myself but because of my color."

The summer had turned tragic when a little Black girl drowned in Lake Michigan, and the residents blamed the volunteers for her death. Some engaged in a mini protest, throwing rocks and shouting, "VISTA, VISTA, VISTA," referring to the white staff from Volunteers in Service to America, a federal anti-poverty organization created in 1964, who trained at the housing project during the prior winter. Mrs. Wexler saw their anger as another frustrating example of being unfairly singled out because of her race.

Later, back at college, Mrs. Wexler made friends with a young Black man. It's not clear from the interview whether he was a college student or, more likely, a local resident. They sometimes went out together in town, strictly on a platonic basis. Another student told her that she was very brave to be seen in public with a Black man. Mrs. Wexler was horrified to learn secondhand that a group of boys had brought up her interracial friendship when exchanging gossip about the girls on campus.

"They said that they would never go out with me because they didn't want to have anything to do with a girl . . ." Mrs. Wexler paused. "And here I'm going to have to use their language—who's had a 'Negro cock in her.'"

Mrs. Wexler returned to Chicago the following summer. She had visited the racially mixed Hyde Park neighborhood while working at the housing project and wanted to spend more time there. A friend referred her to a family who offered her room and board in their house at Fifty-Second and Kimbark in exchange for babysitting. She found a job as a day camp counselor at the Hyde Park YMCA. Another counselor at the camp was William Wexler, who would become her husband. Charlotte oversaw the six-year-old boys, and he supervised the ten-year-olds. The two met when her little boys came running to her in tears after being bullied by the older ones. The story brings back memories of my childhood summers. I attended summer programs at the Hyde Park YMCA and my sister Helen met her first boyfriend when they were counselors at Camp Martin Johnson, the Y's sleepaway camp.

Charlotte and Bill parted at the close of summer. She went back to college in Nebraska, and he returned to college in New York. After two trips to Nebraska to see Charlotte, Bill proposed in March 1968, and they married in September that year.

Mrs. Wexler gave an "it was like any romance" response to my father's inquiry into how she and Bill fell in love.

"By this time, I had had enough contact with Negroes, there was no mental barrier at all," she elaborated. "And to me he never seemed like a Negro, he seemed just like Bill, that's all."

My father seized on her answer as a chance to probe what he had raised with Mrs. Wolff: Which is more of a barrier to romantic relationships—cultural or racial differences? He asked her the very question that troubles me: whether she meant that Bill didn't seem like other Negroes to her.

"I thought of him as being a person, not of being a race," she replied, evading the question.

"I see. But I mean in his speech, in his mannerisms, in his tastes—you know, his general demeanor—did he appear an Anglo-Saxon?"

"Well, he definitely doesn't have the sociocultural attributes of the majority of Negroes," Mrs. Wexler replied.

This response bothers me. It seems that Mrs. Wexler fell in love with Bill because he acted more like a white person than like most Negroes. My father tackled the issue from another angle. He asked Mrs. Wexler to compare her feelings for Bill to her feelings toward the Negro man she met in the college town. She responded that she never became serious about the man in Nebraska because he, unlike Bill, was the "sociocultural-majority type," which made him incompatible with her.

"It wasn't a color difference at all," she emphasized. "I don't think I ever reacted to color. I just react to culture."

I put down the transcript, unsettled by the exchange. Offended, even. I begin to worry about my father's *culture versus race* argument—his interview with Mrs. Wexler had taken it in a troubling direction. Before, he had emphasized the cultural similarities between Black and white people as the foundation for harmonious interracial marriages. He never suggested that Black people should become more like white people to make those unions possible. But now the conversation had veered into something more insidious—evaluating which Black people were culturally close enough to white people to be deemed suitable spouses. Mrs. Wexler's comments implied that Bill, whose father was white, was sufficiently Anglo-Saxon to be acceptable, while "the sociocultural-majority type" of Black people were not.

Then I wonder if I'm judging Mrs. Wexler too harshly. Maybe she was simply saying that she and her husband got along, regardless of race, because they shared similar cultural backgrounds. After all, don't most people marry someone socially and culturally compatible with them? Still, her comments make me question something deeper: Did Daddy choose Mommy, at least in part, because she could move so seamlessly in white, academic circles—despite her dark skin? I don't know whether to see that as elitism or as the foundation of their lasting marriage.

When I was very little, I subscribed to my father's hope in interracial marriage—the motivation behind his years of research. I can recall how my five-year-old chest would swell with pride when I skipped down the street in Kenwood between my pale father and dark-skinned mother. I wanted people to see us, to notice our three-toned family. To me, we were evidence that people could love each other across racial boundaries. My family represented in its very physicality the solution to the racial battles that were raging around me in the early 1960s. We were a living symbol of racial harmony.

But it wasn't just outward symbolism. My parents had created a harmonious home for me and my sisters. Both my parents were kind people. The sort of people who didn't want to hurt anyone's feelings or see anyone suffer. There was never any violence or yelling in our house. I never heard either of my parents utter a curse word. Ever.

We did everything apart from school and work as a family of five.

Mommy and Daddy rarely went out together without us. I now know that for two years while I was growing up they conducted interviews together. But I don't recall them ever going to a movie or a restaurant or a party and leaving us behind. All our activities revolved around the family theme: the equality and unity of all human beings, which was closely tied to Daddy's mixed marriage project. They also revolved around my parents' shared love for travel, a passion they instilled in me and my sisters. Travel was part of our family roots—Daddy's trip to India and around the world as a teenager; Mommy's move from Jamaica to Liberia and the United States in her twenties; our stay in Liberia as babies. Later, during my first two years of high school, we would live in Egypt.

One of my family's favorite pastimes at our house in Kenwood was watching movies my father had filmed of scenes of our family and tribal life in Liberia. The five of us, sometimes accompanied by visiting relatives or friends, would often gather on couches and chairs in the living room. My father would set up a portable screen on a tripod stand, unrolling it by pulling it upward and securing it at the top with a clip. He would remove a large projector from its case and mount a 16-millimeter cylinder of film. The projector whirred and emitted a beam of light across the room onto the screen, sometimes catching someone's face in its glow as the film began to roll. The central footage of my childhood was shot in the Liberian interior among the Indigenous people. Although my sisters and I viewed the images more times than we could possibly count, we never tired of them. My father dressed in a Liberian robe commiserating with tribal chiefs. Bare-breasted women in grass skirts dancing so furiously they kick up dust as the bells on their bronze anklets shake to the beat. Women pounding rice outside thatched huts, carrying babies bound to their backs with colorful cloths.

In an especially memorable scene, three girls around our ages, dressed in matching beaded attire, approach the camera. My father places a coin between each girl's lips, like a priest administering a Communion wafer, a payment for their dance performance. I always flinched when the movie reached a traditional trial by ordeal in the center of a village. The chief has accused one of his wives of infidelity. The inquisitor brings a long knife to a blazing bonfire. He holds the dagger in the flames until it is red-hot, then carries it toward the accused, and presses it against her leg. The woman hops in pain as two men restrain her. "If her leg blisters," my father told us, "it means she is guilty." If she is found guilty, her lover must pay the chief a hefty fine. Daddy would explain every custom to us so many times and so matter-of-factly that we didn't perceive them as peculiar. While we might have thought it was unjust to treat the woman so cruelly, we were taught not to judge Liberian forms of justice and culture as inherently more bizarre than American ways of life.

Some of the scenes from Liberia are the stuff of typical home movies, only with a West African backdrop. My pregnant mother, dressed in a baby-blue smock and matching skirt, is sunning with me, around nine months old, on a blanket at the beach on the Monrovian shore. I am wearing a coordinated blue outfit and bonnet. It looks like a Kodak moment. My aunt Violet approaches, spirited and shapely in a one-piece swimsuit. She takes my little hand and waves it vigorously at the camera. At my first birthday party, I am dressed in a frilly tutu surrounded by the dark-skinned children of my parents' Liberian friends and the blond-haired children of our Dutch neighbors. The movie cuts to me peering curiously into a crib placed in the yard under swaying palm trees to examine my two squirming baby sisters.

My sisters and I were too young when we left Liberia to have real memories of living there. But watching the movies over and over made it seem that we could recall what it was like. My parents spoke of Liberia not as a distant foreign nation, but as an essential part of our family narrative. We grew up in Chicago and the city shaped us, but the tales of our early years in Liberia imbued us with an indelible sense of connection to West Africa.

The Liberian films were often preceded by slides from our trip to Jamaica—the visit intended to introduce me to my grandparents before we moved to Liberia. In hindsight, I realize it must also have been the first time they met my father. They didn't attend my parents' wedding and, as far as I know, there was no Jamaican honeymoon. My mother never spoke about her parents' reaction to her marriage to a white American, but I suspect that, while they may have been surprised, they didn't object. I never sensed any disapproval from her side of the family; her Jamaican relatives always received Daddy with open arms.

As my father narrated the Jamaica segment, we arrived at Accompong, a secluded Maroon village nestled in the island's interior hills. At the village's entrance, there was a crudely handwritten sign, but I can't recall its message. My father explained that it was a place where enslaved people had escaped from plantations and built an independent community of free Black people. The Jamaican men we saw on the screen were descendants of rebels who resisted enslavement and colonial domination for centuries. Given that watching my family's home movies is among my earliest memories, the scene from Accompong must have been my first awareness of slavery. Even before I began elementary school, my parents had instilled in me a profound sense of my heritage through the story of the Maroons. They taught me that I had roots in the enslavement and resistance of Jamaican people. The moment that I comprehended that white people enslaved Black people, my mother's people, my ancestors, I was aware that Black people rebelled and established their own sovereign territories.

All five of us would pile in our sky-blue Rambler to head to the Field Museum of Natural History to watch the latest feature-length documentary during its annual educational series. Each film transported us to a different part of the world—an Arctic expedition one week, a voyage down the Amazon the next—typically narrated live by the filmmaker. My parents also took us to lectures and films at the University of Chicago's International House. I was never reluctant to go. I imagined traveling to all those places when I grew up, and I looked forward to each new journey as eagerly as a rare trip to the movies. Looking back, I see how aligned my parents were in their belief that the world was something to be explored, valued, and embraced—an outlook that must have helped them navigate their own marriage across cultural lines.

Every summer we took road trips. A common destination was Montreal to visit Mommy's brother, Uncle Carlton, a tall distinguished man with a melodious Jamaican accent. My sisters and I played with our cousins Pam and Claudette, called Sissy, who were around our ages. They had two younger brothers, Bobby and baby Donald, a peculiar family dynamic for the three of us girls. We stayed twice with my father's cousin Bill Reinert and his family in Newport, Rhode Island—enjoyable visits, though far less frequent than those with Mommy's relatives.

On the way to Montreal, we might stop at Chief Poking Fire's Indian Village on the Mohawk reserve. There, we watched powwows, peeked into tepees, and browsed the clothing, trinkets, and pottery for purchase from residents. My parents bought my sisters and me moccasins made of soft tan leather, beautifully decorated with colorful beads, which became our favorite slippers. I can picture Chief Poking Fire, fabulously adorned in a traditional tribal costume and giant headdress made of red, blue, yellow, and white feathers that rose above his crown and flowed to the ground. My father added lessons of his own, turning the visit into a mini anthropology course. In hindsight, I recognize how limited that portrayal of Indigenous culture was, but it reflected my parents' efforts to counter the mainstream stereotypes and offer us a fuller picture than the cowboy and Indian movies that Hollywood was showing at the time.

Back from Montreal, we frequently went camping in Michigan, Wisconsin, and rural parts of Illinois. Sometimes the camping trip was on our own; sometimes it was with an organization called Funference, a multiracial social organization founded in 1945 that combined civil rights discussions with family-oriented outdoor activities. In the summer, Funference organized outings to camps or cabins near Chicago. A favorite spot was Herrick House in Bartlett, Illinois, where my parents had stayed while courting and we spent our days swimming and canoeing in a nearby lake. In the winter, we would slide down snow-covered hills in large toboggans. I wonder if Daddy discovered Funference while conducting research before he met my mother. It may have been where my parents became friends with the folk singer Ella Jenkins, who was also a member.

In a way, camping was an accommodation my mother made to my father's American lifestyle. I doubt she would have seen pitching a tent and sleeping outdoors in sleeping bags as a fun family activity. But each summer, she helped Daddy unfold the heavy canvas tent and secure it to the ground, while my sisters and I pounded the silver stakes through the loops. She cooked over a portable Coleman stove, bringing her creative touch even to chili made with canned kidney beans. She told my sisters and me that she had been a Girl Guide when she was growing up in Jamaica and didn't have an indoor toilet. So maybe our family camping trips weren't so much of a stretch.

Our road trips were also lessons in global citizenship. When we visited the 1964 World's Fair in New York, Daddy introduced us to our first Indian restaurant. He ordered lamb vindaloo for the table. I'll never forget watching him devour it without flinching, while I, overwhelmed by the heat, felt like my mouth was on fire. In Montreal at Expo 67, the message was the same: we are citizens of a shared world.

Every time Daddy pulled into a gas station, he took a tiny slip of paper from the glove compartment and meticulously recorded the odometer reading, the amount of gas pumped, and the total cost. I never found those slips among his archives, but I remember them, each one filled with rows and rows of numbers in his distinctive script.

Summers also meant trips to Riverview Park, where Daddy took us on the Bobs, a towering wooden roller coaster that terrified us over three thousand feet of track. I can still see his arms raised high, squealing with delight, while I screamed beside him, clutching the bar for dear life. He must have ridden it three times in a row to give my sisters each a turn. I thought it was fitting that the wildest ride in the park shared his name.

Dinners in our Kenwood house were elegant affairs. Mommy rang a little brass bell to summon us, and we ate at a lace-covered table in the dining room under a chandelier. We used cloth napkins, kept in ivory rings from Liberia that Mommy marked with Roman numerals, identifying each family member. My sisters and I rotated dinner duties—setting the table, clearing plates, washing dishes.

Mommy was a fabulous cook. Meals blended her Jamaican roots and British upbringing with touches of my father's German palate. She served saltfish and ackee, poached eggs on toast, and oxtail stew. She stocked the fridge with jars of sauerkraut and rolls of liverwurst for Daddy. My most memorable birthday party was when she made spaghetti and meatballs for the first time so I could offer something "American" to my friends.

Fish was her specialty. We shopped together at Jesselson's, a Jewish seafood market, where she insisted on wild ocean fish—never from lakes or rivers. She served the whole fish on a large green oval platter with a fish painted along the center. When everyone else was done eating and excused from the table, she stayed behind to savor the fish head. She taught me to eat whole fish, bones and all, to draw out the spine and navigate each bite. Still, I never mastered her skill with a fish head. On special occasions, Mommy roasted leg of lamb. She couldn't understand why anyone would serve turkey, which she considered bland and unattractive. She studded the meat with garlic cloves and herbs, wrapped it tightly with string, and roasted it until the savory aroma filled the house. I always made sure to stand beside her when she took the sizzling roast from the oven. As soon as she unwound the string, she would hand it to me so I could suck on the garlicky bits that clung to it.

Unlike our friends, my sisters and I weren't allowed to eat candy bars or drink Coca-Cola. But Mommy indulged Daddy's sweet tooth. He loved vanilla ice cream drenched in Hershey's chocolate syrup. We had it for dessert so often that he called it "the same ole thing." After dinner, he'd ask, "Who wants the same ole thing?" and our hands would shoot up. With Mommy's permission, he sometimes served black cows—root beer poured over vanilla ice cream in tall glasses. The symbolism of those desserts strikes me now. Could Daddy's fixation on mixing black and white have extended to his favorite desserts? For anyone else this would seem absurd. But knowing what I've discovered about my father, it's entirely plausible.

Once, when I got hold of a nickel, I secretly bought a 3 Musketeers bar and snuck it into my bedroom. I took one glorious bite, then hid the rest in my dresser. The next morning, I woke up with a terrible stomach-ache. I threw the bar away and reaffirmed my loyalty to Mommy's rules. Even now, the bright orange Halloween pails filled with miniature candy bars hold no appeal.

Mommy hosted dazzling dinner and garden parties for my father's academic colleagues. Her appetizers and entrées rivaled the refined fare I would later find at Ivy League receptions—lamb roast, curried shrimp, large slabs of salmon, and fruit salad served in a hollowed-out watermelon, its rind scalloped in decorative edges. My sisters and I helped pass around hors d'oeuvres and, once in pajamas, listened from the stairs to the spirited conversations below. My mother performed the role of professor's wife with remarkable grace and ease. Daddy relied on her not only to present a delectable meal with impeccable artistry but also to add delightful charm to the conversations that went on for hours afterward. I always knew she was essential to the world they built together—now I know that included his research, too.

A photo I cherish evokes memories of those parties at the Kenwood house. It shows me as a little girl, about eight years old, in a pretty sleeveless dress with two tiers flowing from the waist. I am standing behind four adults, who are relaxing together in our backyard. My father's colleague St. Clair Drake is leaning forward in his chair as if engaged in conversation. Next to him is Janheinz Jahn, the influential German scholar of African culture. He is stretched out on a plastic outdoor lounge chair, legs crossed, hold-ing a cigarette to his mouth. Daddy, seated in an outdoor chair, is talking to the men, his face directed toward them. Mommy is sitting on his lap, leaning back against him. She is wearing a checkered dress and a string of pearls that form a collar around her neck. Daddy's left arm is wrapped around her, his hand grasping her arm.

The two men in the photo stand out the most among my father's colleagues. Whereas we always called St. Clair Drake solely by his last name, Drake, we called Janheinz Jahn by both his first and last names, correctly pronouncing the *J*'s as *Y*'s. Never Professor Jahn, or Jahn, or

Janheinz. Always Janheinz Jahn. Drake was a frequent guest at my parents' parties, and my father often spoke about their academic collaborations at Roosevelt. He was a striking character, with his authoritative voice, natural hair standing tall above his head, square mustache, and beard that grew longer every year.

I found extensive correspondence between my father and Drake in my father's papers and in Drake's archives at the Schomburg Center for Research in Black Culture. One letter my father wrote to Drake, dated December 30, 1953, suggests an affectionate but at times trying relationship. The letter began with my father reporting receipt of Drake's special-delivery letter that morning and hoping it contained Drake's completed #296—likely, Drake's questionnaire for my father's interracial marriage study. Drake was not only Daddy's colleague and friend but also his research subject. Instead, Drake was requesting that my father retrieve his passport from his office at Roosevelt College and mail it to him. Thirty minutes later, my father received a telegram that explained Drake's need for a passport. Drake reported good news about an overseas project, likely the Ford Foundation grant he won to support his research in Liberia and Ghana in the 1950s. My father expressed his mixed emotions in terms I find both overly dramatic and humorous.

> *At first, upon reading the telegram and after rejoicing that you finally are about to find one of your dreams come true, I debated as to whether to go to R.C. before Monday, for I have been so far behind in my work that I can ill afford dropping everything for a half day and I had made a firm resolution not to set foot in the college during the vacation period. I also wondered why in the world you didn't have the passport when you knew a month ago that you might need it and I saw you have it in your hands at that time. I thought to myself that if the situation were reversed and I asked you to find something for me I could consider myself more than lucky if the mission were accomplished by 1955.*

A true friend, my father ultimately relented. He continued, "After I had mentally punished you for half an hour by pretending (yet knowing that it was only pretense) to ignore your request, I decided to dash off to the school."

At Roosevelt, he shared Drake's good news with colleagues and the dean. His letter went on.

*By now I was getting excited. I was celebrating with you and even
wishing that you had room in your suitcase for me. I almost felt
guilty for having had the thoughts expressed in the first paragraph.
(I should really have thrown this sheet in the basket and started
over after the first paragraph, but I have done this too often and
want you to realize that you often try my patience and that I almost
found myself heading for the Rialto theatre to cool off—this would be
rationalized as a last-hour field study before the Rialto closed its doors
New Year's Eve to be torn down and replaced by a store.)*

I am struck by how Daddy could frame a trip to the movies as
fieldwork—just as he had woven his mixed marriage research into the
fabric of his personal life, including his friendship with Drake. He located
Drake's passport in a desk drawer and mailed it by special delivery before
noon. Although not requested, he included Drake's wife's passport in
the package. What stands out to me most is my father's loyalty to his
friend, a loyalty that ran even deeper when it came to my mother, my
sisters, and me.

Janheinz Jahn also had a memorable appearance and personality. His
wild shock of blond hair, pronounced eyebrows, and something about
his eyes gave him a feral look. Once, when he stayed at our home on a
visit from Germany, my sisters and I excused ourselves after dinner to go
upstairs to our rooms. When my mother reminded us to brush our teeth,
our guest interjected that he didn't believe in that form of hygiene. "My
children never brush their teeth, and they have never had a cavity," he
retorted. I thought that out of all the various and sundry people who came
to our house from all corners of the earth, he was the strangest.

When I was fifteen, my family visited Germany on a summer trip
across Europe when we returned from our stint in Egypt in 1971. There,
my father reconnected with Janheiz Jahn, who took him, my sisters, and
me on a high-speed drive on the Autobahn in his cool French Citroën.
I don't picture Mommy being with us. When we were saying farewell at
the Volkswagen my father bought in Germany, Janheinz Jahn told him
that he had beautiful daughters. I can't recall why, but I thought he was
referring to our racial mixture.

Just before getting into the car, I turned to say goodbye to him, and
he reached out his hand and wrapped his fingers around my neck. He
squeezed my neck lightly only for a second, no more than the time it would
take to give me a kiss on the cheek. It was as if he were examining the

beautiful object he had praised to my father. I felt a sensation I had never felt before. The titillation of being admired by a man for my looks was foreign to me. The queasiness of being grasped that way without permission was also unfamiliar. My mother had guarded me from any experience like that. I wondered if my father had seen his colleague's hand around my neck. It was a fleeting moment, nothing worth bringing attention to. But the impression of his hand grasping my neck stays with me.

My mother loved to shop in Chicago's fanciest department stores. With me in tow, she would often take the elevated train, known as "the L," from Hyde Park to the Loop, the bustling business district in downtown Chicago, where enormous department stores stood among tall office buildings, hotels, restaurants, and theaters. The L tracks that gave the Loop its moniker circled above, and the roar of the trains intensified the thrill of walking beneath the towering skyscrapers. When a train rumbled by on the tracks overhead, the vibration shook the city below like the tremors of an earthquake. Mommy and I would walk swiftly with the wave of pedestrians, weaving underneath the tracks and through the streets, to the revolving doors of Marshall Field's, Carson's, or Stevens. In my memory, I am always alone with Mommy, but my sisters must have tagged along sometimes and had their own special days with her.

On those shopping trips, barely able to see above the counters, I clung to Mommy's black patent leather pocketbook, gripping the thin gold bar that hung from the top. We entered an elevator with a uniformed attendant, and Mommy asked for the designer floor. A white saleswoman greeted her eagerly, sometimes having called ahead to alert her that something special had arrived. Mommy stepped out of the dressing room to model each chic outfit for me, and we always left with a new addition to her wardrobe.

A famous photograph from 1956, the year I was born, centers a slender young Black woman standing with a little girl on a city street in front of a building entrance. The woman is dressed elegantly in a mint-green dress that is fitted at the top and flares in gossamer pleats like cotton candy to just below her knees. She is adorned stylishly with large round white earrings, a white clutch purse, and white patent leather pumps. The girl at her side, about eight years of age, is as elegant as she. Her white dress with three tiers of chiffon blossoms above her black patent leather Mary Jane shoes and white ankle socks. She wears a white ribbon in her hair. They are the epitome of 1950s elegance. A model of maternal care. Directly above the stunning pair hangs a neon sign blaring in block red letters "COLORED ENTRANCE." The contrast between the vulgar sign and the graceful woman and girl standing beneath it is jarring, its appalling contradiction unmistakable.

Department Store, Mobile, Alabama is one of the iconic photos taken by Gordon Parks while on assignment for *Life* magazine to document the everyday lives of Black people enduring nobly under the thumb of Jim Crow segregation laws in the South. When I look at the photo, I see my mother and me. The woman in the photo looks strikingly like Mommy—her dark skin, short hair, and slim figure, as well as in her fashionable outfit. In the photo I see the indignity of their forced positioning under the sign, the very indignity that I now realize my mother was defying when she took me shopping with her in downtown Chicago. Perhaps Mommy loved to go shopping in fancy department stores in part because she was treated by white people there with the respect she deserved.

Mommy dressed me exactly like the little girl in the photo when we went shopping together. For special family or school photos, downtown outings, or parties at the Kenwood house, my sisters and I were decked out in beautiful dresses. When we played outside, we usually wore crisp cotton pedal pushers, pants that stopped just below the knee, and matching shirts. My mother assigned each of us a color. Mine was blue, Evelyn's pink, and Helen's yellow. Although she didn't follow the color scheme absolutely, she tended to buy us clothes in our designated hue.

Whatever the outfit, Mommy decorated our hair with matching ribbons. Styling our hair was an essential part of her meticulous grooming. She kept our hair natural. My hair was shorter and kinkier than my sisters' tresses, but Mommy never suggested there was anything wrong with mine. We grew up before the Black Is Beautiful revolution took hold, before Afros were commonplace and Black women felt at liberty to wear their hair in natural styles. Black people still referred to "good hair," meaning hair that was naturally straight enough not to require much improvement. Most Black women and girls we knew and saw on television or in magazines pressed or permed their hair. So, Mommy's insistence that no hot combs or chemicals touch ours was unconventional. Instead, Mommy oiled, combed, and braided our hair with tender fingers every morning and adorned each braid with ribbons tied in a bow.

Daddy expressed his gratitude to my mother daily. Every evening after dinner, he would fold his napkin, place it back in its ivory ring, and say, "Thank you, dear, for the lovely repast." He praised her looks and talents often. I can't recall Daddy ever shouting at her. But he was annoyed by Mommy's affection for shopping.

Mommy bought luxurious stockings, each pair reaching her thighs. She fastened them to her girdle with little tabs. The stockings were silky and weightless like a gossamer scarf that slips through your fingers and colored mahogany to match her skin. They came in a slim glossy white box and were folded in delicate white tissue paper. I can feel distinctly the mystical sensation of my mother lifting the cover and carefully pulling back the tissue to reveal the ethereal apparel enclosed inside.

I would watch Mommy put on her girdle, a thick white contraption, that required her to wriggle back and forth as she hoisted it up over her waist. Then she would sit on the side of her bed to pull on the stockings and stand to clip them to her girdle. I would watch her step into a beautiful dress. Sometimes I would climb on the bed to help her zip it up. My gaze stayed on her while she applied red lipstick, then dusted her face with a powder puff dabbed in brown powder, both kept in a round metal case, golden with a colorful design. I can remember imitating the entire ritual in front of her bedroom mirror when she was downstairs. I can remember thinking that Mommy was the most exquisite woman in the world.

Once, my father questioned my mother's need to buy such an extravagant accessory. "My mother never even wore stockings," he told her. "I'm not your mother," Mommy retorted. That's when my mother decided she would get a job so she wouldn't need my father's approval to buy whatever she wanted. I recall this conversation clearly because my mother used to recite it to me and my sisters. It was one of her many anecdotes meant to hammer in the importance of being independent from a man. Looking back on the incident, I find my father's objection curious because he would note in virtually every one of his early interviews whether the wife was wearing stockings.

Unlike Mommy, my father was punctual and penny-pinching. One of his favorite sayings was "Don't put it in the waste; put it under the waist." The adage applied to more than wasting food. It meant not to waste money on anything. My father would have been fine wearing the same inexpensive suit to work every day. He concluded his "Psychological Autobiography," the essay he wrote for his college class, by emphasizing the frugal habits that I recognize so well. "My thrift remained a strong trait in me, and I never spent money foolishly," he wrote. "I doubt if I spend a dollar a year on candy, and one of the reasons I don't seek the company of girls is that they are too expensive." I laughed out loud. Wait until you meet Iris, I chuckled to myself.

While rummaging through my father's papers, I frequently found his handwritten notes scribbled on the back of advertisements, letters, and envelopes that he had received in the mail. When I was growing up, he used to keep old pieces of paper on a clipboard for reuse. In hindsight, I think my father's habit of noting the odometer reading and cost of gas on our road trips, likely scrawled on secondhand paper, was to calculate a way to save money. The funny thing is, I have a similar habit—jotting down notes on leftover pieces of paper. The frugality I inherited from my father is tempered by the fashion sense I absorbed from my mother. I am neither as extravagant as she was nor as stingy as he could be. Even so, I will never match the zenith of Mommy's elegance.

Dorothy's one-year-old birthday party, Monrovia, Liberia, March 8, 1957

CHAPTER 17

The Sixties

Eighth-grade class photo, Shoesmith School, Chicago, 1969. Dorothy is fourth from right in first row.

Mr. Atkins
June 1, 1964

As I continue to read the transcripts from the 1960s, I begin to see a new phase in my father's research emerge. Now a full professor at Roosevelt, he had started assigning his graduate students to visit the homes of the Black-white couples participating in his study. Just as he had begun his own research in the 1930s as part of the Warner-Cayton graduate team, he had now reached a point in his career where he could delegate some of the fieldwork to his students. He often sent them out in pairs—one man, one woman—mirroring the dynamic he had followed with my mother.

On the first day of June 1964, two of my father's graduate students interviewed Mr. Martin Atkins, a Negro man married to a white woman, at his home in Hyde Park. He was attending Roosevelt, where he would earn a bachelor's degree three years later, and was likely one of my father's students, another university recruit to the study. The students began by asking him about his parents' reaction to his marriage. Mr. Atkins responded that his parents were relieved, hoping that married life might settle him down no matter his wife's race. I am surprised to read that he told the students that, at the time of his marriage, he had a grueling schedule working for "S.N.I.C."

"As chairman it was necessary to spend days and days traveling for a couple of years straight. I was living and working in the South, particularly in Mississippi and Georgia," Mr. Atkins recalled.

Could the students have mistakenly misspelled the acronym for the Student Nonviolent Coordinating Committee (SNCC), perhaps confused by its pronunciation as "Snick"? I was puzzled—almost disbelieving—by the suggestion that Mr. Atkins had once directed this pivotal civil rights organization. In my understanding, the leadership of SNCC in the 1960s had been synonymous with figures like Marion Barry, John Lewis, and Stokely Carmichael. None of these iconic Black leaders, as far as I knew, had been involved in my father's research project, and none had married a white woman.

Curious, I quickly search the history of SNCC's leadership and realize I had overlooked someone. Charles "Chuck" McDew had served as the organization's second chairman, leading from the fall of 1960 through the summer of 1963, his tenure bridging the leadership of Barry and Lewis, with Carmichael following after. My skepticism vanishes when I see McDew's birthplace: Massillon, Ohio—the very place Mr. Atkins had told the students he was born in 1938.

This unexpected encounter with a prominent civil rights leader, a man whose personal life defied expectations, added an entirely new dimension to my father's research. It was a revelation I was eager to explore.

Mr. Atkins recounted how he grew up in Ohio and didn't experience full-blown white supremacy until he left for South Carolina State College, his father's alma mater, in 1959. His parents had insisted that he and his siblings attend a historically Black institution so they could become more familiar with accomplished members of his race. He soon encountered, as well, the regular subjugation of Black people under the Jim Crow regime.

"I was arrested three times before I went home for Christmas," Mr. Atkins recalled.

The first arrest occurred when Mr. Atkins was on his way back to campus with his roommate after spending Thanksgiving break at the roommate's home. A police officer pulled the car over. Mr. Atkins was driving and didn't have his license with him. "When we answered, we didn't say 'yes, sir' and 'no, sir,' so he socked me, and we were arrested and put in jail." Mr. Atkins had to borrow $100 from his roommate's mother to be released. According to his obituary in the *New York Times*, dated April 13, 2018, McDew had suffered a broken arm and jaw in the struggle with the officer.

The second arrest occurred on the train heading back to school after the incident.

"I was told to go to the back because the train was crowded. I refused to go to the baggage car on the segregated train. I sat down in the white car, and I was arrested again," Mr. Atkins explained. "That was twice in less than twenty-four hours."

Mr. Atkins told my father's students that he was arrested for a third time as he prepared to take a bus home for the Christmas holidays. While waiting at the bus station in Columbia, South Carolina, he ran into a white friend, a young man with whom he played handball. The bus wasn't scheduled to arrive for several hours, perhaps it was delayed, and they decided to go to the local YMCA to pass the time. But their plans were thwarted at the door. The white man could enter, a YMCA employee told them, but Negroes were not allowed.

"We didn't know that there were segregated Ys," Mr. Atkins said. "Since we were young, when we were told that we couldn't enter together we threatened to burn our cards and rub the ashes in their faces. As we were leaving, we were arrested for fraternizing, which is a form of race mixing."

Citing an interview with a Smithsonian Institution oral history project, the *New York Times* obituary reports a different account of a third arrest, occurring only a day after his arrest for riding in the whites-only train car. According to the paper's retelling, McDew took a shortcut when he returned to campus through a public park reserved for white residents. "So, I'd been arrested for the third time in two days," he is quoted as saying, "and that sort of started it."

Adding the story he told my father's students, McDew was arrested at least *four* times during his first semester at South Carolina State. His father relented and released his son from finishing out the year in the South. He had experienced enough southern hospitality. Despite his father's permission to leave, McDew remained at South Carolina State to participate in the student protests against segregation that were erupting across the South: sit-ins at lunch counters, wade-ins at public swimming pools, demonstrations and marches in the street.

McDew was one of more than three hundred students at the Youth Leadership Conference held at Shaw University in Raleigh, North Carolina, over Easter weekend, 1960. Organized by Ella Baker, executive director of the Southern Christian Leadership Conference (SCLC), the convening brought together student leaders from historically Black colleges and universities to enlist their activism in the Black Freedom Struggle. The discussions there led to the founding of SNCC and to sixteen student activists, including McDew, volunteering to leave college to work full-time as grassroots field organizers in the Deep South. A few months later, McDew found himself back in jail, this time arrested for refusing to leave the segregated lunch counter of a local five-and-dime Kress department store. This arrest wouldn't be his last.

Mr. Atkins told the students that he met his wife when he spoke at a conference at Sarah Lawrence College, where she was student body president and assigned to be his campus host. I imagine that gave the white student leader and the Black civil rights activist a chance to spend several hours getting to know each other. When the Roosevelt students asked Mr. Atkins about his friends' response to his mixed marriage, he replied that, although most had no problem with it, some disapproved.

"Because here was a big Negro leader marrying a white woman. They thought I should marry my own kind, but they were definitely in the minority. However, we were fighting for people to do what they want, so eventually they came around," he explained.

While Mr. Atkins was visiting a Mississippi town recently bombed by white supremacists, the white police chief brought up his marriage during their encounter.

"Hi ya, Martin," the police chief said, walking up to him. "Haven't seen you around for a while."

"No."

"Read in *Jet* that you got married."

"Yes."

"Everyone in the South reads *Jet* to keep up on the Negro news," Mr. Atkins informed my father's students.

I discover from the 1960s transcripts that my father—often accompanied by my mother—and his graduate students interviewed several other Black political activists who had married white women. These interracial unions put my father's antidote for racial hatred to a provocative test. It was one thing for ordinary mixed-race couples to ignore racial politics, to insist that race didn't matter to their love. It was another for Black men widely known for fighting Jim Crow to marry women perceived to be from the oppressor's ranks rather than women from their own community.

The tension between civil rights activism and interracial marriage ran just as prominently throughout the 1960s interviews as did the belief that they were tied together. While Mrs. Wolff remarked that many leftists saw their mixed marriages as a path to racial equality, others in the movement saw these unions as antithetical to the cause. Historian Renee Romano explores this paradox in depth, dedicating an entire chapter to "Talking Black and Sleeping White" in *Race Mixing*, her book on Black-white marriage in postwar America. She highlights the irony of Black nationalists and Black power advocates attacking interracial marriage at a time when the number of Black men marrying white women was steadily rising. "It was a particularly difficult time for interracially married political activists, who found their commitment to the black struggle questioned because of the choices they had made in their personal lives," Romano writes.

While some Black leaders married to white women succumbed to the pressure, their relationships unraveling, others, like McDew, largely escaped scrutiny, having already proven their allegiance to the freedom struggle. Even Malcolm X seemed to accept McDew's commitment, sending him and his bride a set of sherry glasses as a wedding gift.

Malcolm X's criticism of Black leaders who married white women surfaced in another interview. A month after the Aktins interview, two other Roosevelt students visited the home of George Hallis, another prominent civil rights activist, and his white wife. Hallis, the head of the Chicago Urban League, led one of the city's foremost organizations dedicated to Black social and economic empowerment. Founded in 1916, the affiliate of the National Urban League had long been at the forefront of the fight for racial justice. When I read that the Hallises lived in a cooperatively owned apartment building in Kenwood, it strikes me that they must have been my neighbors.

When the students arrived, a Black housekeeper answered the door and escorted them through the hallway, where the walls were checkered with framed photographs. In image after image, Mr. Hallis stood beside Dr. Martin Luther King Jr. and other towering figures of the movement. One of the students paused, mistaking a youthful photo of Mrs. Hallis for that of Lauren Bacall. Now in her forties, the activist's wife was a freckled redhead with a poised demeanor. She greeted them with an apology— her husband was away and hadn't completed their questionnaires. The demands of the civil rights movement consumed him entirely, she explained. The year before, he had delivered nearly four hundred speeches.

"Even his free time isn't his own," she added, perhaps with a weary smile.

She offered them an alternative resource. A recent article about him had been published in *Ebony* magazine, and reprints were available at the Urban League's office.

"They are yours for the asking," she said.

Mrs. Hallis told the students that she had become involved in the Chicago Urban League to pursue her passion for racial equality, at first as a volunteer, then joining the staff in 1953. She met Mr. Hallis when he interviewed for the job of director. They began to date after he assumed the position in 1956 and soon wed.

"What were some of the things people told you about interracial marriages when you and your husband became serious about each other?" the students asked.

"People told me the same things they tell everybody else; that you won't have any friends and that you'll be cut off from the community and so will he," she replied. "And then one of the board members told me that he had just started this job here and that he will be run out of town, and that the Negro women wouldn't have anything to do with me and they would resent him and he couldn't do his job."

Mrs. Hallis chalked up these concerns to ignorance about interracial relationships. "They have fear about it because they don't know anything about it, which is where most fears are based." Besides, she added, she had made friends with many Negro women. "I don't believe this old line, that Negro women would hate me, at all." She went on, "To me, it wasn't interracial. It was just somebody that I liked and wanted to see."

"Because Mr. Hallis is the leader of the Negro community, have you been put down at all?" one of the students persisted.

"Only once. Malcolm X said that Mr. George Hallis could never be a leader because he's married to a white woman. But I didn't let that bother me very much. I haven't experienced it in Chicago."

When the students continued to press her on whether it was a disadvantage for a Negro civil rights leader to be married to a white woman, Mrs. Hallis vehemently disagreed.

"I think the facts deny this to be true," she protested. "My husband has been very successful and has been able to reorganize a dead Urban League and bring it to a point where nobody ever dreamed it would be. In fact, Chicago Urban League is the largest League in the country now."

A quick dive into online research leads me to uncover the true identities of Mr. and Mrs. Hallis. Edwin C. "Bill" Berry served as the executive director of the Chicago Urban League from 1956 to 1972. A photo from the Urban League's records on Flickr captures Martin Luther King Jr. kissing Bill's wife, Betsy Berry, on the cheek—confirming for me that she was white. Standing to the right, the tall and lanky Bill Berry watches with a broad, laughing smile, a controversial moment of civil rights history frozen in the snapshot.

Mrs. Hallis's portrayal of her husband's transformative work at the Urban League is echoed in every tribute to Berry, who passed away in Chicago in 1987 at age seventy-six. Before coming to Chicago, he had been the first Urban League director in Portland, Oregon, until the Chicago board—determined to take a more aggressive approach—recruited him after shutting down the local office. "Berry fundamentally reshaped the League by reenergizing its fund-raising activities and by bringing the League into Chicago's increasingly militant civil rights movement," notes a Black research consortium.

At the time my father's students interviewed Mrs. Hallis in 1964, the Urban League had just secured a long-fought victory: the passage of a Fair Employment Practices law in Illinois. Meanwhile, Berry was forging ties with King, an alliance that would solidify when King launched the Chicago Freedom Movement in the summer of 1965. Like Mr. Atkins, Berry's long-standing commitment to the civil rights struggle seems to have largely insulated him from criticism for his marital choice.

I feel a strong connection to Mrs. Hallis when the conversation turned to living in Kenwood.

"This neighborhood is an interracial neighborhood," she said. "We're integrated not only racially, but economically pretty much so, too. There are lower-, middle-, and upper-class people."

She also described Kenwood as a politically active place. "Most of the people in the area know each other and they're involved in various things like the Urban League, SNCC, and CORE, and Committee to

End Discrimination in Hospitals. Most of the people in the area, white and Negro, are pretty busy in civic projects," she went on. "If I could live anywhere I wanted, I wouldn't want to live anywhere else."

Growing up in Kenwood during the 1960s, I absorbed the activist spirit Mrs. Hallis spoke of. It seemed as if everyone on our block was engaged in one social movement or another. Apathy was simply not an option.

At the heart of my budding political awareness was St. Paul & the Redeemer Episcopal Church, located three blocks from our house at the corner of Dorchester and Fiftieth Street. My mother, sisters, and I attended Sunday services there, and it became more than a place of worship. It was a foundation for my early sense of social justice and political struggle. Daddy opposed organized religion because he believed it divided human beings. He didn't come with us to church, but he never tried to stop Mommy from taking us.

Among my father's papers, I found a postcard from my second-grade Sunday school teacher at St. Paul's with a handwritten message on the back. There was no postage stamp on it; she had handed it to me herself. On the front, beside a stock drawing of white families leaving church in their Sunday best, was a printed certification that I had attended Sunday school. On the back was a note thanking me for being an asset to the class.

It seems I was active in Sunday school and fond of my Sunday school teacher—but I have no memory of her. Years later, in the summer after my second year of college, I would find myself compelled by the teachings of Jesus, studying them on my own and ultimately deciding to follow them. His message of love for all humanity, compassion for outcasts, and liberation from oppression spoke to me. Maybe her class set the stage for my spiritual journey and how it intertwined with my political commitments.

What I do remember are the activist meetings I attended at St. Paul's, where we discussed support for the civil rights struggle and opposition to the Vietnam War. These were the years of the Chicago Freedom Movement, led by King from 1965 to 1967, which fought against segregation, economic injustice, and discriminatory housing policies. My sisters and I spent hours at St. Paul's, stuffing envelopes in support of the Chicago campaign and the civil rights foot soldiers who traveled south to protest and dismantle the Jim Crow regime. I don't recall exactly what we placed inside those envelopes, but I imagine they contained leaflets announcing meetings, calls for donations, or updates on ongoing crusades.

In October 1963, we took part in Freedom Day, a mass boycott against Chicago's public schools. Despite the Supreme Court's *Brown v. Board of Education* ruling, Chicago's schools remained as segregated as those in the South—Black students were crammed into underfunded, over-crowded classrooms, while white schools received ample resources. That day, Shoesmith closed in solidarity, urging its students to join the protest by attending the Freedom School set up at St. Paul's. I remember gathering at the church with my sisters. Mommy had packed our lunch boxes with a special treat slipped inside—Fannie May turtles, delicious clusters of caramel and pecans covered in milk chocolate.

St. Paul's was not only a hub for civil rights organizing—it also hosted meetings with members of the Blackstone Rangers, the Wood-lawn street gang. I remember attending at least one of those meetings, which was likely connected to Oscar Brown Jr.'s efforts to curb gang violence in Chicago.

Like most of my neighbors, I opposed the Vietnam War. I threw my support behind Minnesota senator Eugene McCarthy, the Democratic candidate with the strongest anti-war stance, and wanted him to win the 1968 presidential election. Determined to help his campaign, I went door-to-door in Kenwood, handing out flyers in support of McCarthy's bid. I'm fairly certain I chose him over Bobby Kennedy when they were locked in a tight race for the Democratic nomination.

Still, I was devastated when I heard the news that Bobby Kennedy had been shot at the Ambassador Hotel in Los Angeles on June 5, 1968. That night, I lay in bed, tears soaking my pillow, as I desperately prayed to God to spare his life. "*Please, God, don't let Bobby die,*" I remember pleading. My grief wasn't even about his presidential run—it was the image of him clinging to life that haunted me.

Once the nominees were decided, my fervor shifted into something else—a deep-seated desire for Richard Nixon's defeat. I recall no particular affection for the Democratic nominee, Hubert Humphrey, the incumbent vice president, who seemed milquetoast compared to McCarthy. But Nixon evoked an antipathy that I can still feel today.

On November 6, 1968, I recorded the devastating outcome in my diary, scrawling in large capital letters:

"NIXON WON"

I covered the page with drawings of teardrops.

One day in August 2012, shortly after I first opened my father's boxes in my sociology office, I received the obituary of Jack Fertig, who had died of liver cancer at age fifty-seven, from a listserv. I immediately recognized the name of my childhood playmate on Kenwood Avenue. The photo of a man with bright red hair quickly confirmed my hunch. The Fertigs lived in a brick house across the street. There were three children in the family—Jackie, the oldest; a brother, who bore the distinction of missing a finger; and a little sister the parents had adopted from Korea. Jackie was only a year older than me, and we became inseparable. We spent our days playing in the sandbox and climbing the wooden jungle gym in his backyard. They remain in my memory because Daddy captured scenes of us playing together in our home movies. I distinctly recall Jackie telling me with an air of authority that extra-ripe bananas tasted best because the brown spots were sweet as honey. Looking back, it seems he was echoing how his parents persuaded him to eat the overripe bananas left maturing in the fruit bowl. The Fertigs moved away, and I lost touch with my redheaded friend.

The obituary called Jack Fertig "one of the first Sisters of Perpetual Indulgence—best known as Sister Boom Boom a.k.a. Sister Rose of the Bloody Stains of the Sacred Robes of Jesus." "In his persona as Sister Boom Boom, Fertig was the best known and most flamboyant of the Sisters," it stated. At age fifteen, Jackie told his parents he was gay, and when he died, he was a celebrated activist in the gay liberation movement in San Francisco. I was surprised he claimed San Francisco as his native city, though the obituary noted his birth in Chicago. It described his parents as civil rights activists and Jackie as becoming an activist at a young age after attending political demonstrations with them. I imagine we might have gone to some of those protests together.

My best friend for most of elementary school was Lisa Knauer. I think of us as both fun-loving yet overly earnest for our age. A vivid memory of our friendship is eating potato latkes at a local Jewish diner with her grandmother, who lived close by in Hyde Park. Her grandmother on her father's side was Austrian and Jewish, whom I got to know; mine was German and Christian, whom I never met. I remember us working together on crafts, trying recipes, discussing books, exploring museums, and experimenting with invisible ink. Sometimes we were entertained by her little brother, who was several years younger than us.

Lisa and I lost touch when her family moved away to Pennsylvania after sixth grade, though we exchanged letters for a year or two afterward. We reconnected decades later, in the 1980s. I was an associate attorney in Manhattan when a law student whose last name was Knauer came to the firm for a summer position. Sure enough, he was Lisa's little brother. He told me that Lisa was living in New York City, too. She had become a Marxist and was a director of the Brecht Forum, a Marxist education and cultural center in Brooklyn, where she taught classes and helped to organize the collective's workshops, lectures, and performances.

When Lisa and I met for lunch, we discovered that our kindred spirits had grown in surprisingly parallel ways despite the years that separated us. Lisa was the only person I ever met who immediately recognized the origin of my daughter's name, Yaosca. She, too, had read about the Sandinista rebel profiled by Margaret Randall in her book *Sandino's Daughters* based on her interviews with female revolutionaries in Nicaragua. I had named my only daughter after a brave freedom fighter, and Lisa understood why. She also understood my marriage to my radical husband and invited me to speak at the Brecht Forum about government suppression of political activism.

Lisa and I lost touch again until, about a decade later, I ran into her at an annual meeting of the American Anthropological Association. She had earned a PhD in anthropology, her dissertation on Afro-Cuban music, and was now a professor at the University of Massachusetts, "a tenured radical at a public university," as she describes herself. Her research, teaching, and activism focused on Indigenous struggles for land and water in Guatemala and immigrant worker organizing in the United States. The Brecht Forum had dissolved, but she continued to teach classes with the Marxist Education Project. My heart warmed when I read her bio on the university's website. It begins:

> Dr. Knauer's teaching, scholarship and community service are closely linked. They are rooted in her passion for social justice and the idea that anthropology—the study of human culture and difference—can provide tools to understand, engage with and help foster change in a transforming world.

It was as if she learned the same lessons my father taught me about being an anthropology professor. No doubt she heard some of the lectures he gave me and my sisters when she visited our Kenwood house.

What are the odds that the two people I called my best friends as a child would grow up to become such strong and committed champions for justice? I marvel that all three of us built lives rooted in struggles for human freedom and equality. But it wasn't by chance. It was the spirit of Hyde Park–Kenwood in the 1960s—a community that, along with our parents, instilled those values in us from an early age. Like Mrs. Hallis, I wouldn't have wanted to grow up anywhere else.

Dorothy and Jackie Fertig, in my Kenwood backyard, June 14, 1959

CHAPTER 18

Black Girl

Bob, Dorothy, and Iris, Harvard Law School graduation, Cambridge, Massachusetts, 1980

Mrs. Palmer
February 5, 1969

It's my last week in the Kenwood rental flat. The August heat presses in from outside, but the air conditioner is keeping the study mercifully cool. I walk the now-familiar path from the dining room to the study, a cup of green tea in one hand, the final stack of transcripts in the other. I switch on the ceiling fan and settle in.

At the end of the 1960s, my father began reaching out to some of the couples he had first interviewed decades earlier, in the 1930s, when he was a master's student and they were young activists in the Communist Party. As I near the end of my own work on his project, it feels fitting that he, too, was circling back, returning to the conversations that started it all. Part of his purpose was practical: he hoped to track down the couples' children. His research had entered a new phase, focused on the biracial children of the mixed marriages he had once documented. I can't help but wonder if raising my sisters and me played a part in that shift—if we inspired him to study other children like us or if, in studying them, he was also trying to understand us better.

Daddy made sure to grill each former interviewee about the whereabouts of other members of their interracial communist network as well as any children their unions produced. Helen Raymond, who had directed my father to her aunt, Mrs. Rose, back in 1938, served once again as a helpful scout. She gave my father the phone number of her best friend, Agnes Palmer, another interracially married white woman in their circle. Mrs. Palmer, now in her fifties, was divorced from her Negro husband, Fred, and lived alone in Rogers Park on Chicago's North Side. When my father reached her by phone, she said the intervening decades had erased her memory of their previous conversation, but she agreed to meet with him at her home, thanks to Mrs. Raymond's recommendation.

My father arrived at Mrs. Palmer's apartment just before eight o'clock in the evening. Her three-story building was in a predominantly middle-class Jewish neighborhood, and he observed that most of the mailboxes bore Jewish names. Mrs. Palmer, a somewhat short and stout woman wearing an "at-home" dress and slippers, invited my father into the nicely furnished living room. They begin their conversation by discussing the student strike at San Francisco State College, led by the Black Students Union and the Third World Liberation Front, which began in November 1968 and lasted for five months, becoming the longest student-led protest of its kind in the history of U.S. higher education.

My heart skips a beat when I recognize the strike, not because I recalled it from my childhood (I was twelve years old at the time), but because my former husband, then in his twenties, had graduated from San Francisco State and joined the protesters. The protest marked the launch of his life as an activist and he frequently talked about it. It was how he had become close to the actor Danny Glover, also a San Francisco State student, to whom he had introduced me when we were married. I realize that the strike was ongoing when my father had discussed it with

Mrs. Palmer. It would end a month later, in March 1969. The students won their chief demand—the establishment of the nation's first ethnic studies program.

Mrs. Palmer told my father about an argument she had with her sister on a recent visit to her home in San Francisco. Her sister, who supported the Black Panthers, accused her of being too complacent because she was not in complete accord with the student demonstrators. Mrs. Palmer said that King gained widespread support for the civil rights movement because of his nonviolent philosophy and methods. She feared that the more militant tactics favored by Black activists were turning people away from the struggle.

It seems that Mrs. Palmer had become more conservative over time, considering that she was a member of the Communist Party three decades before. I wonder how my father responded to her criticism of Black activists' militancy. Was he the one who brought up the student strike and raised the issue of movement strategy in the first place? Did he argue with Mrs. Palmer or nod his head in agreement? My impression from reading the interviews my father conducted over the intervening decades is that he, too, had become less radical. My mother, it seems, had been a moderating force in his adulthood. I am confident that Mommy would have voiced assent to Mrs. Palmer's preference for Dr. King over the Black Panthers. My father left no clue as to his position in his notes. Instead, he asked Mrs. Palmer for permission to write down her remarks. *As she had no objection, I wrote as rapidly as possible in a shorthand notebook, but found it difficult to keep up with Mrs. Palmer, who had no difficulty talking with few interruptions for the next five hours.*

My father asked Mrs. Palmer to summarize her life since they last spoke thirty years before. She recounted how, two years after the interview, she and her husband left the tenement where they resided and moved into her parents' apartment in a Jewish section of Woodlawn. This must be a rare instance at that time of an interracial couple living in a white neighborhood, I think. Most of the couples my father interviewed in the 1930s reported being confined to the areas reserved for Negroes, like the neighborhood where the Palmers began their married life. Perhaps her parents' Jewish enclave was more tolerant than other ethnic communities. Shortly after their move, World War II broke out. Fred enlisted in the Signal Corps, the army's communications branch, where he received training in electronics. Agnes went to work at a war plant at night so she could attend college classes during the day.

The war intensified Mrs. Palmer's simmering disenchantment with the Communist Party. She disagreed with the Soviet's nonaggression pact with Nazi Germany. She was disappointed in the Party's failure to build a mass movement in the United States. She felt that its members related to each other more like cogs in a machine than as caring human beings. "I discovered after I was married that just because somebody was in the left-wing movement didn't mean they would be less prejudiced," she added.

After transferring for her last year of college to the University of Illinois at Urbana, she graduated in 1946 with a BS in biology. That same year, Fred left the army, angry at spending four years in the service with no savings to show for it. Still living with Agnes's parents, Fred found a job as a salesman for a candy company, later trying his hand at his own vending machine business. Agnes began working as a microbiologist at a hospital. Both had strayed away from the Communist Party and left-wing activism. "We had lost all the values we had in common," she said.

Fred was hemorrhaging money from his vending machine business despite the long hours he devoted to it. He lacked the required business acumen. "He couldn't figure out the liabilities," Mrs. Palmer complained. "I remember once he bought a lot of Christmas cakes that were half moldy." Their marriage, already worn thin, frayed further when she became friends with a woman at work, a parasitologist named Ruth, who traveled frequently and told tantalizing stories about her journeys. Mrs. Palmer spent four weeks on vacation with Ruth in Alaska, stoking her wanderlust. She began to feel trapped in her parents' home and in her marriage. She told Fred that she wanted to end their union. "He acts like he is totally shocked and totally unaware that anything is wrong," she recalled. "He isn't moving, and he isn't budging out the house." In January 1950, Mrs. Palmer walked out of her parents' home, leaving Fred behind.

At first, Mrs. Palmer blamed the interracial nature of her marriage for the frustration she was feeling. "I felt that if I had not married Fred, I could have done all kinds of exciting things, that I could go places and do things if I was not married to a Negro," she told my father. She recalled a time when they had planned to drive to the East Coast and considered the possibility of being turned away at hotels on account of Fred's race. She proposed driving straight through, but Fred was not willing to take the risk of having to stop and being refused service. They were forced to cancel the road trip.

"Now I realize that if we really had a basis for a marriage and if we really wanted to live together, it would have worked," she admitted. She did not regret her marriage at all. Her experience expanded her understanding of racism, an understanding she could not have gained solely from being in left-wing movements.

"I got to know a lot of Negro people almost as an insider. You get to know the innermost feeling and frustrations which you don't see as an outsider," she elaborated. "When you live in a community and face the same problems, there's a bond that grows and draws you together. It's not the same as when you come into a community and try to solve their problems."

My eyes widen when I read that Mrs. Palmer had become acquainted with the renowned writer Richard Wright through the communist network. "He was a very good close friend of Mrs. Cadwell," she explains. I recognize Mrs. Cadwell as one of the communists my father interviewed in 1937. Her husband was the Negro leader who had been jailed many times, but once famously slipped from the hands of the police. "She used to help edit his books," Mrs. Palmer continued. "When I was first married, I used to visit her and often found Richard right there going over a manuscript. I heard that it was a Russian ballet dancer that he married." My quick search of Richard Wright's biography confirms that he joined the Communist Party in 1933, remaining a member until 1941, lived in Chicago until 1937, and married a Russian Jewish dancer named Dhimah Rose Meidman in 1939.

It was Mr. Palmer who eventually started divorce proceedings, in 1952, when his Serbian girlfriend became pregnant and they wanted to tie the knot. Mrs. Palmer ran into her former husband twice. Once, at a party, Fred and his wife walked in and the host started to introduce them. "I said, 'We have met before,'" Mrs. Palmer recalled. The second time was at a peace rally connected to Dr. King's visit to Chicago.

"Don't misunderstand me," Mrs. Palmer clarified. "Because I left the left-wing movement doesn't mean I don't have liberal beliefs. I left the movement because I felt the way the Communist Party was moving wasn't going to lead to anything. You need a more practical approach."

Mrs. Palmer told my father that her postdivorce life had been downright exhilarating. She left Chicago with Ruth to explore New York City and Baltimore, finding the former too dirty and crowded and the latter too southern. At the Baltimore hospital where she worked as a microbiologist, there were two blood banks, one for Negroes and one for whites. When she questioned the practice, her supervisor retorted, "Over my dead body would they mix these bloods." She and Ruth returned to Chicago within a matter of months. There, she bought a two-flat, where her parents lived downstairs and she lived with Ruth upstairs. "She was like a sister to me, and she really introduced me to another way of life," Mrs. Palmer reminisced.

Mrs. Palmer went back to the University of Illinois to obtain a master's degree, was promoted to chief bacteriologist at the hospital, and had been active in her profession, traveling around the world to present papers at microbiology conferences. When her father died three years before, Ruth purchased the building with another friend, and Mrs. Palmer and her mother moved out. Mrs. Palmer bought her current apartment in Rogers Park, where she lived by herself, as well as one for her mother located a block away. She remained close friends with Helen Raymond, the last of the circle of communist wives my father interviewed in the 1930s. "It boils down to Helen," she said.

"Have you had any romances since your divorce?" my father pried.

"No. I had several near escapes," Mrs. Palmer quipped. She said she was satisfied with traveling to bridge tournaments with a younger male companion, a German chemist. "I don't feel any need to marry."

My father directed the conversation to the network of communist white women with Negro husbands he had gotten to know in the late 1930s.

"What has become of these interracial marriages in the left-wing movement?" he asked. He was particularly interested in learning the whereabouts of any children they produced.

"The group that I knew personally, it seems to me that many separated before they had any children, except Mrs. Raymond and Mrs. Rose and Mrs. Cadwell," Mrs. Palmer replied. She explained that many left-wing marriages failed because the partners wed for "immature" reasons. "I think they had an overidealized picture of what they were doing."

As I read the 1960s interviews, I notice other participants using language similar to Mrs. Palmer's to describe the precarity of interracial relationships among young people during the civil rights era.

In December 1967, my father met with Kenneth Gambos, a white man with light brown curly hair, born in Hungary and nearing the completion of his master's degree in psychology at the University of Chicago. Gambos was candid from the start: he and his wife were separated.

"It's up in the air now," he confided. "We are seeing a marriage counselor, and it may go either way."

My father asked Mr. Gambos why the divorce rate among mixed couples seemed to be rising. Applying his psychoanalytic training, Mr. Gambos opined that many interracial relationships emerging from the civil rights movement were unrealistic attempts by idealistic students to revolt against the meaninglessness of their lives. "They still seem to stereotype Negroes as noble savages, sexual athletes, et cetera," he said, apparently referring to white women's views of Negro men. He speculated that some white women "are motivated by the myth of Negro sexual prowess" and perceived Black nationalists to be more "strenuous" lovers.

"I think much of the motivation of those that date and marry Negroes is very, very immature, precisely among students," he continued. "My first hunch or guess is that many are people who marry for some fantasy reason."

Another of Mr. Gambos's remarks also catches my attention. He observed that the number of white women and Black men seeking to date each other on campus had noticeably increased since 1960. He added that "computer dating" had helped facilitate some of these connections. I was taken aback. A quick search confirmed Gambos's surprising claim. An article in *The Cut* recounts how a group of Harvard undergraduates launched Operation Match in 1965, attracting ninety thousand applicants in just nine months. "By 1967, *Life* magazine wrote that New York singles had half a dozen computer-dating services to choose from," the article notes. The digital age of romance—and of using computers to fulfill racial preferences—began far earlier than I had assumed.

Similar skepticism about people marrying interracially for the wrong reasons was echoed by Toby Landau, a white man pursuing a master's degree in social work, who was married to a Black schoolteacher. Two students from my father's sociology course interviewed the couple in January 1965 at their apartment in Lake Meadows.

Before diving into their questions, one of the interviewers, a Roosevelt student named Claudia Evanchuk, recalled a point my father had made in class.

"Roberts made some remark about the stability and happiness of an interracial marriage—remember what he said last week?" she asked her classmate. Then, turning to the Landaus, she summarized his argument: "In most cases, the couples that do get married interracially, there is no reason to think they will be unhappy together or have a lot of problems."

My father, she explained, believed that interracial couples, having already weathered intense social pressures and hostility, entered marriage better equipped for conflict than their same-race counterparts. I can picture him teaching this optimistic view to his students, trying to persuade them not only that interracial marriage was not uniquely difficult but that it had an extraordinary formula for success.

But Mr. Landau wasn't convinced.

He said my father must have been describing the ideal interracial couple, but in reality, he had known plenty who had married for the wrong reasons—for "immature" reasons.

That word again.

"I can see just as many people joining hands and looking at each other's complexions and saying, 'Let's get married, life will be one big civil rights demonstration. Let's show them,'" he responded.

Mr. Landau advised the students that interracial marriages would last only if the partners married for reasons that have nothing to do with race, the same reasons for marrying someone whose race you share.

"But if they are getting married to raise a social question or lead a crusade or be some sort of social martyr, forget it," he continued. "That is not what marriage is for."

I reflect on how Mrs. Palmer, Mr. Gambos, and Mr. Landau all pointed to *immaturity* as the flaw in leftist students' interracial marriages. I hear them warning that marrying to make a political statement rather than for love is a surefire path to breakup. Yet, I also recall how many of the 1930s and 1950s couples seemed to ignore the racial politics that inevitably shaped their choices and lives. The white immigrant wives who regretted marrying for love spring to mind once again.

It seems that both types of interracial marriages—those formed for love without political awareness and those formed for politics without loving devotion—were equally vulnerable to disillusionment and dissolution. Perhaps the secret to longevity lies in a shared commitment both to love each other and to confront the realities of racism with clear-eyed resolve. I think that was my father's optimistic prescription to his students.

It is past midnight when my father prepared to leave Mrs. Palmer's apartment, putting away his pen and notebook. *I spent about fifteen minutes trying to head for the door, while Mrs. Palmer continued to talk about the reduction of segregation during the past thirty years and other topics.* Another hour elapsed after Mrs. Palmer retrieved my father's coat and held him hostage as he donned it, launching into a condemnation of Israel's occupation of Arab lands. I figure she was reacting to the 1967 Arab-Israeli war, when Israel defeated Egyptian, Jordanian, and Syrian forces and gained control over territory four times its previous size, including Sinai, the Golan Heights, the West Bank, Gaza, and East Jerusalem.

When my father finally made his way to the front door, Mrs. Palmer issued a parting plea.

"I don't want you to write that the reason that all these left-wing marriages broke up was interracial," she said. "At that time there was so much ferment and many were not ready for marriage."

On June 12, 1967, the Supreme Court delivered its landmark ruling in *Loving v. Virginia*, striking down state bans on interracial marriage. At the time, sixteen states still clung to anti-miscegenation laws, and federal jurisprudence upholding these laws had remained unchanged since 1883. *Loving* was the final blow in the Court's dismantling of the Jim Crow regime. The Court's language was unequivocal: Virginia's law existed for one vile reason—"to maintain White Supremacy." *Loving* shattered centuries of racist doctrine and tore down a long-standing pillar of racial hierarchy—though it could not erase the structural forces that continued to discourage and punish interracial relationships even in Chicago.

I don't recall the *Loving* decision making any waves at our Kenwood house. Maybe it was because my parents' marriage—and those of all the couples we knew through my parents' mixed marriage project—felt so familiar to us. Or maybe it was simply because the ruling came down on my sisters' tenth birthday, and we were too busy celebrating to take much notice.

That same year, when I was eleven years old, another seismic event shook my life far more than the *Loving* decision. That was when the activist Stokely Carmichael (later known as Kwame Ture) published *Black Power: The Politics of Liberation in America*. His coauthor was Charles V. Hamilton, who graduated from Roosevelt in 1951 and was a colleague of my father. He taught in Roosevelt's political science department when *Black Power* was released. That must be why I found a copy of the book on my father's desk. Carmichael and Hamilton introduced the influential concept of institutional racism—the idea that systemic inequalities persist beyond individual bias—and argued that mainstream civil rights strategies, with their emphasis on integration, had failed to dismantle these structures.

Instead, they advocated for a more radical approach to Black liberation, rooted in political mobilization and economic self-determination.

Although my parents never spoke in terms of Black liberation at home, I was riveted by Carmichael and Hamilton's argument, absorbing every page. I still remember presenting a report on *Black Power* to my Shoesmith class, my notes carefully written out on index cards, eager to share the revelations I had discovered about our shared commitment to racial equality.

In my memory of those last years at the Kenwood house, reading *Black Power* looms as a milestone in my changing identity, a middle point between my pride as a little girl in having a Black mother and white father and my desire to erase my white "side" in college. I'm not sure that I can attribute my shifting perspective primarily to one book. I also recall the time we lived in Egypt during my first two years of high school and reading *The Autobiography of Malcolm X* as critical turning points. But I had already begun to identify solely as a Black girl by the time we left Kenwood.

It helped that there were few definitive signs of my mixed parentage. I never had the confusing experiences reported by some biracial people of being "too dark to be white and too light to be unquestionably Black." Most Black people in America are mixed to one degree or another, so my tan skin alone was insufficient to disclose my father's race. More significant, my hair has an unmistakable African texture, and my mother never straightened it or did anything else to downplay my African heritage. Most of the children of the interracial couples who came to our house looked different from me. Mr. Alberti's daughter had lighter skin and wavy blond hair and could have been mistaken for white. The girls with a German mother, one of the war brides whom Daddy interviewed, seemed to take after her. I was not a mixed girl like them. I had begun to identity as a Black girl with a white father.

Inside my head, I favor my mother. I identify with her brown skin and short kinky hair. My image of myself for as long as I can remember has been closer to the girls with dark skin like hers than the lighter girls whose complexion may appear closer to mine. Once, when my sisters and I were in high school and traveling home on the bus, my mother banged on the door when it stopped at a traffic light. Apparently, my parents had been trailing the bus in their car and my father pulled up alongside it when it halted. They had plans for us that afternoon and thought it would be easier to pick us up along the route rather than wait for us to get home. I heard my mother telling the bus driver she wanted my sisters and me to get off the bus and join her in the car. It was embarrassing enough that my mother was addressing the bus driver in her proper semi-British accent, but it got even worse when I heard her describe us as "three light-skinned girls." I was mortified. Until that moment, I had never heard my mother characterize us by skin color. I didn't want to be singled out by my color, distinguished both from the other Black girls on the bus and from my darker-hued mother. I slunk off the bus with my sisters, ashamed, my head hung low, as if on a perp walk to the paddy wagon.

Another time, when we were adults, I was waiting in my car to pick up one of my sisters. I can't remember the circumstances, but I have a vague recollection of being on a college campus. A Black woman with beige skin and hair pulled back in a bun passed by and I paid her no more than a fleeting glance. Then I realized it was my sister! For that split second, I saw a woman I didn't associate with my internal image of myself. I remember thinking, *Do I look like that to other people?* Yet, when my sisters and I hold our monthly Zoom calls and our faces all appear together on the screen, it's remarkable how much we look alike.

Mrs. Hamilton, a white wife my father interviewed in June 1938, had made a troubling comment about the children born to members of the Manasseh Club, whose mothers were almost exclusively white women with Black husbands. She told my father that some of the Manasseh children wished their mothers had not married Negro men. "I guess they thought they would have been white if their mother had married a white man," she mused. "Most of them resented it, I believe. I think that was because their mother could do so many things they couldn't do, that they felt restricted."

Perhaps Mrs. Hamilton was projecting her own feelings onto the biracial girls with white mothers—less resentment than regret, a recognition that her own children would inevitably be less privileged than she was. I think about how the Manasseh Club, with its predominance of white mothers, may have affected how their colored daughters saw themselves. I wonder if they internalized the club's rejection of colored women, absorbing its disparagement as a reflection of their own worth.

And then, a more difficult question arises.

Would the Manasseh girls have longed to be white if their mothers—instead of their fathers—had been Black?

I prefer to believe they would have embraced being Black like their mothers, valuing their mothers the way I do mine—and myself. I can't imagine what it would feel like if my mother were white. I hope she would have been the kind of white mother who affirmed my Black identity and fought fiercely against anyone or anything that tried to demean it.

Even as a child, walking proudly between my parents, my pride wasn't so much in my being biracial as in what the three of us represented—a vision of interracial harmony for the world to see. Since then, I have bristled at the terms "mixed race" and "biracial," at least as applied to me, as if they placed me in a category separate from Black. I've grown to respect how others choose to define themselves, even if their terms don't fit me.

The flip side of the eugenicist claim that racial mixing contaminates the white race is the equally insidious notion that white ancestry somehow improves Blackness. I never wanted any part of the idea that whiter features or heritage made Black people more attractive, intelligent, or intriguing. I admit it sometimes irks me when biracial women complain about having no sense of belonging, feeling excluded from both Black and white circles. I know I should be more sympathetic—I have never experienced that sense of isolation. Still, my empathy tilts toward dark-skinned girls, whose experiences of discrimination far outweigh any slights for being too light. Over time, I not only came to identify as Black but also to despise the fetishization of biracial children.

My parents sold the Kenwood house in 1969 when my father received a Fulbright fellowship to teach for two years at the American University in Cairo. He proposed to study interreligious marriages between Christians and Muslims in Cairo and compare them to the Black-white marriages he had investigated in Chicago. To my father, the distinctions between Black and white Americans were superficial. They were created by false stereotypes invented by powerful people to separate them. In reality, Black and white Americans had basically the same culture, he would say. I remember him reporting when we lived in Egypt that his research on Christian-Muslim marriages confirmed his position. "Christians and Muslims in Egypt are more culturally distant than American Blacks and whites," he told me. "If they can marry successfully, there is no reason that Black and white people in America can't."

I think back to how Mrs. Wolff said the problems in her marriage stemmed more from her husband being white than his being Jewish. She believed that racial differences were harder to overcome than differences between faiths. "I think it is easier to change religion than to change race or background," she explained. "I would prefer the interfaith marriage where there is a struggle over beliefs. It is easier to discuss this than trying to discuss differences that you almost have no control over." My father must have bristled at Mrs. Wolff's words. He told me the opposite— that religious differences should be harder to overcome than racial ones.

My mother found an administrative position at the university and soon learned basic Arabic, making friends with students and shopkeepers, as she had in Chicago. My sisters and I attended Cairo American College, an international K–12 school taught in English that enrolled the children of visiting professors, foreign ambassadors, Yugoslavian consultants, and white Texas oil company executives. I was starting high school, and my sisters were two years behind me.

Among the students from all over the globe, the Texans seemed the most foreign to me and I didn't make close friends with any of them. Instead, I hung out with the daughters of ambassadors from Liberia and Tunisia, a white girl from Evanston whose father was an engineer, and the boys from Yugoslavia. One of my best friends was named Hoda, the daughter of the Tunisian ambassador, who lived in a glamorous home in a fancy part of Cairo. Hoda insisted on holding my arm, drawing me close to her, as we walked across the schoolyard together. I could sense the heat of stares from the Texans, unnerved by the display of affection between two girls. I felt awkward and rebellious all at once. Even now, I can still remember the rush of defiance that surged through me when I chose to hold on to my friend's arm instead of placating the more popular white girls.

My parents never owned another house again. I don't know exactly what happened—why they had no savings. They never discussed the family's finances with my sisters and me, but we picked up whispers of a financial disaster tied to Daddy's investment in the Occidental Petroleum Corporation. For years, I remember him speaking about the company with excitement, his enthusiasm spilling onto countless scraps of paper filled with market calculations—just like the ones he kept in the glove compartment of our family car, scrawled with odometer readings. He must have invested too heavily, and the company must have taken a sudden, devastating turn. In a letter to Drake a few months before we departed for Cairo, he confessed, "I am in a state of depression now as the house is still unsold, and I don't know how I can manage without selling it before leaving."

It wasn't just the failed investment. There was also the book—the one he had been writing our entire time on Kenwood Avenue—left unfinished. And then there was Mommy's extravagant shopping. In the end, it all added up to catastrophe. Leaving it all behind, our move to Cairo served as a welcomed escape.

My parents never recovered financially. When we returned from Egypt two years later, they rented a brick center-hall colonial house in a predominantly white section of Evanston. Mommy wanted my sisters and me to attend the public high school, which had a solid reputation for sending its top students to highly ranked colleges. The house was owned by a wealthy doctor, who was happy to lease it to my family at a substantially discounted rent. We lived comfortably while I completed high school, but the glamour of our years at the Kenwood house had evaporated. My parents did not leave me a financial inheritance, but I would not trade my memories of Kenwood for a mountain of gold.

Back in Kenwood with all my father's boxes, I pass my childhood home every morning on my early jog. The house, like the others on the block, still looks the same, though its market value had soared over the years. I am heartened to see a sign in the front yard declaring "Hate Has No Home Here." One morning, I notice the current owner, a white physician, chatting with a neighbor out front. I introduce myself and he graciously invites me inside. In the hallway, I am struck by a large family portrait. His family looks uncannily like mine—a white man of Polish descent, married to a Black woman, raising three children. I imagine how gratified my father would have been. The house where he had once worked so passionately on his mixed marriage project is now home to the very kind of family he hoped his work would help make more possible. To see it occupied by a family that embodied his vision would have meant the world to him.

The doctor and his wife had practically gutted the inside for a massive renovation. Although I recognize the main contours of my childhood home, many of its features have changed. The butler's pantry and TV room have disappeared to make way for a stunning kitchen expansion. The scenes of African wildlife that used to grace the walls have been painted over. The dressing room mirrors are gone, as is the secret passageway from the closet to the hallway and a small second-floor balcony that was likely considered a hazard to children. The basement has been refinished to create an enormous recreation room with couches and a giant-screen TV. In some ways, the Kenwood house is now more magnificent than ever, but it has lost the eccentric charms that enthralled my sisters and me when we were growing up.

⁓

The only time I ever heard my parents have a full-blown argument, with voices raised in anger, was during my senior year of high school. My first choice for college was Yale, but my father wanted me to go to Northwestern, whose campus was walking distance from our rented house in Evanston, so I could live at home and avoid the cost of housing. Daddy had taken me on a road trip to visit the three colleges I applied to besides Northwestern—Yale, Swarthmore, and Oberlin.

Even that trip could not escape his research. At Oberlin, we met with the Black sociologist Calvin Hernton, who had recently joined the Black studies department and was known for his controversial book *Sex and Racism in America*, published in 1965. Professor Hernton argued that white men's obsession with political and sexual dominance was so intertwined that "all race relations tend to be, however subtle, sexual relations." The conversation in Professor Hernton's office centered more on the two scholars' mutual interest in interracial intimacy than on my interest in attending the college. I was an awkward presence at the sidelines of a discussion about race and sex between my father and a man who could become my professor.

Now Daddy was insisting that I forget the other schools and choose Northwestern for financial reasons.

It was getting down to the wire for reporting my decision and Daddy had not relented despite my pleading with him. One evening, I heard my parents arguing on the first floor and I went to the top of the stairs to listen. My mother was chastising my father for his cheapness at the expense of my academic aspirations. He should be proud that I got into such a prestigious Ivy League university, one that I had aimed and worked so hard for, she was saying. My father defended his position, pointing out that Northwestern was an excellent school, and he couldn't afford the high cost of tuition and room and board; I could go to the Ivy League for my graduate studies. My mother ended the quarrel with words I will never forget: "You are dashing Dorothy's dreams!"

The saving grace came in the nick of time when my high school counselor disclosed that I had been selected for the Rebecca Kranz Crown Award, given to a graduating student for excellence in scholarship and leadership, which came with a sizable scholarship that renewed for each year of college. My father had no leg to stand on. With the scholarship, student loans, and salary from my summer jobs, he had to contribute only a manageable amount toward my college expenses. Mommy and I prevailed. I enrolled at Yale.

Looking back on that argument, I feel a pang of shame at my sense of entitlement—demanding that my father fund my education at an elite, expensive college when he was teetering on the precipice of financial ruin. Yet I was grateful for my mother's defiant love for me in that moment—and the memory still moves me. My father, the lenient professor, was the one trying to tether me to home, while my mother, the strict homemaker, insisted I spread my wings. All those rules she imposed, the ones I chafed at growing up, were aimed at preparing me to branch out when it was time. She had always been the ambitious one, determined that I would reach my highest potential.

Within a week of arriving at Yale in 1973, the Black students came together and formed a closely knit community that carried us through all four years of college. I was in awe—everyone seemed so brilliant and talented, with a dazzling range of passions from music and poetry to medicine and political thought. We gathered often at the Afro-American Cultural Center, affectionately known as the House, for programs, celebrations, and conversation. It also became a rehearsal space for those of us who joined the newly founded Yale Gospel Choir. Henry Louis Gates—whom we all called "Skip"—was a graduate student then and a constant presence there. For the first time, I felt like I had found my people in this vibrant community of young Black students.

One of the first things we did as a group was to pair off into couples. A tall, sharp, and magnetic freshman from New York City caught my eye—and I caught his. It didn't take long for him to become my first boyfriend.

When I arrived at Yale, I was still wearing my hair in braids. Everyone else had Afros, which had become in vogue. With boyfriend secured, my next mission was clear: a new hairstyle. I made my way to the dorm room of a classmate named Michael Jackson, who was known around campus as a talented barber. With his large, perfectly round Afro, thick mustache, and bell-bottom pants, he was as cool as the famous singer. As I sat cross-legged on his dorm room floor, Michael cut my hair down to a teeny Afro. I left transformed from a geeky teenager in braids to a sophisticated young woman with a fashionable hairdo. By the time we graduated, Michael had changed his name to Onaje, which means "sensitive one" in Yoruba. I thought that suited him perfectly.

After my first semester was over, I flew back to Evanston for winter break. When my mother met me at the airport, she nearly cried at the sight of my shorn head. "Dorothy, what have you done to your hair?" she shrieked, as if I had dyed it neon green. At the time, I regarded my mother's reaction as another exasperating instance of her old-fashioned propriety. Now, as I reflect on her patient devotion to combing my hair, I can understand her heartbreak over the plaits that lay lifeless on the dormitory floor.

I wore my hair in the same short natural for the next three decades. After an expensive Manhattan stylist snipped my ear, I started cutting my hair myself with an electric razor. When I turned fifty, I decided to let my hair grow into dreadlocks. By then, my mother had suffered a paralyzing stroke and was bedridden. She lived with Evelyn in Pennsylvania at first, but as her condition worsened, my sister didn't have the skills or physical strength to care for her even with the help of aides we hired. So, my sisters and I moved Mommy to a nursing care facility in Chicago, just over the border with Evanston, where Helen and I could visit her every day.

The day an African stylist divided up my hair and twisted each section into tiny peaks, what would mature into long locs over the years, I drove to the nursing home to spend time with my mother. When I entered the room, she looked up at me from her bed, nose skewed in her signature look of disapproval and amusement. "Why do you have little worms growing all over your head?" she asked sardonically. Mommy chuckled as she mocked the little worms on my head every time I visited her until my hair reached a respectable length. The stroke may have confined her to bed, but it didn't diminish her wicked wit.

Sorting through the 1960s transcripts, I see that in September 1964, my father paid a return visit to Mrs. Green, a Negro woman married to a white man she had met as activists in CORE, a decade after he interviewed the couple in the summer of 1951. My father judged Mrs. Green to be *unmixed*, as she was *very dark brown with quite Negroid hair which was combed back and seemed to lack beauty parlor treatment*. Mr. Green, the son of Jewish immigrants from Poland and Lithuania, was a sociology master's student at the University of Chicago back then. Mrs. Green, who migrated with her parents from Macon, Georgia, at age three, was an undergrad at DePaul. Rather than orchestrate a wedding that incorporated Mr. Green's Jewish heritage and Mrs. Green's Catholic faith, they decided on a simple civil ceremony at Chicago City Hall. Besides, their parents opposed their marriage. Only Mrs. Green's mother attended, though she was not thrilled with her daughter's choice of a spouse.

Mr. Green, now a University of Chicago professor, was at work when my father arrived. The couple lived with their two young daughters in a co-op apartment they owned in the diverse, middle-class Hyde Park neighborhood, walking distance to campus. "Interracial couples are so very common today that there are many residences available to them, and most can reside where they wish," she told my father, noting the scarcity of such housing a decade before. Their parents on both sides had become more accepting of their mixed marriage once the couple had children. Other interviewees also reported that grandchildren had that effect.

Mrs. Green resisted when my father pushed her to identify any difficulties the couple still encountered. She considered the question to be unfair, as it implied that mixed marriages produced extraordinary problems. "I personally don't consider our interracial marriage to be any kind of a challenge," she said, adding, "At least I can't say that it's any more of a challenge than it would have been if I had married a Negro." In fact, she emphasized, the deliberate effort she undertook with her husband to iron out any major disagreements prior to getting married had made their union especially harmonious. Mrs. Green went on to school my father on the secret to a happy marriage, one she learned, ironically, because of the perceived racial gulf between her and her husband.

As a result of the compromises they reached, "my husband and I have something that is very significant to a good marriage, and that is compatibility," she explained. "The difference in our features, the color of our skin, and the texture of our hair is very insignificant to us. We are indifferent to these things. The important thing is to agree on the vital issues of marriage, and this we have been able to do. The important thing is that we respect one another and value each other as human beings, as two individuals."

Although I usually find comments about not seeing race as naive or disingenuous, Mrs. Green's words resonate with me on a deeper level. They remind me of a conversation I had with a friend, a married Jewish man, earlier this summer at the Kenwood rental. We ran into each other by chance, and I learned he had grown up on Kimbark Avenue, just around the corner from my childhood home, and was still living in the neighborhood. Though we'd connected as adults over a common dedication to racial justice, we'd never realized we shared roots in Kenwood. His father had been a professor at the University of Chicago, he explained, so he attended the Lab School instead of Shoesmith.

When I told him about my father's research, the conversation turned to relationships—and how to sustain them. We agreed that any lasting partnership requires each person to recognize the other's individuality. Your partner isn't an extension of you—they have their own body, history, perspective, thoughts, and feelings. And that's exactly how it should be.

Like my father, he suggested that interracial couples might come to this realization more quickly: they start out forced to contend with society's assumption that they are fundamentally different. That idea stayed with me. I hear the same insight in Mrs. Green's words: she and her husband confronted their differences—both racial and religious—before they married, and had consciously come to terms with them to build a life together. Their happiness wasn't in spite of those differences; it was shaped by the work of acknowledging and honoring them.

I try to remember this wisdom whenever my husband is irritated by something I did that seems entirely harmless to me, or when he can't fathom why I'm upset over something he did—like when we clash over the meaning of a scene in a movie, when we debate the best approach to ending homelessness, or when we disagree about whether my ever-growing piles of paper are a functional system or just unnecessary clutter, even when we see an interracial couple through different lenses. Despite both being Black, I've found Mrs. Green's advice applies just as much to us.

My first husband was born in Nacogdoches, Texas, but as a baby moved with his family to San Francisco, part of the broader migration of Black farmers from Texas to California. Thirteen years older than I was, he was already active in the Black liberation movement when I met him at Harvard. We married soon after I graduated and moved to New York City. My parents had never told me who I should marry. It was understood he should have a college education, but they never expressed a preference about race. My husband not only met that expectation—he also met my mother's condition that I get my advanced degree before marrying. It was a JD instead of the PhD in anthropology I had planned for until my senior year of college, but that would do.

In our first year of marriage, I clerked for Judge Constance Baker Motley, the trailblazing civil rights champion, and my husband helped to organize a group of radical Black activists centered in Brooklyn. He called himself a revolutionary. At his core, what most defined him was his fearless love for Black people. He often ended conversations, even with our young children, by declaring, "Freedom or death!" Though my parents didn't share his radical politics, I believe they respected his conviction and strength.

In 1984, Rudolph Giuliani, then U.S. attorney for the Southern District of New York, charged my husband, who was leading the group of Black activists in Brooklyn, and seven of his comrades with federal racketeering offenses. Using a criminal statute designed to convict mob bosses and drug kingpins, he accused them of conspiring to break fellow activists out of prison. My husband was arrested and held without bail in the city's federal detention center. At the time, I was a junior lawyer at a Manhattan law firm and the mother of two small sons—a toddler and a three-month-old infant. When I refused a subpoena to testify before the federal grand jury, which would have meant cooperating with the unjust prosecution, I was threatened with jail. It was the first truly existential decision of my life, one that forced me to weigh my loyalty to my husband and my principles against the possibility of devastating consequences. I stood firm.

My parents came immediately from Evanston to help with the children and give me moral support. My mother never questioned how I'd ended up in such a predicament. In her eyes, I had run afoul of one of the rulers she believed power had corrupted. My firm provided me with a prominent criminal defense attorney, and the subpoena was soon withdrawn. The defendants were victorious at trial: the jury acquitted them on the conspiracy charges. The ordeal drew us closer together. In time, we had two more children—a daughter and then, fourteen years later, a son, born when I was forty-four. We called him our miracle baby.

Not long after my daughter was born, I began to question how I wanted to live and the kind of impact I wanted my work to have. I left legal practice to pursue my passion for teaching, writing, and activism centered on Black women's reproductive lives. After an eight-year detour as a practicing attorney, I returned to the path I had imagined since childhood: becoming a professor, just as my parents had always envisioned for me. A decade into my academic career, when I was appointed as a professor at Northwestern—where my mother had given up her PhD for me—she was overjoyed. "It's divine intervention," she told me, beaming with pride. It felt like I had repaid a debt I owed her. Yet, fulfilling my parents' dream as an adult—with my own convictions, following my own path—made it feel more like answering a calling of my own, though one shaped by their lessons, principles, and care.

Then, after thirty-five years together, my husband and I decided to separate. Disillusioned by what he saw as the failure of the Black liberation struggle in America, he had decided to move to Zimbabwe, where he had been embraced as a dignitary. But my life—my children, my work, my community—was here. He was determined to move on, and I suspected he had already started a new life in Africa. We were at an inescapable crossroads. It was time to part.

Not long after our divorce, I met the man who would become my second husband—a creative, kind, and steady presence who reminded me of my distinguished Jamaican relatives. He proposed on my sixtieth birthday. I was fortunate. Like me, he had come through past relationships with hard-won wisdom about how to live compatibly with difference and love. Though we met in Philadelphia, we both grew up on the South Side of Chicago. "We have good roots," he told me on our first date. Our shared experience as Black children raised in 1960s Chicago is an important connection that overrides the differences in our parents' backgrounds. He is the product of the Great Migration: his father traveled north from Memphis and his maternal grandparents from Mississippi. Although I have no ancestral tie to those migrants from the South, I still feel they are my people. That sense of connectedness may have something to do with the men I married and my Chicago upbringing.

I think about my Jamaican mother and white father, whose backgrounds diverged even more than most mixed-race couples. Yet, somehow, they remained compatible. They disagreed on everything from finances to going to church, to proper attire, to child-rearing, but sustained a solid marriage for five decades, until my father's death. What bound them together was their deep respect for each other, their shared belief in our common humanity, their love for travel, and more than anything their devotion to their three daughters. It's only now that I also see their investment in the mixed marriage project as an irresistible incentive to stay together. Divorce would have meant not only a failed marriage but also a failed mission—and dealt a humiliating blow to my father's theory.

After returning to Philadelphia from my summer in Kenwood, I am even more curious about my father's failure to publish his book. One day, I sort through the boxes in my sociology office, searching for records of my father's efforts to find a publisher. My initial goal is to locate the Simon & Schuster contract I remember from childhood. When I finally uncover a manila folder stuffed with relevant papers, I sit at my desk, the cluttered office silent except for the faint sounds of students passing outside my window. As I flip through the letters and documents, one piece catches my eye. It's printed on long, eight-by-fourteen-inch paper that has yellowed at the edges, enclosed in a cover made of heavy, light blue paper that has also aged with time. At the bottom, in bold black letters, I read: "SIMON & SCHUSTER, INC., PUBLISHERS. 630 FIFTH AVENUE, NEW YORK, NEW YORK 10020." The document, dated May 23, 1969, is signed by executive editor Richard Kluger and my father.

I gingerly set aside the blue cover and begin to read its contents, as though I've unfurled a sacred scroll. Under the title "Publishing Agreement," the terms outline that Robert E. T. Roberts will deliver a literary work tentatively titled *Interracial Marriage* in final form by November 1, 1969. The date surprises me because our family had moved to Cairo that fall for my father's two-year fellowship. It seems almost reckless for him to commit to completing a manuscript while adjusting to a new position in a foreign country. I imagine my father thought—unrealistically—that he could make momentous headway over the summer months, free from teaching responsibilities, when he could fully concentrate on writing.

Turning the page, I'm startled again to see that Simon & Schuster had agreed to pay my father a $2,000 advance—$1,000 upon signing and $1,000 upon delivery and acceptance of a "complete and satisfactory manuscript." That amount, nearly ten times as much in today's dollars, makes me wonder if our family's precarious financial situation had pressured him to rush the manuscript to receive the partial payment.

In that same folder, I also came across earlier letters from Cornell University Press and the University of Minnesota Press, both expressing strong interest in publishing my father's work. Daddy had turned down their offers in favor of Simon & Schuster's more lucrative deal. Clearly, he had high aspirations for his book. Among his correspondence are letters to Herbert Hill, addressed to a personal residence or private office on Riverside Drive, discussing the book proposal, a sample chapter, and negotiations with Simon & Schuster. At the time, Mr. Hill, a civil rights activist and labor scholar, was national labor director of the NAACP, a position he held until he joined the University of Wisconsin's Department of Afro-American Studies in 1977. Simon & Schuster had commissioned him to edit a new series on Black studies.

"I would want to reserve motion picture and television rights should interest in the subject lead to a film based on my research," Daddy wrote in one letter about the contract. In another, he compared his book to *The Children of Sánchez*, the acclaimed and controversial 1961 work by anthropologist Oscar Lewis, which explored the struggles of an impoverished Mexican family. That book not only garnered widespread attention but was later adapted into a major motion picture starring Anthony Quinn—a trajectory my father must have imagined for his own project. I suspect he shared his fantasy with my mother, building up her hopes for the fortune and prestige his book might bring.

A year after missing the deadline, my father was still corresponding with Herbert Hill, now from his office at the American University in Cairo, about the book's introductory section. As more months went by without receiving the manuscript, Simon & Schuster lost patience. It canceled the book contract and requested that Daddy return the advance.

Among the papers is another publishing agreement—this one with a yellow cover—dated October 22, 1971, between my father and G. P. Putnam's Sons. The new book, tentatively titled *Study of Interracial Marriage*, was slated to be part of a series, New Perspectives on Black America, once again edited by Herbert Hill, the scholar who had shepherded my father's arrangement with Simon & Schuster. The manuscript was due in January 1973. Perhaps, after grappling with the project while in Egypt, my father had returned to Chicago with a renewed determination to complete his life's mission. And perhaps Hill, unwilling to let the project die, rescued it by moving it to a new publishing house.

Still, the shadow of debt to Simon & Schuster hung over my father. The $1,000 advance promised by G. P. Putnam's Sons slipped through his fingers before it could provide any relief. "Will this amount be paid to me, or will it go toward canceling my obligations to Simon & Schuster?" he asked Hill. Either way, he had to repay Simon & Schuster. I can feel his distress at watching this income evaporate. My parents were already under financial strain—forced to sell our Kenwood home before leaving for Egypt and unable to afford another house when we returned to Chicago. My father's renewed push to complete his manuscript may have been as much about financial survival as it was about fulfilling his scholarly ambitions.

Apparently, even financial strain and a second chance at publication weren't enough to drive my father to complete the manuscript. Among his papers, I found a letter from Herbert Hill dated February 25, 1974—more than two years after their initial agreement—confirming the arrangement they had discussed in a recent phone call. The letter feels like the culmination of numerous attempts to prod my father into delivering the manuscript, now titled *Sex and Race: A Study of Interracial Marriage*. Hill's frustration is palpable, his stern tone practically leaping off the page as he warned that failing to deliver the manuscript by September "will cause cancellation of the contract and a return of all moneys received."

In August, as the September deadline loomed, my father wrote to Hill pleading for a six-month extension. He had secured a half-year paid leave from Roosevelt, hoping it would give him the time he needed to complete the book. "At the moment, I am heavily in debt, and with one daughter in college and two about to begin their senior year of high school, my only hope for getting through the inflationary years ahead is to complete the book and add to my income through royalties," he explained. Despite his financial and writing struggles, he sounded resolute: "With this goal in mind, I am confident that I will be able to complete the task in hand during the next six months." A handwritten note scrawled on a green scrap of paper reads "Herbert Hill phoned—Jan. 11, 1974: Extension of deadline to April 1, 1975. Concentrate on interview material. Write a conclusion."

But even the extended deadline slipped by. A year later, my father wrote to Drake, revealing a devastating setback. Hill had asked him to significantly reduce the historical section of the book—a section my father had devoted nearly a decade to writing. "This is such a blow to me," he confessed. "After spending years ferreting out quantities of data on in-termarriage and non-marital cross-racial sexual encounters in the U.S.A. over a 350-year period, I found myself almost unable to proceed." The disappointment proved insurmountable. He never submitted a revised manuscript to Hill. On March 9, 1976, one day after my twentieth birthday, G. P. Putnam's Sons officially terminated the publishing agreement and demanded the return of the advance. My eyes well with tears as I read my father's heartbroken response to Hill written the following week. "Some day, with or without help, I intend to complete my book which represents enormous investment of time and effort," he vowed. "I had just whipped up renewed enthusiasm when I received the contract termination letter from G. P. Putnam's Sons."

I assumed that was the point when my father gave up on completing his book—until I stumbled across a 1981 profile of him in Roosevelt's newspaper, *The Torch*. The article recounted details of his decades-long research and ended with an exciting announcement:

"A Century of Interracial Marriages," Roberts' book, will be the culmi-nation of 40 years of painstaking, intensive research. And since he has information dating back to 1882, all that is needed is a marriage in 1981 to complete 100 years of marriages. Roberts has already written several hundred pages on the book and said, "After 40 years, it's time to get on with it."

Yet he didn't "get on with it." I found no trace of the hundreds of pages he claimed to have written—unless he was referring to his PhD dissertation or the lengthy historical introduction Hill had once asked him to abandon. In the manila folder, I found later letters from Rutgers University Press and Temple University Press expressing interest in publishing his work. I couldn't help but laugh at a senior editor's observation in one of them: his proposed work encompassed three books—a comparative study of interracial marriage, a social history of one hundred years of interracial marriages in Chicago, and a study of the children of interracial marriages. "Wouldn't any one of these make a significant and marketable book?" the editor asked.

Taking this advice to heart, my father wrote to Drake that he had finally decided to abandon the book on the couples he had interviewed. "I think that I will start with a book on the children," he explained, "as there are a dozen or more books on intermarriage but almost nothing on the children, except for those in transracial adoptions." He never published a book on the children, either.

While he was still alive, I failed to ask my father why he never finished his book. I didn't want to add to the disappointment I sensed already plagued him. But after reading the interview transcripts I have my suspicions as to the reason. It certainly wasn't because he lost interest in his research on interracial marriage. Daddy was still collecting the narratives of hundreds of Black-white couples throughout the 1960s, either in interviews that he conducted himself, sometimes with my mother's help, or that he delegated to his graduate students at Roosevelt. He continued the interviews upon our return from Egypt in 1971. Then he began interviewing the couples' mixed-race children and amassed hundreds more interviews of them. No, it was not apathy that doomed my father's book. He remained devoted to his interracial marriage project for half a century, as dogged in reaching mixed couples and their children in the 1980s as he was in the 1930s. And that, I came to conclude, was the source of his writer's block.

In a December 1953 letter to Drake, Daddy indicated the same hindrance to completing his PhD dissertation. He described a lunch at the University of Chicago's Quadrangle Club with the faculty on his dissertation committee, including Professor Warner, where he "was strongly urged to halt or interrupt my continued field work and write a conclusion to my dissertation and turn it in this spring." He promised to avoid new cases and to wrap up interviewing in the next few weeks. "Last night I got to bed around 2 a.m. after a busy day in which Iris and I visited four mixed couples in our windup effort," he wrote. But Daddy didn't wrap up his interviews—he met with the Albertis, for example, throughout the 1950s—and failed to submit his dissertation until 1956. I think Daddy didn't want to end his mixed marriage project, a project that had become synonymous with his life and my family's life together.

Then, in one box, I find hundreds of index cards linked somehow to the interviews. Each card has tiny holes punched in it in different patterns, like secret messages written in braille. I remember my father referring to coding the interviews when I was growing up. He would leave the dinner table to go up to his office to code them. We would have to be quiet because Daddy was coding the interviews. He had to hire a student to assist him with the coding. This was before the advent of high-speed computer programming, which allows for quick analysis of qualitative research data, such as interviews, on a personal laptop. In the 1960s and 1970s, researchers had to input much of the work manually.

My father contributed a chapter to a 1978 textbook on ethnicity that documented trends in interracial marriages in Chicago based on his study. From 530 couples he interviewed between 1937 and 1969, he extracted various demographic findings, presented in eighteen numerical tables—ancestry and skin color of the Negro spouses, ethnic or national origin of the white spouses, age at marriage by race, years of schooling and occupation by race, and so on. He must have used the index cards to tabulate these statistics. As far as I know, however, my father never used the cards in the service of his book. Could it be that the sheer volume of coded cards overwhelmed him? He was drawn to conversing with his research participants, getting to know them, and bringing them together and into our family. He wanted to tell their life stories, not analyze the variables that represented their lives.

I feel a weight of sadness thinking about all those years my father poured into writing his book. I can imagine the mounting disappointment with each missed deadline and canceled contract. And yet that sadness is outweighed by the extraordinary adventure my parents' research gave our family while I was growing up. I wonder if, in the end, my father felt that the joy he found in interviewing couples over half his life was worth letting the book go unwritten. The world was deprived of the text he worked so long to finish. But I've had the gift of reading the stories he gathered, and of carrying with me the lessons they taught about love, race, and family. As I place the folder filled with contracts and letters back in its box, my heart is full of gratitude for the mixed marriage project, which shaped who I am and is still a defining part of me.

Research Participant No. 224

Bob and Dorothy at home, Evanston, 1973

When summer comes to a close in the rental apartment in Kenwood, I have completed my mission, reading all my parents' interviews with interracial couples. Back in Philadelphia, I turn to a set of boxes that had remained in my campus office—nearly a hundred folders filled with transcripts and notes from my father's next research project: interviews with the children of interracial couples. I'll put off the daunting task of reading them all for now, but I can't resist at least taking a glimpse at what they might hold. There's still a week or two to lose myself in the interviews before fall semester pulls me back into classes and faculty meetings.

As I leaf through the papers, I come across a file that jolts me into an entirely new dimension of Daddy's research, shaking up once again the kaleidoscope of its connection to our family. I pull out a manila folder,

marked only with a research participant number, as all the interviewees
had: 224.

Inside are four documents. A college paper I submitted for a sociology class. Two versions of an essay I wrote, one in longhand, the other
typed. And a typed letter my father wrote to me. I feel dizzy as the realization sets in: I am research participant number 224.

Daddy had created a file on me and placed it among the folders containing notes and transcripts from his interviews with other children of
interracial couples. By now, I know that his fascination with interracial
families began long before he started one of his own. I have long understood that my mother, my sisters, and I were inextricably tied to his
scholarly obsession—woven into his lifelong pursuit of interracial intimacy. But discovering that he considered me an actual subject of study?
That was a whole new level of entanglement.

I begin to wonder: Was I born entirely from his love for my mother,
or was I, in some way, an extension of his mission to document and pop-
ularize mixed marriages? It unsettles me to think that my sisters and I
may have been unwitting guinea pigs in a social experiment designed to
prove the viability—perhaps even the superiority—of interracial unions.

I decide to read my father's letter first, eager to examine this forgotten memento of our relationship. It is two single-spaced, typed pages,
produced on a manual typewriter, and appears to be an original copy. At
the end, after "Sincerely," my father signs "Daddy" in blue ink, a vivid
contrast to the black type.

The letter is dated April 25, 1994. I had just turned thirty-eight and
was an associate professor at Rutgers University Law School in Newark,
deep into work on my first book, *Killing the Black Body*, which would be
published three years later. By then, I was married with three children.

```
Dear Dorothy:
I am writing in response to your request of yesterday
evening. My feeling that biracial children (referring
to persons who have one White and one Black parent) tend
not to be more maladjusted than others is impressionistic
and not based on psychiatric or psychological research.
As a social anthropologist my research on children of
interracial marriages in Chicago was concerned mainly
with social and cultural rather than psychological
factors. But I did have contact with more than a hundred
```

**such children and nearly all appeared to me to be
"normal."**

Apparently, I had asked my father about his research on the children of interracial couples—whether it refuted the tragic mulatto trope, the enduring stereotype of the biracial child, caught between two races, belonging to neither. At the time, I was studying the history of eugenics in the United States. I remember a pivotal moment in my research for *Killing the Black Body*, when I wrestled with how to articulate why the devaluation of Black women's childbearing was central to America's history of reproductive violence. How could I convey that the mass sterilization of Black women—denying them the right to give birth—was as unjust as abortion bans that stripped them of the right to end a pregnancy? Investigating eugenicist ideology helped me understand how government-imposed standards for reproduction reinforce white supremacy and other oppressive hierarchies. Later, I would work alongside other Black feminists to develop the framework of reproductive justice—one that encompassed both freedoms, the right to have children and the right not to.

On the evening before he typed the letter, my father and I may have discussed the eugenicist claim that race mixing was biologically dangerous, that the so-called hybrids it produced were destined to be defective.

My father continued his response with what reads like a mini treatise—an analysis of historical views on biracial children, followed by a review of the latest literature on the subject, complete with citations. It feels less like a personal letter to his daughter and more like a scholarly article. In a way, it's a sequel to the tutorials on interracial marriage Daddy gave me as I was growing up in the Kenwood house—only now, it's in written form, addressed to me as a fellow professor. He critiqued the lack of well-constructed studies based on broad samples of biracial individuals, dismissing psychologists' skewed conclusions drawn from interviews with troubled clients seeking therapy.

"Historically, a major argument against interracial marriage was that the children would suffer psychologically," he wrote, referring to the "mulatto inferiority theory." He gave the example of a play by Langston Hughes, *Mulatto*, performed on Broadway, which "told the story of an angry young mulatto who killed his white father and then killed himself as he was surrounded by a lynch mob." He mentioned that Hughes also wrote a poem from the perspective of a troubled mulatto, "Cross," and quoted his lament of "being neither white nor black."

My father also cited an 1883 Mississippi court decision, *State v. Jackson*, that upheld the state's law prohibiting interracial marriage. He quoted the court as ruling, "It is stated as a well authenticated fact that if the issue of a black man and a white woman, and a white man and a black woman, intermarry, they cannot possibly have any progeny, and such a fact sufficiently justifies those laws which forbid the intermarriage of blacks and whites." The myth that the children of Black-white unions would be incapable of reproducing was so commonly believed that it generated the label "mulatto," after the sterile mules produced by mating a horse and a donkey. I couldn't find a record of the court's opinion, but it foreshadowed the Mississippi Constitution of 1890, which provided: "The marriage of a white person with a negro or mulatto or person who shall have one-eighth or more of negro blood, shall be unlawful and void." Although *Loving v. Virginia* struck down state bans on interracial marriage in 1967, Mississippi did not repeal its constitutional provision until 1987—twenty years later.

When my father began studying interracial marriage in the 1930s, eugenicist theories of "defective hybridity" were considered mainstream science. Decades later, not much had changed. Even in the 1960s, some sociologists and psychologists still promoted the belief that mixed-race children were destined to struggle with social and personal problems. A central goal of my father's research was to disprove this argument— to show that children of interracial unions experienced no more difficulties than those born to same-race parents. But in our home, if not in his scholarly letter to me, he went even further. He believed biracial children weren't just *equal* to their white peers; they were *advantaged*.

Daddy told my sisters and me that we were exceptional. He insisted that children with one Black and one white parent not only measured up to white children but possessed intellectual advantages over them. He rejected biological theories of racial inheritance—he was adamant in his opposition to that unfounded and dangerous science. But he did believe that being raised by parents from different racial backgrounds gave children unique strengths. Their ability to move between racial worlds made them *more*, not less, socially well-adjusted. He dismissed entirely the idea that biracial children suffered from identity confusion—and he set out to prove it.

For my entire childhood, even as the contours of my identity shifted, I never thought of it as a psychological problem.

Like everything else about our relationship, my father's high expectations for me were related to his research. He loved to boast to his colleagues about the top grades my sisters and I received. His crowing was more than fatherly pride in his children; it was the pride of a scientist who had proven a path-breaking theory. Our academic achievements were evidence refuting the myth that interracial mating produced innately flawed offspring.

I have a distinct memory of attending the funeral of one of my uncle Alfred's children, an older cousin I'd never met, who died in a motorcycle accident. When my father approached his brother at the church, with me by his side, he had barely expressed his condolences when he began to brag about how well I was doing in school. I remember feeling that I was on display, how inappropriate it was for Daddy to sing my praises when his brother was mourning his son. It's only now I see that he might have felt an extra compulsion to vindicate his decision to marry my mother to his family members who were skeptical, if not disapproving, of it.

I decide to read my paper next, curious about this relic from my college years. It is titled "Being Ethnic: The Individual Reality of Ethnicity in America (Term paper for Sociology 16b, Yale University, April 24, 1974)." I took the course during spring semester of my first year and had turned eighteen years old the month before. I must have handed the paper to my father when I came home for the summer.

I framed the paper as a criticism of sociological studies of ethnicity for focusing on the group as a whole and neglecting how individual members of the group deal with their identity. Both the assimilationist and Marxist theories of ethnicity, I wrote, are based on the goal of the loss of ethnicity and failed to consider that individuals often choose to identify with an ethnic group. Ethnicity is not "a title pinned on the individual at birth," I argued. Rather, "an individual's ethnicity involves a great deal of personal choice." I elaborated these points with evidence I gathered from remarks by fellow students in a study group for the course, a form of participant observation, giving examples of their varied approaches to self-identification. I also drew from in-depth interviews I conducted with two classmates, Lilian, a Tlingit Indian, and Jo, a male student of Lithuanian descent. And I wove reflections on my own identity throughout the paper.

In a section on "Mixed Self-Identification," after noting that "an individual may choose an identity which is associated with more than one group," I wrote:

When I was younger, I too chose a mixed identification. My mother is black, my father is white, and I made a point of my mixed parentage for philosophical reasons. Growing up in a time when liberals were busy proclaiming that all people could live together in peace, I was proud to present myself as the embodiment of this ideal—the offspring of the union of two races. When the emphasis of the day was the harmonious melting pot rather than stressing one's ethnicity, a mixed identity seemed the most appropriate choice.

I continued in a section on "Ignoring Part of One's Heritage":

As times changed, my ethnic self-identification changed. With the growing acceptance of ethnicity and the increasing popularity and pressure to be ethnic, and as I became more aware of what it meant to be black in America, I began to ignore the white part of my heritage and to stress the part with roots in Africa. Now, I identify solely as black and have even found myself taking measures to hide the fact that my father is white. The white "side" of me will never come into the discussion of my ethnicity unless I am asked specifically about it.

I addressed my Jamaican "side" in a section on "Change According to Context":

My mother is actually Jamaican, but among Americans I do not make this distinction and usually identify myself simply as black. When I am with Jamaicans, usually relatives, however, my "Jamaicaness" suddenly takes on importance and is emphasized.

My professor was impressed. He gave me an A+ and wrote in longhand on the last page, "This is one of the most insightful undergraduate papers (probably also graduate) on ethnicity that I've ever read. Absolutely great." My father must have been filled with pride when he read that. I can hear him saying to himself, "I trained her well."

Finally, I turn to the essay I wrote. One copy is in longhand on lined, three-hole paper. My handwriting is in curly cursive, and I drew daisy petals around the holes on the side. The playful style suggests that I had recently started college. The essay reads like a diary, a confession, so it can't be a class assignment. My only explanation for its presence in my father's file on me is that he asked me to write it. I suspect that I wrote it while I was home for the summer after my first year, shortly after I wrote the paper for my sociology class. Perhaps my father requested a more candid elaboration of my college submission. It's likely that I gave him the handwritten draft and he typed the second version.

The essay rehearsed many of the things I wrote in my sociology paper about my changing self-identification, except in harsher, unvarnished terms. "When I was a little girl I believed in the fairy tale that all people—black, white, or whatever were alike," I began. "They only looked different. Labeling people racially, in fact, used to make me feel very uneasy." I recounted an incident from my childhood that I no longer recall.

> *I remember once hearing Muhammad Ali on the radio speaking out against associations between whites & blacks. He claimed that the difference of skin color was God's sign that blacks & whites belonged apart. I was outraged. I wanted to phone the radio station and point to the example of my parents as proof that blacks and whites could live together.*

I traced my gradual departure from that view and growing identification as a Black girl.

> *While in 6th grade I wrote poems on the equality of all men—"It's good to be different; color doesn't count. It's what's inside that really amounts"—in 8th grade I wrote a poem of the great accomplishments of black people to be presented to any white man who thought he was superior to blacks.*

Still, I faulted myself for not identifying enough with Black people: "I was still too busy feeling a sense of belonging to mankind." I wrote that it wasn't until my family moved to Egypt that I experienced "a great change in my attitude." I became more aware of my Blackness when thrown among the white Texan and European students who attended my international school in Cairo. I read *The Autobiography of Malcolm X* and wrote a paper on the Black liberation movement for my social studies class. "I remember writing in my diary that I was ashamed of my previous attitudes and from then on would become more involved in 'blackness' and the struggle of black Americans against racial discrimination."

I am stunned by how I describe where my changing sense of identity had landed. I repeat my renunciation of my white "side," but in terms that seem overly severe to me, especially considering that I wrote them for my father's eyes.

> *As far as I am concerned, the white "part" of me is insignificant. I consider myself as a black person and I want others to consider me this way, too. The greatest problem being the child of an interracial couple presents itself at this point of my life: I often feel a fear of rejection by my black brothers and sisters because my father is white. In conversations when it has happened to become pertinent that my father is black, I never object to the assumption that he is.*

I went on to describe a "close call" that brings back a clear memory. It happened in the study group I joined for my sociology class during my first year at Yale.

> *I was participating in a group session on ethnic symbols for a sociology paper I was writing during which each participant was asked to guess the ethnic identity of the others. Everyone identified me as black except one person who thought I might be partly white. I was asked to verify his fancy guesswork. I couldn't bring myself to admit that my father was white, esp. since one of my black schoolmates was in the room. I finally said one of my grandmothers was white and that I never met her.*

I can still feel my stomach clench as I recall that moment in my sociology study group, when a white male student found me out. Ironically, it may have been his lack of familiarity with Black people that made him question my racial identity. Maybe he didn't realize that we come in a spectrum of shades, features, and mannerisms. Or maybe he wasn't challenging my Blackness at all—just speculating that I had some distant European ancestor and unintentionally blowing my cover.

The story evokes another recollection from that year. I am showing my boyfriend a photo that my father took of me while I was home over the holidays. In the photo, I am wearing a red knit dress, my hair is cut short in its new style, and I have taken off my glasses, trying to look more attractive, I suppose. I am standing in my parents' bedroom in front of their dresser that is topped by a large mirror. I have kept another photo taken at the same time with my father, who is standing close to me with his arm over my shoulder, my arm wrapped around his waist. He looks distinguished, sporting a full salt-and-pepper beard, glasses, and a red silk robe with what appear to be Japanese symbols etched in black. He must have set up the camera on a tripod and timed it to snap the photo of us together. That photo of me and my father now sits on a bookshelf in my home office. In the photo, I am smiling broadly, looking happy. Daddy bears a more subdued smile, one of pride in his daughter.

I deliberately refrain from showing my boyfriend the photo of my father and me. As we are gazing together at the photo of me by myself, I realize that the reflection of my father taking the photo is visible in the dresser mirror behind me. A jolt of panic shoots through me like a lightning strike. Did he notice my father's image? Could he tell that my father is white? I quickly pull back the photo and put it facedown on a table. I would later introduce him to my parents, when he stayed at our house in Evanston over spring break. He told me he was surprised when my father opened the front door. But at that earlier stage of our relationship, I was fearful of revealing my full racial ancestry, a composition that didn't represent my true identity, one I worried might ruin my newfound affiliation with him and our tight group of Black classmates.

I can still conjure up the panic that struck me during those incidents in college, but it makes no sense to me now. I no longer fear the perception that having a white father makes me any less Black than anyone else. My Black mother, my embrace of my Black features, my love for Black people, my commitment to our struggle for liberation are my indisputable credentials. No one can tell me that I am not Black. So, I was infuriated, along with many other Black Americans, when then–presidential candidate Donald Trump questioned whether his opponent, Kamala Harris, was Black because her mother was Indian. As a boy, Barack Obama understood that he was regarded as Black, and he came to embrace that identity as his own—a Black man with a white mother. Even when I worried about other people's assessment of my identity, I never questioned my own self-determination as a Black woman.

Still, when I became a professor, I made a deliberate choice never to mention that my father was white. I avoided the topic of interracial marriage altogether, believing it was irrelevant compared to the more pressing struggles I was engaged in—reproductive freedom, criminal justice, and child welfare. It wasn't until my 2006 review of Paul Gilroy's *Postcolonial Melancholia* in the *Boston Review* that I briefly mentioned that my identity as a Black woman was not defined by my genetic makeup. I revisited that point in *Fatal Invention*, published in 2011, where I examined the resurgence of false biological concepts of race. By referencing my own identity as a Black woman with a white father I meant to underscore a more fundamental truth: race is a political construct, not a biological one.

After I gave a talk about *Fatal Invention* at Oberlin College in October 2012, a group of students offered to drive me to my next engagement at Ohio State University. During the trip, the students peppered me with questions about my writings on race. I waxed on about how Europeans invented the concept of race to oppress other groups, how it is a completely political category, how our ideas about racial divisions aren't natural, but made up. "So how do you deal with the privileges you gained by having a white father?" a young man asked from the back seat.

The question caught me completely off guard. "How do you know I have a white father?" was my knee-jerk reaction, forgetting that I had disclosed it almost as an aside in the book we were discussing. My second, more profound, reaction was to realize that I didn't have an answer to his question. Why was it only late in life that I realized I never confronted the privileges I had growing up because my father was white? Despite focusing my academic career on exposing structural inequality based on race, I had never questioned whether I had experienced structural advantages owing to my father's race. I had devoted so much effort to denying the white half of my parentage that I had failed to grapple with the implications of having it.

I thought it was enough that I identified with my mother—as a Black girl. As a young adult, I thought I could magically erase my father from my identity. My biggest fear was not so much that Black people would think I wasn't Black enough. It was that I didn't want anyone to think that I thought I was special because my father was white. It never occurred to me that I might have to acknowledge him to truly face the reality of my place in America's racist society.

Something as simple as Daddy checking into motels without the rest of the family to me reflected anti-Black racism. But I never thought about how his being white allowed us to stay at the motels once he obtained the keys. During the years we lived on Kenwood Avenue, we were one of the few Black families on the block. Would I have grown up in that magical house if my father weren't the white man who inherited a two-flat in Logan Square and applied for a mortgage?

Now I was wondering if it was wrong to ignore the benefits that came from having a white father, dishonest to downplay my father's involvement in my life.

Then my essay went even further to reject my father—and my mother's decision to marry him:

> *There are few topics I feel so emotionally opposed to as interracial marriage. Any black person who marries a white person is pulling himself or herself away from other black people to some extent. I think this is a foolish thing to do. Furthermore, I believe the minds of Americans are too saturated with racial stereotypes & prejudices for any love between a black and a white person not to be negatively affected by them. It is unrealistic to believe that all interracial couples have overcome stereotypes & prejudice.*

I can hardly believe I wrote those words—so dismissive of my father and of my parents' marriage. I recognize in my opinions as a teenager the skepticism I feel today toward interracial intimacy as a palliative for white supremacy. But their virulent opposition to it is unrecognizable to me now as is their disregard for my father's feelings. Perhaps the words didn't seem cruel to me at the time, for I regarded them as objective input to a research study. When I wrote the essay in response to my father's request, I was answering as a research participant as much as a daughter. Even as I ponder this exchange with my father, I don't imagine him feeling devastated by what I wrote. I see him reading my narrative just as he had listened to the responses of hundreds of people he interviewed for his interracial marriage study.

Putting down my essay, I reflect on how Daddy never forced his ideas on me. He presented them as arguments, carefully laying out facts, statistics, and logic in an effort to persuade, not dictate. He accepted my disagreements—even hurtful ones—without any hint of disapproval. Even as a little girl, I felt free to consider his ideas and decide for myself. He wanted me to think critically, to come to my own conclusions.

For years, I believed he had instilled his promotion of interracial marriage in my impressionable mind. But looking back, I see that it was persuasion, not indoctrination. Remembering our conversations, I now recognize how much respect he had for my intelligence and judgment, even when I was very young. I owe him a debt of gratitude—not just for nurturing my critical perspective on the status quo, but for teaching me *how* to think, not *what* to think.

Reflecting on the folder marked 224, I realize that my disagreement with my father over interracial marriage was never as significant as I once believed. Far more important was the deeper mission my parents instilled in me: to dedicate my life—my politics, my scholarship, and my personal decisions—to uplifting our shared humanity.

Reading the file my father kept on me does not diminish what I knew of his love. If anything, it deepens my understanding of his lasting influence on me. The intertwining of our relationship with his lifelong research project didn't devalue, either. It only meant that I was woven into every part of his life.

In January 2002, while I was teaching at Northwestern, I was invited to give a talk in Philadelphia. My parents had moved to Pennsylvania by then, and the event's proximity to their home made it the perfect opportunity to visit them and Evelyn, who was living with them at the time. Helen and my one-year-old son came along for the trip. We arrived to find my father in bed, weakened but alert—and overjoyed to have all three of his daughters by his side. A year before, doctors had discovered that the wires connected to the pacemaker in his chest were infected. After several surgeries to treat the infection and replace the device, Daddy's health was devastated.

The very evening we arrived, Mommy summoned us to the bedroom. Daddy's breathing had grown increasingly labored. We called an ambulance and gathered around his bed, holding hands, praying. Within the hour, with the family he cherished surrounding him, Daddy passed away. It was as if he had waited for his daughters to come together beside him before letting go.

My father had wanted to be cremated and his ashes laid to rest in the cemetery in Chicago where his parents and grandparents, the Reinerts, were buried. In his family's time, it was called German Waldheim Cemetery, established in 1873 by German Masonic lodges as a nondenominational burial ground for German-speaking immigrants. Although open to all religions, like most cemeteries in Chicago, it was racially segregated. It wasn't until 1969 that it merged with Forest Home Cemetery, by then having shed its restrictions on national origin and race. We honored Daddy's wishes. There was no funeral, just a peaceful ceremony at his burial site. Mommy, my sisters, and I stood together, holding hands, crying, and speaking of how much Daddy meant to us.

After several strokes that left my mother partially paralyzed, her health failed for the final time in 2009. At the hospice center near Evanston, Evelyn and I kept vigil by her side. We reached Helen, who was living in Liberia, and held the phone to Mommy's ear so she could say goodbye. Moments later, Mommy took her final breaths. Evelyn and I held her, crying and praying, as her life slipped away. My entire body filled with the most blissful sensation of pure love I had ever experienced.

At her funeral service in Evanston, friends and family shared stories of her faith, her compassion, and her acts of care. My uncle told of how, as a girl in Jamaica, she once nursed an orphaned baby goat back to health. A pastor recalled how he and his wife had spent years trying to conceive until Mommy placed her hands on his wife's belly and prayed for her fertility. Within a year, they had their first child. When I spoke, struggling to hold back sobs, I recounted the time she made spaghetti and meatballs for my birthday party.

We buried my mother next to my father's ashes and our German ancestors at Forest Home Cemetery—my parents' final crossing of Chicago's color line.

"At funerals—that is the time you feel those things," Mrs. Pratt, a white wife, had told my father in 1937 when he asked about objections to her marriage to a Black man. "When my sister died, my children could not go to the cemetery. That makes you very sad."

I regret that I didn't explore my parents' mixed marriage project until after they were gone. I had always known my father was researching interracial marriage throughout my childhood, but I never truly understood its scope or reckoned with its impact on my life.

Living with the interviews changed me. They reframed my understanding of interracial intimacy. They altered the way I saw my own identity. The stories of hundreds of mixed couples made me see them—made me see my family, made me see myself—in a different light.

If I could go back in time, I'd slip a letter into file 224—one that didn't try to erase my father from my identity, but instead expressed my appreciation. This time, I would tell him that both he and Mommy were essential to the Black woman I am today.

I loved my father intensely. As a child, I revered him—even through my recalcitrance and aggravation. I can still sense the comfort of resting against his soft body, sucking my thumb and rubbing his elbow. I can still recall the thrilling camaraderie of hurtling down the Bobs roller coaster side by side. I can still feel the bond we forged through endless discussions about interracial marriage and racial equality. I remember the countless hours our family spent together—lingering over Mommy's sumptuous meals at the dining room table, taking summer road trips, watching home movies. Daddy was always there.

His lessons about human equality, his dedication to his research, his mission to challenge the racial caste system—all of it is embedded deep within me. It helped make me who I am. And yet, I spent years denying that he was part of me in the way my mother was woven into my being. I tried to distance myself from him. But he never distanced himself from me. He never denied I was an essential part of him. I often cite the way white enslavers disowned the children they fathered with enslaved women as a despicable illustration of how race can shatter family ties. But in rethinking my own callous treatment of my father, I have to ask myself: Was I also guilty of allowing race to disrupt our bond?

I now realize that Daddy was always an inextricable part of me. It was his *whiteness*—not *him*—that I could not make part of my identity. Coming to terms with his influence on my life did not negate my mother's importance or my affiliation with Black people.

I still hold to my belief that interracial intimacy alone will not dismantle white supremacy. But as I read the interviews, I began to see that the couples my parents met had something to teach us about what it takes to make love across the racial divide possible. Some of the couples who braved violence and scorn to marry I even grew to admire. And yet, their stories—of legal restrictions, of terror, of families who disowned them—also reinforced my view that racism will not be vanquished through personal relationships alone. On the one hand, their experiences exposed the immense barriers erected by segregation and prejudice. But on the other hand, they proved those barriers weren't impenetrable.

Chicago's color line kept people apart, but some still crossed it.

As I began to read the interviews, my once-firm position on the relationship between interracial intimacy and racial equality started to waver. I began to wonder: maybe intimate relationships *do* count for something in the struggle for liberation.

I think back to the 1980s, when a husband and wife I knew from the Black liberation movement in New York City were interviewed on the radio. At one point, they broke away from political rhetoric to talk about how they fell in love. Later, at a meeting I attended, a strident leader of the group ridiculed them for mentioning their love. She called it emotional weakness. She said they should have stuck to a political discussion about Black freedom.

I understood her caution against mixing personal affection with political analysis. But I also felt she was too harsh. Could they really separate their love from their activism? It seemed to me that their love was not only a product of their political commitments but that their love and politics were also mutually reinforcing. In fact, I felt that way about my activist husband at the time. But we were Black couples whose love and politics were intertwined. I was still wrestling with how that understanding applied to interracial couples.

Interdisciplinary scholar and writer Imani Perry reminds us: "The ethics of building a just society begin at the place where you can touch another person." If we want to create a world built on care and shared humanity, we must start with ourselves—even in our most intimate relationships. We can't wait until racism ends to relate to each other as equals. We have to practice that equality now, even as we continue to live in a world governed by racial hierarchy. We must learn to exist within the tension of both realities—to *grapple* with it—while envisioning a future in which racial hierarchy is unimaginable.

As I delved into the interviews, all my curiosities—about the marriages my parents studied, about my parents' own marriage, about my own childhood—kept leading me back to one fundamental, agonizing question: Is it possible to love each other as equal human beings across the chasm of race?

I came to realize that, even as I avoided the topic that consumed my father's career, all my own scholarship had been circling this same question. I called race *a fatal invention* because the lie that human beings are naturally divided into races has wrought incalculable devastation. My deep grappling with racism left me skeptical that we could traverse its minefield unscathed—that we could love one another with pure hearts, untouched by the structures that divide us, by the stereotypes that both attract and repel us.

And yet the reason I have spent my life asking this question is because I *do* believe in our common humanity. I *do* believe we can collectively dismantle the seemingly unbreakable structures, ideas, and stereotypes that deny it. All this time, I have been trying to understand, more than anything, how to love in a racist society.

My parents' mixed marriage project forced me to wrestle with that question more intensely than ever before. It brought me closer to the elusive space between the lovers who claim they never see race and those who are consumed by it.

I didn't find any definitive answers.

But I did find reconciliation.

ACKNOWLEDGMENTS

My academic home at the University of Pennsylvania, in the Department of Africana Studies, the Department of Sociology, and Penn Carey Law School, has been an invaluable source of support from start to finish. I'm immensely grateful to the deans, chairs, faculty, and staff for the many ways they encourage and facilitate my work. Silvana Burgese, Director of Faculty Support, and Timothy Von Dulm, Associate Director for Research Services, at Penn Carey Law, answered every request with speed and grace. I'm especially thankful to my colleagues and friends Sophia Lee, Serena Mayeri, and Barbara Savage for their enthusiasm for the history in my memoir and Tobias Wolff for lending me his Palm Springs house as a writing retreat. I owe a debt of gratitude to the MacArthur Foundation for its unexpected financial support and to the Black mamas fighting to end family policing for their unwavering moral support.

I'm also indebted to the dozens of undergraduates, law and PhD students, and postdoctoral fellows I've worked with since arriving at Penn and launching this project—too many to name. Special thanks to those who helped organize my father's archive and sift through the hundreds of interviews and other papers—Sarah Adeyinka-Skold, Dawn Androphy, Emily Bleiberg, Maddy Carter, Cayla Kaplan, Jordan King, Hazel Millard, Alex Moon, Madeleine Morales, and Jackson Sauls. Ashleigh Cartwright provided excellent research assistance in the final stages of preparing the manuscript even as she completed her own dissertation.

My literary agent, David Halpern, has been a steady guide throughout my career as an author and at every stage of this book project. When I first told him about my father's interviews, he suggested I write a memoir. His confidence and encouragement helped carry this project forward.

Thanks to the team at One Signal for making this book a reality.

My editor, Alessandra Bastagli, believed from the beginning that I could write a memoir. She helped me shape my uncertain ideas about weaving multiple stories together into a coherent whole. Rola Harb masterfully shepherded the manuscript through production; Katie Rizzo and Rob Sternitzky's meticulous copyediting sharpened its clarity and accuracy. Thanks also to James Iacobelli and Chelsea McGuckin for a stunning jacket design that captures my parents' love for each other.

I'm eternally grateful to my remarkable husband, Donald Ellis Moore, whose steadfast love keeps me centered and sustained me throughout my work on this book, including my marathon summer spent reading all the transcripts. My beautiful children, Amilcar, Camilo, Yaosca, and Dessalines, are my greatest joy. They are forever lifting me up and cheering me on. I'm blessed to have two wonderful sisters, Evelyn and Helen, who have loved and cared for me nearly my entire life. They helped create the memories in this book and reminded me of those I had forgotten. Thank you for trusting me with this story of our life together.

Most of all, I am indebted to my incomparable parents, Iris and Bob—Mommy and Daddy—who loved me completely and taught me all the best lessons in life. They gave me a fascinating childhood, which I recall fondly every day. Words can't possibly carry the depth of my gratitude. This book is a tribute to them, from the bottom of my heart.

NOTES

CHAPTER 1: ORIGINS

10 *published in 1795*: Johann Friedrich Blumenbach, *On the Natural Varieties of Mankind* (London: Longman, Green, and Co., 1795).

12 *families building new lives in the city*: Chris Bentley, "The Tale of the Two-Flat," WBEZ Chicago, August 20, 2014, https://www.wbez.org/curious -city/2014/08/20/the-tale-of-the-two-flat; Carla Bruni, "The Chicago Brick Two-Flat (and Its Cousins)," Chicago Bungalow Association, August 30, 2023, https://www.chicagobungalow.org/post/chicago-two-flat.

14 *out of a population of 114,174*: Louis Wirth, et al., *Local Community Fact Book, 1938* (Chicago Recreation Commission, 1938), 43.

15 *"an authentic part of Masonry"*: Lynn Dumenil, *Freemasonry and American Culture, 1880–1930* (1984; Princeton University Press, 2016), 10.

16 *away from her family and friends*: Ethan Michaeli, *The Defender: How the Legendary Black Newspaper Changed America* (New York: Houghton Mifflin Harcourt Publishing Company, 2016), 44–45.

16 *a witness reported him declaring*: Michaeli, *The Defender*, 45.

16 *"language and culture in the United States"*: Frederick C. Luebke, *Bonds of Loyalty: German-Americans and World War I* (Northern Illinois University Press, 1974), xiii.

23 *"homes to become tenement yards"*: Vinette K. Pryce, "Jones Town: Once Kingston's Oasis Now 'Wasteland,'" *Caribbean Life*, August 29, 2017, https://www.caribbeanlife.com/jones-town-once-kingstons-oasis-now -wasteland/.

CHAPTER 2: THE MASTER'S STUDENT

31 *"some roomers had to sleep in shifts"*: Isabel Wilkerson, *The Warmth of Other Suns: The Epic Story of America's Great Migration* (Random House 2010), 272.

31 *a third was Jewish*: Lynn Y. Weiner, "Pioneering Social Justice," *Chicago History* 43, no. 2 (2019): 32.

37 *Virginia state legislature in 1924*: "An Act to Preserve Racial Integrity," in *Acts Passed at a General Assembly of the Commonwealth of Virginia 1924* (David Bottom, 1924), 534, https://babel.hathitrust.org/cgi/pt?id=njp.32 101073363507&seq=7.

37 *laws criminalizing interracial marriage unconstitutional*: Loving v. Virginia, 388 U.S. 1 (1967).

38   *claimed to be hereditary*: "An Act to Provide for the Sexual Sterilization of Inmates of State Institutions in Certain Cases," in *Acts Passed at a General Assembly of the Commonwealth of Virginia 1924* (David Bottom, 1924), 569, https://babel.hathitrust.org/cgi/pt?id=njp.32101073363507&seq=7.

38   *"Three generations of imbeciles are enough"*: Buck v. Bell, 274 U.S. 200 (1927).

38   *"both the man and woman"*: "An Act to Preserve Racial Integrity," 534, sections 1 and 4.

38   *letter to prominent eugenicist Harry Laughlin*: Quoted in Philip R. Reilly, *The Surgical Solution: A History of Involuntary Sterilization in the United States* (Johns Hopkins University Press, 1991), 78.

38   *"intermarriage of the white race with mixed stock"*: W. A. Plecker, "The New Virginia Law to Preserve Racial Integrity," *Virginia Health Bulletin* 16, no. 2 (1924): 2, https://babel.hathitrust.org/cgi/pt?id=mdp.39015 067921166&seq=20; Dorothy Roberts, "Race," in *The 1619 Project: A New Origin Story*, ed. Nikole Hannah-Jones, Caitlin Roper, Ilena Silverman, and Jake Silverstein (One World, 2021), 45, 48.

39   *"a crime worse than treason"*: Trevor Noah, *Born a Crime: Stories from a South African Childhood* (Spiegel & Grau, 2016), 21.

39   *"unwritten law of the 'color line'"*: Thomas Lee Philpott, *The Slum and the Ghetto: Immigrants, Blacks, and Reformers in Chicago, 1880–1930* (Wadsworth, 1991), xi.

39   *"social and racial crime of the first magnitude"*: Madison Grant, *The Passing of the Great Race*, 4th rev. ed. (Scribner, 1923), 60.

39   *"every American should read"*: William H. Tucker, *The Science and Politics of Racial Research* (University of Illinois Press, 1994), 93, quoting "The Great American Myth," editorial, *Saturday Evening Post*, May 7, 1921.

41   *"and literally tears the pair apart"*: Quoted in Angela Onwuachi-Willig, "A Beautiful Lie: Exploring *Rhinelander v. Rhinelander* as a Formative Lesson on Race, Identity, Marriage, and Family," *California Law Review* 95 (September 2007): 2393, 2454.

CHAPTER 3: FINDING MANASSEH

45   *by the University of Chicago Press*: Chicago Commission on Race Relations, *The Negro in Chicago: A Study of Race Relations and a Race Riot* (University of Chicago Press, 1922), 1–52.

45   *in Our National Life*: George S. Schuyler, *Racial Intermarriage in the United States: One of the Most Interesting Phenomena in Our National Life* (Haldeman-Julius, 1929).

46   *"medical men and quacks"*: George S. Schuyler, "Quantity or Quality," *Birth Control Review* 16, no. 6 (June 1932): 165, 166.

48   *to stop a fascist takeover in Europe*: During the civil war, Langston Hughes sent harrowing dispatches from Spain that were published in the *Baltimore Afro-American*, reporting on Black Americans' participation in the struggle to stop the dictators Franco, Mussolini, and Hitler. Matthew F. Delmont, *Half American: The Epic Story of African Americans Fighting World War II at Home and Abroad* (Viking, 2022), 8–9. Historian Robin D. G. Kelley calls the volunteer brigades that fought fascism on Spanish soil as a prelude to World War II "a significant episode of international solidarity." Kelley,

"Preface," in William Loren Katz and Marc Crawford, *The Lincoln Brigade: A Picture History* (Wipf & Stock, 2013), 5.

CHAPTER 4: EXCLUDED FROM THE HIGHER ELEMENT

60 *"according to the condition of the mother"*: "Negro Women's Children to Serve According to the Condition of the Mother," Virginia General Assembly, Act XII, 1662, https://encyclopediavirginia.org/primary-documents /negro-womens-children-to-serve-according-to-the-condition-of-the -mother-1662/.

61 *sins into financial gain*: Quoted in Estelle B. Freedman, *Redefining Rape: Sexual Violence in the Era of Suffrage and Segregation* (Harvard University Press, 2013), 29; Roberts, "Race," 50.

CHAPTER 5: THE COLOR LINE

65 *"every other corner of America"*: Wilkerson, *The Warmth of Other Suns*, 9.

65 *it had surpassed 200,000*: Janet L. Abu-Lughod, *Race, Space, and Riots in Chicago, New York, and Los Angeles* (Oxford University Press, 2007), 51–52; Allen R. Kamp, "The History Behind *Hansberry v. Lee*," *U.C. Davis Law Review* 20, no. 3 (Spring 1987): 483.

66 *designated to contain Black residents*: As Drake and Cayton observe in *Black Metropolis*, "Negroes, regardless of their affluence and respectability, wear the badge of color. They are expected to stay in the Black Belt." St. Clair Drake and Horace R. Cayton, *Black Metropolis: A Study of Negro Life in a Northern City* (University of Chicago Press, 1945), 204.

66 *as adjacent white areas*: Drake & Cayton, *Black Metropolis*, 204.

66 *neighborhoods designated as white*: Al Chase, "Bar 'White Area Sales' to Negro," *Chicago Daily Tribune*, May 5, 1921.

66 *covenant against Black homeowners*: Hansberry v. Lee, 311 U.S. 32 (1940).

66 *a group of white businessmen*: Charles J. Shields, *Lorraine Hansberry: The Life Behind A Raisin in the Sun* (Henry Holt, 2022), 22; Imani Perry, *Looking for Lorraine: The Radiant and Radical Life of Lorraine Hansberry* (Beacon Press, 2018), 12–17.

66 *violated the Fourteenth Amendment*: Shelley v. Kraemer, 334 U.S. 1 (1948).

66 *became segregated Black neighborhoods*: Shields, *Lorraine Hansberry*, 45.

69 *in a different part of town*: Noah, *Born a Crime*, 27–28.

CHAPTER 6: PASSING

78 *racially ambiguous individuals*: Destiny Peery and Galen V. Bodenhausen, "Black + White = Black: Hypodescent in Reflexive Categorization of Racially Ambiguous Faces," *Psychological Science* 109, no. 10 (October 2008): 973–77, https://journals.sagepub.com/doi/abs/10.1111/j.1467-9280.2008 .02185.x.

79 *factors influence racial identification*: "Symposium: Genetic Ancestry and Perceptions of Race: Impacts in Social and Medical Contexts," University of Pennsylvania, May 9, 2024, https://web.sas.upenn.edu/genetic-ancestry -and-race/symposium/.

81 *"raising an interracial child"*: Barbara Kantrowitz and David A. Kaplan, "Not the Right Father," *Newsweek*, March 19, 1990, 50.

81   *Black fathers and white mothers*: @shogentushi, "Modern NBA culture. #NBADraft," X, June 23, 2022, https://x.com/shogentushi/status/154014 3662524399617.

82   *chose his tall, white wife*: LaVar Ball, interview by Val Warner and Ryan Chiaverini, *Windy City Live*, ABC7 Chicago, video, August 2, 2018, https: //www.youtube.com/watch?app=desktop&v=MWySclNxT0Q.

CHAPTER 7: COPPERS

86   *on a summer day in 2019*: Hollie Silverman, "3 Couples Are Suing Virginia after Being Denied Marriage Licenses because They Refused to Disclose Their Race," CNN, September 10, 2019, https://www.cnn.com/2019/09 /10/us/virginia-marriage-license-race-question.

86   *racial-identification requirement unconstitutional*: Rogers v. Virginia State Registrar, 507 F. Supp. 3d 664 (E.D. Va. 2019).

87   *calling him a racial slur*: Nettie George Speedy, "Judge Cook Displays Rank Racial Prejudice in Court Decision," *Chicago Defender*, November 9, 1918.

87   *"someone of a different race"*: Kate Markey, "Unlawful Intimacy: The Criminalization of Interracial Relationships in Progressive-Era Chicago," *Law & Society Inquiry* 49, no. 2 (2023): 1169–91.

88   *my father had apparently transcribed*: Harold F. Gosnell, *Negro Politicians: The Rise of Negro Politics in Chicago* (University of Chicago Press, 1935).

CHAPTER 8: IT IS A HANDICAP

98   *while reducing their benefits*: Benjamin Wiggins, *Calculating Race: Racial Discrimination in Risk Assessment* (Oxford University Press, 2020), 9–28.

101   *a man who is a weakling*: Jonathan Green, *Green's Dictionary of Slang* (digital ed., 2025), https://greensdictofslang.com/entry/qol2kji.

101   *"written all over him"*: George Ade, *The Girl Proposition: A Bunch of He and She Fables* (R. H. Russell, 1902), 3–4.

103   *a friend of Cayton*: *Black Metropolis* was published by Harcourt, Brace. It won the 1946 Anisfield-Wolf Book Award for the best nonfiction book on race.

CHAPTER 9: THE BACHELOR

108   *cultural connection to nudity*: Alice Gregory, "Das Butt," *New York Times Style Magazine*, October 20, 2019.

110   *into my father's interest*: Herbert Nipson, "Nudism and Negroes: Interracialism Is Introduced in Scattered Camps around Nation and First Trickle of Negroes Joins 2,000,000 in Clothesless Cult That Worships Sunshine and Fresh Air," *Ebony* Magazine Archive 6, no. 10 (1951): 93–101, https: //research.ebsco.com/linkprocessor/plink?id=36eaeb69-ce82-318f-961d-099053d7896b.

118   *Black and white communities*: Renee C. Romano, *Race Mixing: Black-White Marriage in Postwar America* (Harvard University Press, 2003), 54–57.

123   *the first to ask him*: Kiese Laymon, *Heavy: An American Memoir* (Scribner, 2018), 93.

125   *they remain relatively uncommon*: Solangel Maldonado, *The Architecture of*

Desire: How the Law Shapes Interracial Intimacy and Perpetuates Inequality (New York University Press, 2024), 2–3.

125 *shape marital choices*: Maldonado, *The Architecture of Desire*, 2–3. According to a 2023 Census Bureau survey, same-sex couples are more likely to be interracial than their different-sex counterparts, with 31 percent of same-sex marriages occurring between partners of different races. "Interracial Couples More Common among Same-Sex Couples," American Community Survey, U.S. Census Bureau, November 8, 2023. See also Ariel Messman-Rucker, "Interracial Couples More Common in Same-Sex Relationships, the US Census Finds," Yahoo News, November 10, 2023, https://www.yahoo.com/news/interracial-couples-more-common-same -143050148.html.

125 *modern dating landscape*: Sarah Adeyinka-Skold, "Dating in the Digital Age: Race, Gender, and Inequality," unpublished PhD dissertation, University of Pennsylvania, January 1, 2020, https://repository.upenn.edu/entities/ publication/4fd99f16-10dd-4662-8193-58b199fb793a.

125 *reach out to Black users*: Maldonado, *The Architecture of Desire*, 133nn 15–16.

125 *"I don't like black guys, sorry"*: Quoted in Maldonado, *The Architecture of Desire*, 80n79.

125 *group they would date interracially*: Jennifer H. Lundquist and Ken-Hou Lin, "Is Love (Color) Blind? The Economy of Race among Gay and Straight Daters," *Social Forces* 93, no. 4 (June 2015): 1423–49.

126 *author of the book* Dataclysm: Christian Rudder, "Race and Attraction, 2009–2014," *Oktrends*, September 10, 2014, https://gwern.net/doc/psycho logy/okcupid/raceandattraction20092014.html.

126 *simply because they are Black*: Sarah Adeyinka-Skold, "Barriers in Women's Romantic Partner Search in the Digital Age," in *Young Adult Sexuality in the Digital Age*, ed. Rachel Kalish (IGI Global, 2020), 113–37.

129 *in the Garvey Mausoleum*: "Photo Flashback: The Rev. Dr. Martin Luther King Jr. in Jamaica, June 1965," *The Gleaner*, https://jamaica-gleaner.com /article/esponsored/20210618/photo-flashback-rev-dr-martin-luther -king-jr-jamaica-june-1965.

CHAPTER 10: UNDESIRABLES

134 *nearly one-third in 1960*: Arnold R. Hirsch, *Making the Second Ghetto: Race & Housing in Chicago, 1940–1960* (University of Chicago Press, 1983), 16–17.

135 *"to keep the walls in place"*: Wilkerson, *The Warmth of Other Suns*, 372.

135 *the Red Summer of 1919*: Wilkerson, *The Warmth of Other Suns*, 372–74.

CHAPTER 11: LIFE IMITATES ART

151 *journalist Era Bell Thompson*: Era Bell Thompson, *American Daughter* (University of Chicago Press, 1946).

153 *seventieth anniversary in 2014*: Laura Mills and Lynn Y. Weiner, *Roosevelt University* (Arcadia, 2014), 8.

153 *from the* Washington Post: Mills and Weiner, *Roosevelt University*, 9.

CHAPTER 12: SERVICEMEN AND WAR BRIDES

159 *equal rights and opportunities*: Matthew F. Delmont, *Half American: The Epic Story of African Americans Fighting World War II at Home and Abroad* (Viking, 2022), 263–76; "Remembering Black Veterans Targeted for Racial Violence in the U.S.," Equal Justice Initiative, November 11, 2024, https://eji.org/news/remembering-black-veterans-targeted-for-racial-violence-in-the-us/?utm_source=chatgpt.com.

159 *"the white Mississippians would"*: Quoted in Delmont, *Half American*, 263.

163 *an uproar back home*: Romano, *Race Mixing*, 21.

CHAPTER 13: SEEKING A HAVEN

174 *President William V. S. Tubman*: "Swift Visit Here Impresses but Tires Liberian President," *Chicago Sun-Times*, October 26, 1954, 13.

181 *in an unpublished memoir*: Warren L. d'Azevedo, *Rebel Destinies: Remembering Herskovits*, PAS Working Paper Number 15 (Program of African Studies, Northwestern University, 2009), 29, https://africanstudies.northwestern.edu/docs/publications-research/working-papers/dazevedo.pdf.

182 *"social mobility and intermarriage are sanctioned"*: Robert E. T. Roberts, "A Comparative Study of Social Stratification and Intermarriage in Multi-Racial Societies," unpublished dissertation (University of Chicago, 1956).

182 *of India and Nazi Germany*: Isabel Wilkerson, *Caste: The Origins of Our Discontents* (Random House, 2020).

CHAPTER 14: KENWOOD

197 *"of Chicago's residence suburbs"*: Jean F. Block, *Hyde Park Houses: An Informal History, 1856–1910* (University of Chicago Press, 1978), 78.

198 *adorned some of the walls*: A 1993 obituary for Christopher R. Sergel in the *New York Times* suggests he may have been the former owner of our house. At the time of his death at seventy-five, he was president of a play-publishing company and a Broadway playwright. A graduate of the University of Chicago, he was described as "an adventurer and a sportsman" who "lived for a year in the African bush while writing for *Sports Afield* magazine." "Christopher Sergel, Publisher of Plays and Playwright, 75," *New York Times*, May 12, 1993, https://timesmachine.nytimes.com/timesmachine/1993/05/12/657593.html?pageNumber=27.

201 *integrated the association's crematorium*: "Richard Clayter," The History Makers, https://www.thehistorymakers.org/biography/richard-clayter-41; "Charles S. Jackson Funeral Homes Records," Bronzeville Historical Society, October 2016, https://bronzevillearchives.com/wp-content/uploads/2017/10/jackson-funeral-home-collection-description-july-23-2017.pdf.

CHAPTER 16: SYMBOL OF RACIAL HARMONY

236 *who was also a member*: "After 50 Years of Social Change, Group Members Remain Happy Campers," *Chicago Tribune*, September 7, 1997, updated August 19, 2021, https://www.chicagotribune.com/1995/09/07/after-50-years-of-social-change-group-members-remain-happy-campers/.

CHAPTER 17: THE SIXTIES

247   *struggle with the officer*: Sam Roberts, "Charles McDew, 79, Tactician for Student Civil Rights Group, Dies," *New York Times*, April 13, 2018, https://www.nytimes.com/2018/04/13/obituaries/charles-mcdew-79-tactician-for-student-civil-rights-group-dies.html.

249   *"made in their personal lives"*: Romano, *Race Mixing*, 225.

251   *frozen in the snapshot*: "Martin Luther King Jr. Kisses Betsy Berry," Flickr, https://www.flickr.com/photos/uicdigital/8026612831?utm_source=chatgpt.com.

251   *Black research consortium*: "Chicago Urban League–Collection Description, 1916–2000," Chicago Collections, https://explore.chicagocollections.org/ead/uic/25/z88n/.

254   *"the Sacred Robes of Jesus"*: Carl Nolte, "Jack Fertig—Sister Boom Boom—Dies," *SFGate*, August 7, 2012, https://www.sfgate.com/bayarea/article/Jack-Fertig-Sister-Boom-Boom-dies-3770649.php.

CHAPTER 18: BLACK GIRL

263   *the article notes*: Hanna Kozlowska, "Before There Was Tinder," The Cut, September 5, 2022, https://www.thecut.com/2022/09/computer-dating-love-stories.html#.

265   Black Power: The Politics of Liberation in America: Stokely Carmichael and Charles V. Hamilton, *Black Power: The Politics of Liberation in America* (Random House, 1967).

271   *"however subtle, sexual relations"*: Calvin C. Hernton, *Sex and Racism in America* (Doubleday, 1965), 6.

280   *in Roosevelt's newspaper*, The Torch: Jean Natalechapter, "Racial Studies Not Just Black and White for RU Prof," *Torch*, April 16, 1981, 10.

282   *based on his study*: Robert E. T. Roberts, "Trends in Marriages between Negroes and Whites in Chicago," in *Perspectives on Ethnicity*, ed. Regina E. Holloman and Serghei A. Arutiunov (Mouton, 1978), 173–210.

EPILOGUE: RESEARCH PARTICIPANT NO. 224

286   *"shall be unlawful and void"*: Mississippi Constitution of 1890, Article 14, § 263 (repealed 1987).

291   *with a white mother*: Barack Obama, *Dreams from My Father: A Story of Race and Inheritance* (Crown, 2007).

297   *"touch another person"*: Imani Perry, *South to America: A Journey below the Mason-Dixon to Understand the Soul of a Nation* (Ecco, 2022), 237.

ABOUT THE AUTHOR

Dorothy Roberts is the George A. Weiss University Professor of Law & Sociology and the Raymond Pace & Sadie Tanner Mossell Alexander Professor of Civil Rights at the University of Pennsylvania, where she directs the Penn Program on Race, Science & Society. The author of five books, including *Killing the Black Body*, a MacArthur Fellow, and member of the American Academy of Arts and Sciences, she lives in Philadelphia, Pennsylvania.

Atria Books, an imprint of Simon & Schuster, fosters an open environment where ideas flourish, bestselling authors soar to new heights, and tomorrow's finest voices are discovered and nurtured. Since its launch in 2002, Atria has published hundreds of bestsellers and extraordinary books, which would not have been possible without the invaluable support and expertise of its team and publishing partners. Thank you to the Atria Books colleagues who collaborated on The Mixed Marriage Project, as well as to the hundreds of professionals in the Simon & Schuster advertising, audio, communications, design, ebook, finance, human resources, legal, marketing, operations, production, sales, supply chain, subsidiary rights, and warehouse departments who help Atria bring great books to light.

EDITORIAL
Alessandra Bastagli
Rola Harb

JACKET DESIGN
James Iacobelli
Chelsea McGuckin

MARKETING
Aleaha Reneé

MANAGING EDITORIAL
Paige Lytle
Shelby Pumphrey
Sofia Echeverry
Abby Borchers

PRODUCTION
Katie Rizzo
Alexis Leira
Rob Sternitzky
Davina Mock-Maniscalco

PUBLICITY
Joanna Pinsker
Annie Probert

PUBLISHING OFFICE
Dana Trocker
Abby Velasco

SUBSIDIARY RIGHTS
Nicole Bond
Sara Bowne
Rebecca Justiniano